MORE PARAGRAPHS ⌣

MULTILINGUAL MATTERS

**Please contact us for the latest book information:
Multilingual Matters, Frankfurt Lodge, Clevedon Hall,
Victoria Road, Clevedon, BS21 7HH, England
http:/www.multi.demon.co.uk**

MORE PARAGRAPHS ON TRANSLATION

PETER NEWMARK

MULTILINGUAL MATTERS LTD
Clevedon • Philadelphia • Toronto • Sydney • Johannesburg

For my sister Monica

Library of Congress Cataloging-in-Publication Data
Newmark, Peter
More Paragraphs on Translation/Peter Newmark
1. Translating and interpreting. I. Title.
P306.N4727   1998
418′.02–dc21 97-51150

British Library Cataloguing in Publication Data

A CIP catalogue record for this book is available from the British Library.

ISBN 1-85359-403-2 (hbk)
ISBN 1-85359-40204 (pbk)

Multilingual Matters Ltd
UK: Frankfurt Lodge, Clevedon Hall, Victoria Road, Clevedon, England
BS21 7HH.
USA: 1900 Frost Road, Suite 101, Bristol, PA 19007, USA.
Canada: OISE, 712 Gordon Baker Rd., Toronto, Ontario, Canada M2H 3RT
Australia: P.O. Box 586, Artamon NSW 2064, Australia.
South Africa: P.O. Box 1080, Northcliffe 2115, Johannesburg, South Africa.

Typeset by Solidus (Bristol) Ltd
Printed and bound in Great Britain by The Cromwell Press.

CONTENTS

Concept • Trials of a Translator • The Translation of Longer
Sentences • The Translation of Colloquial Language

Lauren Leighton • The Moral Universal • *Wie Rafft ich Mich auf in
der Nacht* • The Translation of Idioms • Corfu and Athens • Poetry
Translation • Sexist Language • ESIT • The Law of Titles • The
University of Bir Zeit • Jerusalem and Israel • Sorry • For Tiny Tots •
Componential Analysis Register • Anthony Pym • Technical •
Rouault • Translation Theory as a Comprehensive Frame of
Reference • Theodor Kramer • Four Correlations for Technical
Translation • Some Tentative Remarks on Frames • Amour Propre •
Fauré and His Chansons • Another Latin Tag • Reduction to Prose •
Translation as Text • The Five Direct and the Three Indirect Purposes
of Translation: A Revised Version

Variant Spellings • Golden Advice • Technical Terms • Translating or
Disentangling Zeugmas and Hendiadys • Contemporary Translation
Theories • Theory • Anti-Goethe? • The Nord • The Translator
Intervenes • Interlanguage • The Contracting Apostrophe

PC • Sarcastic • The Deadline • Translation Should (usually) be into
the Modern Language • Limits of Translation • The London
Language Show • Norms and Standards • It is Three O'Clock •
Prescriptivism • Phrasal Adjectives • The Cave • Translation Facts •
Titles of Periodicals • The Poetics of Translation • Howlers • The
Evanescence of Idioms and Clichés • American Judiciary Interpreters
and Translators • Translating Eponyms • Tytler and Nietzsche • Text
and Meaning

The Barber Institute • La Patrie • Translation Studies at Birmingham
University • Translating Metalanguage • Translation Material •
Reception Theory and Hype • Galician Symposium • The Key to
Technical Translation • Evil • An Israeli Translation Theory of Peace •
Greco-Latin Semi-Neologisms • Geographical Features • Etymology
in Translation Again • The Musée d'Orsay • Teaching Translation and
Detecting Allusions • Apostrophes • Literary and Non-Literary
Translation • Paraphrase as a Translation Procedure • The European
School of Literary Translation • The Meaning and Translation of
Dashes • Translation for Drama • The German *Sog.* • Figaro's
Wedding by Jeremy Sams • Translation Theory • La Serenissima • In
Praise of Trieste • Some (additional) Translation Exam-Day Hints

INTRODUCTION

The art and craft of translation may be turned to any account, but in principle it is a noble and truth seeking profession, reflecting true statements or life-enhancing images through another language in another culture. All the degrading remarks about translation, that it is manipulative, parasitic, servile, treacherous, composed at the behest of a patron, subservient to the norms and trends of its time, are in principle wrong, if one thinks of it, as I do, as one person's attempt to wring the truth out of another person's writing.

Furthermore, translation, which must always be differentiated from the ability to speak or write foreign languages, is becoming continuously a more powerful and extensive instrument. It is inextricably bound up with the service industries and political devolution, with foreign travel and with recreational and cultural tourism. As soon as countries 'split' ... Belgium, USSR, Czechoslovakia, Spain, Yugoslavia, Wales, ... more translators are required, even though the separation of Serbian and Croatian becomes more of a philologist's feast than a linguistic reality. As soon as there is a new joint venture, a multinational or an international organization, professionals are required to translate the contracts, the articles and the treaties.

Migrations and settlements, invasions and occupations, and the consequent flight of refugees, have covered the world's towns and cities with multilingual notices and produced the requirement for public service translators and interpreters. Tourism again has filled the public buildings and the monuments and the information offices with translated guides, brochures, handbooks, and leaflets ...

This book carries on where the last one, *Paragraphs on Translation*, left off. Beginning in October 1992, it is a revised version of the articles I wrote for *The Linguist*, the journal of the Institute of Linguists, now in its handsome new offices at 48 Southwark Street, London SE1, every two months till September 1997.

As previously, the book is written for various 'interest groups': first for students – I have my own students in mind, especially the English, the Czechs, the Greeks and the Triestini – translators and teachers of translation, perhaps even a few friendly translation theorists; after reading the book, I hope they will be able to use it as a reference book, where the Index, with its sections on Translation Topics and Words is especially designed for them; secondly for language teachers, linguists and educationalists, who often need a clear view on the autonomous importance of translation, and where it merges and where it does not with foreign language proficiency; thirdly, for the political class, for administrators, and for the staff of town halls, social services, the courts, clinics, hospitals, museums, art galleries, theatres, cinemas, airports, information offices, to make them aware of the translation requirements at their places of work, which have to be regularly updated; and lastly to the general and educated readership, who should be continuously and increasingly conscious that translation is the key to a proper understanding with and of the minorities in their midst.

The content of my 'discourse' remains as in the previous book:

1. Translation topics, many of them sequels, others, such as examining, assessing, capitalization, emphasis, idiolect, grecolatinisms across languages, the small print, eponyms, howlers, and a host more appearing (apparently) for the first time, usually with translation examples to test my propositions. I think that the number of profitable translation topics is infinite.
2. Translation theory. I have increased the number of my correlative statements about translation ('the more . . . the more' . . . 'the less . . . the less', etc.). These have been met with a deafening silence 'in the literature'. I have increasingly insisted on the differences between good and bad translation; good and bad writing; literary and non-literary texts and translations; authoritative and non-authoritative texts and translations; cultural and universal factors, as well as the large number of factors that often govern a translation.
3. The distinctions between translation and foreign language proficiency, and the role of linguistics in both.
4. Translation as a matter of public interest, in the European Union and national parliaments, as well as in museums and art galleries.
5. Critical discussion of recently published books and conference proceedings.

Again, my political and moral interest in human rights is evident in the book.

And again, I acknowledge the helpful advice of Pauline, Liz and Matthew Newmark.

I

SEPTEMBER 1992

Magritte on TV

The flowing mysterious visions fascinate, but what gives David Sylvester, the presenter, the right to change the titles *La clé des songes* ('The key to dreams') to 'The interpretation of dreams', *La femme introuvable* ('The woman who cannot be found') to 'The elusive Woman' or 'The unfindable Woman' (brevity?), *Les jours gigantesques* to 'Titanic days', *L'esprit de géométrie* to 'The mathematical mind', etc. Even if he is following a 'tradition', a 'translation norm' for nice free euphonic translations (cf. *Remembrance of Things Past*), isn't it time to break with it, to try and write simply what the painter wrote? On the other hand, if the titles are not Magritte's (cf. *'The Emperor Concerto'*, i.e. Beethoven's 5th Piano Concerto), the translator can go ahead.

Investments

The sentence: *Une période de désinflation peut être peu propice à l'investissement du fait de l'attrait des placements financiers et du coût de l'endettement* may appear contradictory, as English can barely distinguish *placement* from *investissement*; a contrasting word could be added: 'A period of disinflation may be unfavourable to general (industrial) investment owing to the cost of borrowing and to the attraction of investments that are restricted to the money markets.'

The Three Modes of Reading

I think there are three modes of reading: (1) reading aloud, (2) 'phonic' reading, where, as in thinking, the sounds of what is read remain in the mind, and (3) normal 'efficient' rapid reading, where the sense 'eliminates' the sound. Poetry (and usually drama) always requires phonic reading. The translator, at least, has to be ready to switch (switching the sound on) to phonic reading when faced with conversation in texts and rhetorical writing such as poetry and drama, including journalism and publicity that has sound effects. Often, the more important the words, the more important their sounds. Sometimes, even a semi-assonance such as 'dirty trick' (*schlimmer* rather than *gemeiner Trick*?) can be suggested, but this may be one of the lucky coincidences of translation, though not in de Beaugrande's sense.

Coincidence in Translation

In the later stages of translating, I sometimes exercise my mind as though it were a kaleidoscope to be rotated until a more or less convincing coincidence of meaning with the source language unit of translation (not longer than a clause) comes up. I doubt whether Robert de Beaugrande has this type of coincidence in mind in his stimulating essay *Coincidence in Translation* (*Target*, Vol. 3, No 1, 1991; ed. G. Toury and J. Lambert; Benjamins, Amsterdam). He defines coincidence as a 'dialectic between similarity and difference', but does not pursue the concept. He states that the theoretical groundwork of translation theory is increasingly coming from discourse analysis and text linguistics, which may be true, but it ignores a lot of work to be done in other fields, and leads him to quote seventeen of his own works and none by Ladmiral, Wilss or Toury (all of whose references are often somewhat egocentrically similar, *je vais y consacrer une prochaine étude*), let alone by Nida, Vinay and Darbelnet, Delisle, Koller, House, Reiss, who might merit a place in what is partly a general review of the field. 'As far as I can judge', De Beaugrande states, 'comparative linguistics' (the inverted commas are depreciatory), 'has remained suspended ever since the '60s,' thereby ignoring the vast amount of work done in this field, by for instance Guillemin-Flescher, and now by Hervey and Higgins (see below). De Beaugrande believes that three sources 'vitally' need to receive more consideration to build a more solid and useful foundation on translation theory: (a) professional translators and interpreters, as well as their instructors, (b) experts in subject matters where translation is required (but how are they going to help?), (c) an international collection of special terms, especially for 'burgeoning' technical fields like . . . computer science. But he concludes the essay with a fruitful comparison of his own and a poor translation of the poem *Mi ultimo Adios* by the Filipino poet Jose Rizal, which brings me back to his fine translation of the *Duino Elegies* in *Factors in a Theory of Poetic Translating* (Assen, Van Gorcum, 1978).

Modern Translation

Translation should normally be into the modern language (which may switch over the seventy years covering an *état de langue*), unless the source language text is written in an antiquated style, or the translator has a particular flair for say a period style. Anything else is likely to be artificial. Only modern language is likely to have the maximum impact on readers. That said, it's dangerous to dogmatize. I prefer classical music played on modern instruments, even Bach (Mozart was hampered by the glass harmonica), to authentic music on period instruments, but listening to John Eliot Gardiner or Roger Norrington, Christopher Hogwood or Nicolaus Harnoncourt conduct is always rewarding; they are *innig* (heart-felt, devoted, intimate); they eschew flashy playing, they give a fresh (not a 'correct') insight into whatever they play, and then it's good to return to the modern orchestra. When does one start 'translating' Shakespeare into modern

English? As late as possible; only when one can't feel the language any more.

Loyalty

Loyalty, the concept which Christiane Nord has introduced into the Vermeer 'scopos' theory (see *Scopos,* Loyalty and Translation Conventions in *Target* 3(1), 1991), would not be worth commenting on if it did not include so many misconceptions, e.g. that the initiator or the reader of the translation cannot check on whether the translation conforms to their expectations, and have to rely on the translator doing a fair job. Any professional translation has to be revised before it is delivered. But I don't think this 'loyalty', daringly referred to as a 'moral principle', means anything more than professional competence.

The Reims Museum of Fine Arts

It is strange that the *cité des sacres* and of the champagne barons cannot afford to label its pictures multilingually or to issue more than two-sided summaries in English, German and French to barely mention its magnificent Boudins (swarming figures on the beach, and sailing ships at Rouen), as well as the superb Le Nain *Les Tricheurs* and about twenty Corots.

The Status of the Translator

'Today there seems to be the need to reinstate the translator to the status s/he once had as a member of one of the most time-honoured and highly respected professions known to man', John Dodds writes in his Introduction to the *Rivista internazionale di tecnica della traduzione* (numero 1, 1992, Campanotto Udine), produced by the School of Translators and Interpreters at the University of Trieste, a fascinating journal with contributions on technical and literary translation. John Dodds rightly and abundantly substantiates how greatly translations have enriched the national literatures, but whether translators as such had high status in at least England is not known. Sir Thomas North (Plutarch's *Lives*, read by Shakespeare) did a lot of other things; Florio (Montaigne' essays) was groom to Queen Anne's bedchamber; there were a host of poets who translated, but were not known as translators till FitzGerald (*Omar Khayam*), who was a minor poet. In Europe, there were independent translators (Schleiermacher actually mentions commercial translators, I suspect for the first time ever, in his famous essay of 1813), but it is my impression that say the school of translators at Toledo (13th century) achieved their status as learned men rather than as translators. However I agree with the spirit of John Dodds' statement and there is progress.

Thinking Translation

Thinking Translation: A Course in Translation Method: French-English by Sandor Hervey and Ian Higgins (1992, Routledge, London, ISBN 0-415-07815-6) is a useful, readable, sometimes wordy and donnish record of a third year course at St Andrew's University, taught to 'the Elite', who are named . . . Some texts and cassettes are available for anyone wanting to teach the course, but most teachers would want to make their own syllabuses and choose their own texts, and the outlines of parallel German and Spanish syllabuses are of marginal interest. What is interesting to teachers and translators is the literate and practical discussion of translation topics such as cultural transposition, compensation, language varieties, technical translation, and five chapters contrasting French and English structures in the manner of Guillemin-Flescher. Some texts are too ephemeral, and a few solid literary texts could have been added, but the book is sensitive, civilized and free from the jargon.

Rethinking Translation

Rethinking Translation: Discourse, Subjectivity, Ideology edited by Lawrence Venuti (Routledge, London; 1992, ISBN 0 415 06051-6) is a rich and various collection of mainly American essays which I recommend. Venuti in his Introduction protests against translation as an 'invisible practice', all around us (I see it every day now in the supermarkets and hopefully soon in all the streets and public buildings), 'rarely acknowledged . . . The contemporary translator is a paradoxical hybrid, at once dilettante and artisan.' According to American and British law, translation is a second-order product, an 'adaptation' or 'derivative work'. Translation is marginal and translators do nothing to assert themselves. William Weaver states that 'When a reviewer neglects to mention the translator at all, the translator should take the omission as a compliment to his anonymity, a real achievement'; I believe the contrary to be true. Venuti condemns 'fluent strategies, pursuing linear syntax, univocal meaning, current usage, conversational rhythms, avoiding anything that calls attention to words as words . . . this leads to self-annihilation, to the cultural marginality and economic exploitation of the translator.' Venuti's conclusion is arguable, but I see this as a plea for close and accurate translation, warts and all, for independence from the target language 'polysystem'. Venuti, like his master Derrida, talks much of difference and *différance*, but he has not got the courage to put this plainly, and he produces no translation examples.

Richard Jacquemond discusses '*Translation and Cultural Hegemony: The Case of French-Arabic Translation*'. He begins with a useful set of statistics of French-Arabic and Arabic-English book translations since the 40s, but his conclusions, without examples or evidence, are merely modish: the translator from a hegemonic language culture is a servile mediator through whom foreign-made linguistic-cultural objects are integrated without question into his own dominated language culture, thus aggravating the schizophrenia! Interestingly, he concludes that a critique of 'universality' should be a priority for translation theory, but I suspect that he would simply reject this the concept that most needs affirming. Sherry Simon on '*The Language of Cultural Difference: Figures of Alterity in Canadian Translation*', like Venturi, beneath the jargon, isn't 'otherness' enough? must we have 'alterity'?), discusses cultural differences between French texts and English translations (notably *Maria Chapdelaine*) through pertinent examples and even gently protests against the licences of the translations ('breath-takingly liberal approach'). She includes an interesting section on the translation of *joual*, the language of the French urban working-class. Grisly sentences like 'Translation not only negotiates between languages, but comes to inhabit the space of language itself' are only a slight distraction from her translation criticism. There are also some dreadful essays assimilating translation to coitus, sexual relationships (as in the 17th century by Roscommon and the 18th by Thomas Francklin), gender politics and imperialism. Dreadful because they seem designed to arouse attention rather than to say anything of interest. Thus Jeffrey Mehlman on *Merrill's Valery: An Erotics of Translation*, commenting on Merrill's unpleasant mistranslation:

> What is this delectation
> If not divine duration
> That, without keeping time,
> Can alter it, seduce
> Into a steady juice
> Love's volatile perfume?

of what may be these lines from Paul Valery's wonderful poem *Palme*:

> *Sa douceur est mesurée*
> *Par la divine durée*
> *Qui ne compte pas les jours,*
> *Mais bien qui les dissimule*
> *Dans un suc où s'accumule*
> *Tout l'arôme des amours*

states that Merrill's translation here prepares an ejaculation which the context establishes as masturbatory. (So much for *Le pain tendre, le lait plat*, one of the loveliest lines I know.) George Steiner's: 'There is evidence that the sexual discharge in male onanism is greater than in intercourse' (*After Babel*, p.44) and 'Sex is a profoundly (note the clever word-play) semantic act' (p.38) are quoted approvingly by Lori Chamberlain. Both Eagleton and the egregious Harold Bloom are quoted in the view that 'all poems are translations'; in the essence of their intertextuality, they arise from language rather than life, behaviour, observation, experience, emotion. Sharon Willis indulges in a riot of punning but contrives some criticism, and Samia Mehrez is informative on the difficulties of the Maghreb writers.

Academia
Academia is a strange world. In *Fremdsprachen* 2/3/91, the outstanding GDR translation journal that has now been taken over by Verlag Alexandre Hatier (Oranienburgerstrasse 13/14, 0-1020 Berlin), Monika Doherty writes a quirky piece on *Translation Theory, Linguistics and Style* which, according to her, expresses a similar view to my *Curse of Dogma in Translation* in *Lebende Sprachen* 1/89 (also an excellent journal, published by Langenscheidt) but according to me, has no remote bearing on any view of mine. In *Fremdsprachen* 1/91, as elsewhere, Sergio Viaggio accuses me of 'denying' the difference between 'sense' and 'meaning', which is an arguable, context-dependent difference; in fact, he is confusing 'sense' and 'meaning' with 'sense' (linguistic meaning, the dictionary, the 'Morning Star') and 'reference' (extra-linguistic meaning, the encyclopaedia, 'Venus'), which difference I have been explaining and illustrating for many years.

Foreign Phrases
In the *Sunday Times* of 2.8.92 a correspondent accuses John Carey of élitism for translating 'The deil aye kens his ain' but not *crème de la crème* or 'curriculum vitae.' I think Carey's decision is logical, since the two phrases are in any good dictionary, whilst the dialect components of the proverb have to be looked up individually. Admittedly, the use of many foreign phrases is élitist, but *crème de la crème* can be nicely ironical and anti-élitist, whilst CV is succinct and now indispensable. (Latin has the virtue of concision; most of Latin's social defects are in its supremacist past; now, enthusiasm for Latin teaching as a minority subject is rare and admirable.)

Végétatif
Végétatif relates to the physiological function controlled by the autonomic (F. *autonome, neuro-végétatif*) nervous system. Its activity is reflex and independent of the brain. Hence *signes végétatifs*, 'involuntary movements' (the 'sign', contrasted with 'symptom', is moving, hence here 'movements'). Note that *végétatif*, a commoner word in French than in English, is often translated as 'plant'.

Functional Sentence Perspective
It is significant that the *Introduction to Functional Sentence Perspective in Written and Spoken Communication* by Jan Firbas (Cambridge University Press, Cambridge, 1992, ISBN 0-521-37308-5),

which I warmly recommend, begins with a superb analysis of the emphases (prosodic prominence) in a paragraph and its translations in three languages (E, F, Cz) from Hugo's *Les Misérables*. (Jan Firbas, an outstanding linguist, is (like myself) a native of Janáček's town, Brno.) Functional Sentence Perspective, for which Firbas and his Brno colleagues have devised a comprehensive and suggestive parsing terminology and system, is concerned essentially with linguistic emphasis within the word order of a sentence, which includes its degree of informativeness (i.e. communicative dynamism), its emotiveness (Firbas's 'emotive factor'), foregrounding, and, in speech, its prosodic prominence; together with syntax and lexis, it contributes to meaning, and is therefore an important factor in translation theory; it is usually neglected except by the Leipzig School (Fleischmann and Neubert). Firbas's book is essential reading about every aspect of FSP; and for the translator, it includes useful passages on retrievability (the retrievability span should not normally exceed five clauses), the semantic factor, while meaning is distributed over a collocation ('light flooded', 'tears brimmed', 'swelled his bosom', 'a wave drifted', 'a fly settled' – both collocates should reflect this semantic affinity in the translation), and contrast (e.g. 'I liked the Continental and the Grand ... but I did not like the International'). Contrast is as important in FSP as in translation. It emerges from these studies that the more a word or lexical unit is displaced from its normal unmarked word order, the more emphasis it assumes, and therefore the more emphasis must be put on it in translation. Thus:

Dazzling white the picotees shone.
Blendend weiss leuchteten die Nelken. (G.)
Des fleurettes blanches brillaient éblouissantes. (F.)
Hvozdíky svítily oslnivou belí. (Cz.)

These four sentences appear to be in order of 'strange' or marked word order; the English gives most, the Czech least, emphasis on 'dazzling white'. Should the Czech translator have compensated?

A Tentative Order of Extracontextual Word Class Emphasis

I posit the following descending order of word class emphasis, which is designed to assist translators:

1st. Verbal nouns. (a cry, a drop)
2nd. Adjectival nouns. (loudness)
3rd. Abstract (conceptual) nouns. (capitalism)
4th. Common nouns. (book)
5th. Full verbs. (seize)
6th. 'Empty' verbs. (seize the opportunity, deliver a lecture; usually followed by a verbal noun)
7th. Adverbs. (loudly)
8th. Adjectives. (loud)
9th. Pronouns.

10th. Particles of phrasal verbs.
11th. Pronouns at end of sentences.
12th. Auxiliary verbs.
13th. Prepositions.
12th. Conjunctions.
13th. This, that.
14th. An, a.
Context can vastly change this order of emphasis or importance.

Languages and Tourism

The chairman of the British Tourist Authority is aware that 'if Britain is to be successful as a leading tourist destination, we must learn to speak to people in their own language'. What is equally important is the provision of multilingual brochures, leaflets, manuals etc. in shops, museums (the V and A is a model), galleries and public buildings, which requires a separate skill.

II
NOVEMBER 1992

Values

'What is interesting is the apparently strongly felt need among some of those who look at translations with more than a passing interest to apply labels to them such as 'good', 'bad', 'worse', etc. While such value-judgements may of themselves be interesting, of course . . . one is tempted to ask what they actually mean, from a 'scholarly' or 'objective' point of view. There is of course nothing wrong with having value-judgements; we all have them, after all. However, it does not require a scholar of translation to say that a translation is 'bad' or 'good' (whatever those terms may mean). Surely a more fruitful approach to any 'objective' study would be to accept those translations for what they are (texts which function in a particular way in a particular culture at a particular time) and then, if one wishes to go further than description, to attempt to explain the results; but not, surely, on the basis of 'I think this translation is better than that one'. The goals to be achieved by such an approach are questionable, to say the least (Julian Ross, p.203, *Translation and Literature*, see below).

I find the self-assurance of this passage, with its two 'of course's', its two 'surely's', its 'after all', its 'apparently', its 'actually', which fudge the issues, shallow and nauseating. It is a prime example of Gombrich's 'cultural relativism'. (See *Paragraphs on Translation*, p.165). I think it is the business of scholarship and criticism both to describe and to evaluate, mainly distinguishing the two processes. As for 'objectivity', coyly and puzzlingly twice put in inverted commas, it is Mr Ross's fantasy. Since translation is primarily concerned with truth, I think that 'goodness' and 'badness', which so worry Mr Ross, must be assessed in relation to accuracy.

Translation and Literature

The first number of *Translation and Literature*, edited by Stuart Gillespie (Edinburgh University Press, 1992) should by now be in every university library. It includes some excellent reviews, a fascinating document by Leopardi on the Right Language of Translation, and a typically provocative article by Douglas Robinson on the origins of Western 'translatology' (a lot of which I think he has invented).

The Met

The magnificent Metropolitan Museum of Art on Fifth Avenue in New York appears to be stubbornly monolingual. Not even non-English titles of paintings are given in their original languages, thus inviting confusion. A mysterious Monet entitled *The Mists* is given the alternative title *La Débacle*. The second language, Spanish – there are now more Spanish speakers than blacks in the States – is ignored. Yet the descriptions of the paintings – all in English – are exemplary.

Criticism

It seems obvious to me that what one wants first from a critic of a translation as of anything else, is a personal value-judgement, supported by a reasoned argument with examples. Where sensitivity and intelligence are combined, the objectivity is in the argument and the examples, but it is far from absolute; the subjectivity is a constituent of the judgement.

Eagleton and Literary Theory

'Fascism is a desperate attempt on the part of monopoly capitalism to abolish contradictions which have become intolerable' (*Literary Theory: An Introduction*, Terry Eagleton, Blackwell, p.66). This is a typical example of the sickening rhetoric which for eighty years influenced and tragically misled many idealistic and egalitarian communists all over the world, and Eagleton seriously maintains it, even now. His book is an attempt to replace 'moral' literary criticism (Arnold, Leavis) with the cultural relativism drawn from Foucault, Barthes, Derrida, Lacan, Bloom etc. – the further relation with populist, value-free minimal art and minimalist music (Glass, Nyman) has yet to be considered – and it has for nearly ten years had a strong influence on the heterodox literary establishment, and more recently on the literary 'translatologists'. It is the kind of bright iconoclastic book that liberal intellectuals welcome (they also gave him an Oxford chair for it), in spite of its frequently sneering and smearing attitude to literature as a humanity. The book has many references but virtually no quotations, neither from literature nor from criticism, let alone any literary judgements. (Incidentally, Heidegger is twice smeared ('it is *interesting* that') for his brief association with Nazism, although Eagleton makes no connection between his philosophy and his politics; Paul de Man's collaboration and antisemitism, however, are not mentioned, since he is approved of.)

Eagleton regurgitates everything, racily and skilfully, and since he debunks literature, and sees no qualitative difference between comics and tragic drama, the reader never learns anything about his literary standards, if he holds to any. However, 'it is quite possible that given a deep enough transformation of our [whose?] history, we may produce a society which is unable to get anything *at all* out of Shakespeare. His works might simply seem *desperately* [the italics are mine] alien, full of styles of thought and feeling which such a society found limited or irrelevant.'

This is poppycock. I can take hundreds of lines within hundred of speeches in Shakespeare, say:

Grief fills the room up of my absent child

Through tattered clothes small voices do appear

If you prick us, do we not bleed

which are impervious to time and place and concerned only with human behaviour. The reality is the opposite of Eagleton's vapid ruminations. Increasingly, over space and time, *Hamlet*, the *Flute* and the *Third of May* are being discovered and rediscovered. Eagleton is similarly perverse in his reference to Karl Marx being puzzled by the 'eternal charm' of ancient Greek art; such works have great psychological perception, as both Marx and Engels (who showed a profound appreciation of the Greek tragic dramatists), and Freud noted, however remote their social backgrounds. Lastly, Eagleton suggests that the structuralists, by analysing advertisements as well as 'literature' (as in fact Leavis and the Birmingham English school had done) deprived literature of its 'ontologically privileged status' (p.107), meaning its greatness. They didn't. But soon perhaps the post-structuralists will be deconstructing *Fidelio* into a text in favour of fascism, or of nothing at all.

Footnote: I have attacked Paul de Man's views on translation in two previous issues.

Raw Copy

John Chadburn, a former UN translator and co-author of Marina Orellana's *International Spanish-English English-Spanish* international glossary and handbook for translators, has pointed out to me that vocational translator courses are unwise if they mainly use edited material for their translation practice courses. More often than not, translators have to deal with ill-written, unstructured, often misspelt reports from technical experts who have no pretensions to a good writing style, and as they are translated, they have to be put into shape, by the translators, not the copy-editors.

Puerto Rico

On the occasion of the first international conference on translation in Puerto Rico, the Governor of the *Estado Libre Asociado de Puerto Rico*, literally translated as 'the Associated Free State', officially translated as 'the Commonwealth of Puerto Rico' issued a proclamation on 24 August declaring the day to be 'the day of professional translators and interpreters', and emphasising the importance of translation and the dignity of the profession in the state. It is a pity that the other United States have not yet even begun to take translation (so) seriously.

Quid Pro Quo and Quiproquo

Quid pro quo appears to exist only in English, where it means a 'reciprocal exchange' or 'something given in exchange', and, my helpful correspondent Richard Burrows of Malaga assures me, in Spanish, where it can only mean a 'slip of the tongue'; *quiproquo* exists in all the Romance languages, and in German, and typically means 'misunderstanding' and occasionally 'mistaken identity'.

Esperar
There seems to be some desperate cultural association in Spanish between *mañana* and *esperar*, which takes the future for granted.

The Museums of Florence
In spite of their huge receipts, neither the over-crowded and ill-lit Pitti nor the more active Uffizi have yet started to consider the question of communicating with their visitors, the greater number of whom are not Italian. Note that the name, *Gli Uffizi*, is transferred for English, translated for French (*les Offices*), translated for Castilian (*los Officios*), translated for Catalan (*los Uffizios*), naturalized for German (*Die Uffizien*). As for the Borghese Museum in Rome, it appears to be in such chaos (the staff appeal to visitors to protest against the closure of the first floor), I doubt whether translation has ever been heard of there.

Personification
Animism in languages, following animism in thought, continues to decline. Virtues, countries, rivers, cities, nature (the pathetic fallacy), even ships, tend no longer to be feminine, and translators have to take the trend into account. Nevertheless it appears possible to create personifications in translation quite effectively. On the Rome-Genoa express, there is a railway regulation displayed in four languages where *le mécanicien*, *die Lokomotive* and '*steam*' are respectively the subjects (in the appropriate languages) of a predicate approximately signifying 'propels the train'. Unfortunately I did not take down the complete extracts.

Translation's Role in National Identity
Translation's Role in National Identity is the title of a significant and controversial article by Wolf Lepennies in the *Times Higher* of October 2. Lepennies stresses the importance of translation in 'making the specificity of national cultures more visible and revealing their essential characteristics; translation should be a bulwark against a flood, say, of American English over Europe'. Where he becomes, for me at least, controversial is in his apparent approval of secondary translations (French versions of Livy into Spanish, English versions of Chinese into French). He readily accepts that the infidelity of translations has an important social and intellectual function; this is

undeniable, but he never indicates how much is lost by often unnecessary secondary translation, and that if 'cultures' were to be more accurately translated, nations would understand each other better, which is his expressed hope.

Saint Jerome

The beautiful and fascinating exhibition of 14th to 17th century paintings of Saint Jerome (Hieronymus) continues at the National Gallery till 13 December. St Jerome's (c.331 to 420) great achievement was to translate the Bible used for centuries by the Catholic Church directly into Latin (the Vulgate) from the original Greek and Hebrew. Further, in his Letter or Epistle (*Sendbrief*) 57 to Pammachius, he was the first to set out clearly and at length the principles of translation at the reader's level, that is 'sense for sense, and not word for word', thereby causing 'a storm of protest that followed him through the rest of his life'. (See, for instance, Nida's *Towards a Science of Translating*, p.13).

The National Gallery exhibition includes wonderful paintings by the great Georges de La Tour (candle lit intensity, blue and gold) and the fantastic Joachim Patenier (1524), who amongst many other things was the first landscape painter; furthermore, the generous programme contains an analysis of 15th century Italian art animal symbolism; some animals have contradictory meanings, and the human sense of animals (related to their size and their dangerousness) is usually evident.

Mona Baker

In Other Words: A Course Book on Translation by Mona Baker (1992, Routledge, London, 304pp) is a substantial and original contribution to translation studies. Designed as a coursebook for post-graduate translation students, it has sections on: equivalence at word and above word level; grammatical equivalence; textual equivalence; thematic and information structures; cohesion, and pragmatic equivalence. Each chapter is followed by exercises, most of which appear to assume that the reader will be translating from English; the book concludes with nine English non-literary texts, which are translated into foreign languages, four of them into Japanese, a brief glossary, and three comprehensive indices.

As I have previously indicated, it is not clear whether the book is primarily addressed to readers with English as their language of habitual use, and in fact a lot of it, while interesting, sensible and informative, is more pertinent to the student of linguistics than of translation; thus the section on Functional Sentence Perspective, with its just tribute to Firbas, barely relates the topic to translation, and, unlike Firbas (as I showed in the last issue), has no translation examples. Further, possibly in an attempt to avoid any reference to 'free' or 'literal' translation, there is no discussion of text typology or of the value of the language of the source language text, or of key-words, though Baker admits: 'You simply[!] cannot make any word mean whatever you want it to mean (p.206)'. It is assumed that the translator is only concerned with informative texts or advertisements, so it is rather disconcerting to suddenly find the reader being asked to analyze, adapt and translate an extract from *Othello*, for which she is ill-prepared, in a later exercise. Baker appears to assume that the trans-lator is as ignorant as the average reader, and is incapable of tracing a well-known remark of Clive of India in the *EB* or any dictionary of quotations, which together with dictionaries of collocations, synonyms, neologisms and modern quotations, amongst many others, is an essential translator's tool, as is the *EB* itself. Moreover, the outstanding translator Ralph Manheim, who died a month ago, would have disagreed with her remark: 'A good translator does not begin to translate until s/he has read the text at least once.'

That said, there is much to praise: a detailed and comprehensive discussion of collocations; some just remarks on punctuation, includ-ing the observation that French, like many other languages, does not use italics for emphasis (*'He* did it.' *C'est lui qui l'a fait.*); excellent hints on the translation of many idioms; the poverty of Arabic com-pared to the richness of English lexis; information flow; a discussion of Grice's principles of good communication, from the point of view of an at least cautious 'culturalist'. The book is far from Eurocentric, there are references to about fifty languages, and effective use is frequently made of Tiny Rowland's anti-Fayed diatribe.

Machine Translation and Machine Tools

Computers in Translation: A Practical Appraisal, edited by John Newton (Routledge, London, 1992) is essential, 'state of the art' (dare I coin a phrase?) reading for anyone interested in translation. John Newton, formerly a valued member of the Council of the Institute of Linguists, who eschews the revolting jargon, believes that the emer-gence of international networks of translation companies, tending to favour the spread of translation tools and translator workstations, is the most recent significant development.

Postscript

No one deliberately writes nonsense. There is no such thing as human or non-human nonsense. Everything makes symbolical sense. The more mistakes we sincerely and involuntarily make, the better. We can only genuinely learn (and remember) from our mistakes. Never be afraid of making mistakes. In translation, you have to make sense of everything (misprints, gibberish), particularly what appears o be nonsense. 'There is no such thing as a silly question' (Nida). There are only silly answers and silly non-answers. The story of progress is the story of making sense out of nonsense, or of learning from mistakes. The more questions we ask, the better. The nicest people are the silliest, who provoke the most productive answers.

The above reflections are inspired by Marshall Morris's *With Translation in Mind*, a paper he read in San Juan in Puerto Rico which will eventually be published, hopefully not as late as the average conference proceedings. Morris's paper, like Walter Benjamin's essay *The Task of the Translator*, is the exception to the rule that writing on translation should always include translation examples; in fact it is a conceptual background to translation, and indicates pertinent references to the thought of Saussure (language as one aspect of communication), Marcel Mauss (starting with gifts, the continuous need for reciprocity), R.G. Collingwood, a fine writer on aesthetics, J.S. Bruner, Carlo Ginzburg and the great anthropologist Evans-Pritchard, who wrote on what he called 'the translation of culture'. I also warmly recommend Marshall Morris's 'What Problems? On Learning to Translate' in *New Departures in Linguistics* (ed. George Wolf, 1992, Garland Publishing Inc., New York and London).

III
JANUARY 1993

Halliday

M. A. K. Halliday's *Language Theory and Translation Practice* in the Trieste *Rivista internazionale* (see last issue) marks a welcome return to his writing on translation. (Halliday is the only living British linguist profiled in the indispensable Fontana *Biographical Companion to Modern Thought* (ed. Alan Bullock and R. B. Woodings), which however fails to point out that his capital achievement is to have put semantics at the centre of linguistics, and meaning at the heart of language, at a time when semantics was being banished from at least American and much British linguistics.) Halliday's view of translation theory is refreshingly unorthodox: according to him, a translator defines a theory of translation as 'how you *should* translate; it tends to be normative and evaluative, whereas a theory of translation in linguistics is about what happens *when* you translate, and is explanatory and descriptive.' This is right, and I think one is incomplete without the other, and that the linguist's theory is dependent on the translator's. Halliday states that linguistics cannot offer a theory of translation equivalence [I think any translation equivalence has to take in far more than linguistics] but a theory of context, which he proceeds to unfold in a discussion of three extensive translation examples. The essay is fascinating.

Translation in South Africa

Translation and Interpreting in South Africa, a report by Alet Kruger of the Department of Linguistics, University of South Africa, Pretoria, for the South African Translators' Institute deserves attention. It is comprehensive; here are some extracts:

'English and Afrikaans, the two official languages, and nine African Languages (Zulu, Xhosa, Swati, Ndebele, North Soto, South Soto, Tswana, Tsonga, Venda) have to be accommodated . . . Translation between English and Afrikaans dominates the market . . . The speakers of the African languages tend to favour English as medium of intercultural communication, neglecting their own languages, unlike the Afrikaners . . . If these people want to demand equal rights [*sic*] they will obviously have to develop their languages terminologically . . . In order for these languages to be meaningfully employed in the training of translators, they will have to achieve a level of terminological development akin to that of Afrikaans and English.' This is true, but there is a patronising note in this report which I dislike. I think the difficulties are too large for SATI, and, as I have said before, it is high time the SA government set up a National Language

16

Planning Council. It is intolerable that there should still be only the two official white languages in South Africa.

Modern Art in Rome

The National Museum of Modern Art (*Museo nazionale di art moderna*) is a misnomer, since it mainly displays modern Italian art, to which it is a magnificent introduction. There is a superb variety of pictures by Sironi, Balla, Guttuso, Severini, de Chirico, Morandi (not even one jug!), and two lovely landscapes by Ottone Rosai. However, in the whole building, there only appears to be one translation, viz. the notice on the bar: *E vietato recarsi in giardino con tazze e bicchieri* Close translation: 'It is forbidden! (here again, *das Betreten ist verboten*, see Rupert Brooke's *Grantchester*) to make one's way into the garden with cups and glasses.' Displayed translation: 'Please do not carry glasses and cups in the garden.' My preferred translation: 'Please do not take cups or glasses into the garden.' Note again the warmth and friendliness of the 'untranslatable' English 'please', to which I wrote a hymn of praise in this journal many years ago. There are excellent descriptive leaflets to the main pictures in each room, but why only in Italian?

The Fourth Mode of Reading

The fourth mode of reading (see p.1) is skimming or gisting which typically means reading only headings, sub-titles, first sentences of paragraphs, the concluding paragraph or sentence (or, like John Kennedy, every two lines out of five?) and looking for contrasts and enumerations. (Acknowledgements to Lucio Sponza.)

Linguistic Nationalism

Everything in language is fuzzy, not least the difference between a language and a dialect, which can only be settled politically. After the Catalans and the Castilians, the Czechs and the Slovaks, we now have the Croats furiously maintaining their linguistic differences from the Serbs, which amounts to a few minor vocabulary differences and the use of different alphabets. And so the horror goes on.

Contrast and Continuation

Contrast and/or continuation is the basis of discourse progression, and too many French connectives include both: thus *d'autre part* may be 'moreover' or 'on the other hand'; *alors que* may be 'when' or 'whereas'; *tout en (faisant)* may be 'while' or 'although'. Typically, the paragraph has to be examined to make sense of the sentences.

Satie

Constant Lambert's *Music Ho!* was a fine book, but the nonsense he

wrote about Satie misled me for many years. *Gymnopédie* has become
a musical cliché unless it is exceptionally well played (so has *Parade*)
but listen to the intensely frail and melancholy, wispy melodies, sung
by Marjanne Kweksilber (and to the great *Socrate*); disgracefully, no
translations are provided with the texts (Lamartine as well as Cocteau
in the 1980 Philips record. In my opinion texts and translations are
essential for all vocal music, live as well as recorded. As for Satie,
don't know whether he is a great composer, his range is limited, but
am sure he is an immortal; no one else has ever expressed such deep
pessimism, and his music will be played forever.

Concision

I have long maintained that typically, the qualities of a good full
translation are accuracy and economy. I think that concision, which i
not the same as brevity (it depends how much there is to say), is a basic
element in all good writing, and that it is therefore universal. This wa
recently volubly and expansively denied by some Italian colleagues
who insisted on a thousand tedious variations on the theme that
candidate should not be accepted unless they had the requisite
qualities to be admitted to the shortlist (shortlisted!) for a chair. I think
that a last stage in revision consists of paring down one's translation
getting rid of redundancies and superfluities, intensifiers, inflated
jargon, clichés and cliché metaphors, hyperbole, twaddle, so that what
remains is packed with meaning and has greater force. Some of this i
easier in English than in other languages (e.g. the example in thi
paragraph) but it applies in all languages.

**Ambiguity (see also p. 218 in *A Textbook of Translation*, where I
attempt a comprehensive survey)**

Ambiguity arises when a segment of language has two or mor
meanings, or is otherwise obscure; where the ambiguity is evidentl
due to clumsy writing, the short answer to the translation difficulty i
to offer the most reasonable clarification, and where appropriate t
add a note giving alternative versions and the reasons for the preferre
choice. According to Cobbett, quoted by Fowler, the wrong placing o
words leads to the greatest number of misconceptions: howeve
Fowler's examples (e.g. 'I can recommend the candidate for the pos
for which he applies with complete confidence') would not give
translator any more trouble than a reader.

Other causes of ambiguity are:

1. The use of a word with two senses, both of which might reason
ably suit the context: *Le déficit de la Sécurité Sociale est beaucou,
plus fort que prévu* ('is much larger than expected, foreseen, allowe
for, provided for, scheduled, planned'). Here the translator has t
decide, on the basis of the full context.

2. The use of a word that has a general (hold-all) and a specific sense, both of which are 'possible'. (Most translation moves continuously between the more general and the more specific, between over-translation and undertranslation.) (*Les agents recherchaient une gestion plus efficace de leurs finances*. 'Both parties' or 'The brokers'? The ambiguity is usually ironed out in the context.)

3. The use of an adjective grammatically qualifying either one or more nouns: 'slow neutrons or electrons' (the referential meaning is that only neutrons can be slow); *cliniques et infirmières libérales* ('clinics and private nurses') – *libérales* is used in the sense of 'self-employed', which cannot apply to clinics. (But note *école libre*, 'private school'). In many other cases, the reader or translator can only be guided by common sense, but normally, one assumes that the adjective refers to both nouns.

4. The use of a present participle in an absolute construction with its own subject. (e.g. 'This being so . . .', *Les facteurs de production étant rares, les biens économiques le sont aussi*; 'as/when input is scarce, so are economic goods.') The construction, inherited from Latin, is more common in French than in English, and is therefore usually translated by an adverbial clause, which in principle may be causal (since, as, because), conditional (if), concessive (although), temporal (when, while), contrastive (whilst, whereas). The ambiguity has to be resolved through context and/or fact. In my experience, it is most frequently both a causal and a temporal clause, as in: *L'unité française renaissant, l'opinion pèsera de nouveau* ('As French unity revives (with the rebirth of French unity), public opinion will again carry weight'). When a past principle is used, there is usually no ambiguity (e.g. *Cela fait*; 'when that's done/after that was done') in the context.

5. The use of a word which conceals an obvious lexical gap. How do so many foreign languages carry on without distinguishing 'politics' from 'policy'? In the numerous ambiguous cases I have come across, the only 'tip' I can give is that it is likely to translate as 'politics' if the noun (*Politik, politica* etc.) is qualified by a definite article, and as 'policy' if it is qualified by a determiner (*cette, sa* etc.) or a possessive/genitive (*de, di, des*, etc.).

6. The use of pronouns, where the reader cannot be sure of their referents. This ambiguity is more common in English than in languages that have two or three genders for inanimate nouns. For translation into English, it is quite common to replace the pronoun with a (repeated) noun.

7. The use of the negative, which is intrinsically ambiguous unless the context is clear (e.g. 'The letter was not sent because of information received.').

8. The use of sentences, where the field of operation of a word or

phrase is not clear (e.g. 'He needs more suitable friends.' *Il a besoin d'amis plus convenables; il a besoin de plus d'amis qui lui conviennent*). In long sentences, the sentence should be rewritten, not merely repunctuated.

9. The mention of isolated figures or geographical features. The omitted objects or standard systems have to be specified. Bear in mind that many 'English' geographical features are replicated in various parts of the ex-British Empire, particularly the US (Paris, Winchester etc.).

The Translation of Long Sentences into English
I have already suggested that in non-authoritative texts, English sentences tend to be shorter than those in other European languages, and long French sentences may be recast if they lead up to a final theme, so that in the translation, the initial theme is followed by a passive verb. In other cases, the sentence can be split up and the linear sequence approximately retained (thus also retaining the various emphases), provided the connectives are strengthened. Thus: *Parce que l'indépendance nationale se manifeste par des signes que* (Because national independence shows itself by signs that) *l'Histoire a progressivement consacrés au fil du temps – et la monnaie* (History has progressively established in the course of time – and currency) *est, avec l'impôt, l'armée et le drapeau, un de ces signes – le débat sur* (is, with taxation, the army and the flag, one of these signs – the debate about) *Maastricht bute en permanence sur le problème de la politique monétaire* (Maastricht continually comes up against the problem of monetary policy) *dont les Francais voient mal si elle échappera aux autorités nationales* (in regard to which the French cannot see how it will escape the national authorities). *Ce qu'affirment bon nombre des partisans du 'non'.* (Which is what many partisans of the 'no' affirm.) (A. Vernholes, *Le Monde*).

Suggested translation: 'National independence finds its expression in features progressively established by history in the course of time; currency, together with taxation, the armed forces and the flag, is one of these features. For this reason, the discussion about Maastricht constantly comes up against the question of monetary policy. In fact the French cannot imagine how monetary policy will ever elude the control of national authorities. This is what a large number of the treaty's opponents are saying.' (I avoid using 'problem' as it's a vogue-word in this sense.)

The obvious alternative is to begin the passage with the main proposition and to follow it with two parallel causal clauses: 'The discussion about Maastricht constantly comes up against the question of monetary policy, for two reasons: (a) national independence finds its expression in features progressively established by history in the course of time; (b) currency, together with taxation, the army and the flag, is one of these features. In fact.. (etc.). I slightly prefer the second version, as it is more clearly set out.

The Translation of Songs

It is a pity that compilers of programme notes and inlay cards cannot agree to select sober close 'plain prose', parallel, line by line translations for songs. At a recent 'Young Brahms' concert, the translations varied between (a) these, (b) amateurish rhymes, reducing the lines to unrecognisable inaccuracy (e.g. 'With all thy charms endearing' for *Ich will es selbst dir sagen*), and (c) outright but delightful howlers such as 'You cast immortality on me through your lips, Yet I dread(!) cooling down! for *Du, die Unsterblichkeit durch die Lippen mir sprühte, Wehe, wehe mir Kühlung zu* (close translation: 'You who sprinkled immortality on me with your lips, now breathe, breathe coolness upon me) – typical romantic nonsense, by Ludwig Holty, as it is. Reluctantly, I admit that there is no strict correlation between the value of a *lied's* music and its words, but there are an exceptionally high number of fine *lieder* written by Goethe, Heine and Platen, who are great poets. (Some, but not me, would add Mörike, Eichendorff and Schiller.)

Fear of Literal Truth

Soundbite from BBC interview: *Es mag Länder geben, die sich auf die Füsse getreten fühlen*, interpreted as: 'There may be Länder that feel disturbed.'

Descriptive Terms, Collocations and Technical Terms

It is an unconvincing arugment to maintain that *inflationäre Spannungen* cannot be translated as 'inflationary tensions', simply because 'inflationary tensions' is not a common collocation nor a technical term (any more than *inflationäre Spannungen* is); nor can it be translated as 'inflationary pressures', since 'pressure' is outside the semantic range of *Spannung*; the translation is more likely to be 'inflationary tensions' which is a descriptive term (tensions associated with inflation'), but only a wider context can determine the matter. In contrast, 'inflationary trend' (*tendance inflationniste*) is a standard collocation; 'inflationary gap' (*écart inflationniste*) is a technical term.

Translators as Professionals

'It is impossible, except in extreme cases, to draw a line between what counts as a good translation and what counts as a bad one. Every translation has points of strength and points of weakness.' (*In Other Words*, Mona Baker, p.7) If ever there was a *non sequitur*, it's the second sentence. Would Mona Baker make the same comment on the work of doctors and engineers? How can translators be regarded as qualified professionals and be required to take examinations in the light of such a remark? (Mona Baker is chair of the Education and Examinations Committee of the ITI!) What are 'extreme cases'? How fine is the 'line'? Are there standards of translation or not?

Why Translation Theory

Not to propound theories of translation, but mainly to help people who translate to make decisions by indicating all the possible choices and their merits and demerits, and making recommendations.

Some Teaching Points (more to come)

1. There must be a lesson for the day – at least two or three concrete translation points, rarely the same ones, learned by each student.

2. Start by asking the students what the text is about. The answer should be 'referential', not 'linguistic'. Thus a text entitled *Dix années d'innovations financières* may be about deregulation in the 80s in Europe, not about ten years of financial innovation.

3. A teacher inevitably changes her mind (in moderation) about the translation of one or two segments of a translation she has marked when she goes over this in class, and students should expect this (though they prefer marking certainties). If it happens often, the confidence of the class will be lost.

4. Everything has to be understood, at least by the translator, and not merely translated. No difficulty in translating *la Charte de Paris* (extract from Maastrict Treaty), but not one student had even tried to find out what it was, or had thought that the TL readership might want to know, perhaps in a footnote. (The charter of Paris dotted the i's of the Helsinki Final Act. Acknowledgement to Richard Nice.)

5. You have to look for possible generalisations, and when you find them, quote or invent further examples drawn from your generalisation.

6. It is ironical that while you continually insist on the importance of writing the target language well, and attack the mistrust of 'literature' and its style, you avoid literary language, the faded words of a previous period (a misquotation from T. S. Eliot), the refined genteel register of: bring to the fore, beget, wonder, odour, crave (unless used technically), bound for, destined for, comely. In twenty years of teaching in a technical translation course, I noted that the best translators were usually the most elegant writers of English and the ones most sensitive to language. No wonder I am dubious about translatologist X and translatologist Y.

Die Wahrheit, die Wahrheit – 'Be Truthful, or the Truth, Friend'

The retranslation of *A la recherche du temps perdu* (by D. J

Enright) as *In Search of Lost Time* is not a new ideological turn nor a reinterpretation of Proust by a structuralism-besotted reader but a timely assertion of the truth – albeit not the whole truth, which is something like 'lost/wasted/spoilt time' ('lost' after 'search' being most probable) or 'time lost/wasted/spoilt' but that is due to the imperfect nature of translation. There will be no going back to *In Remembrance of Things Past*, beautiful as that was – but Proust protested against this version and wanted Scott Moncrieff to change it. Ironically, this is at a time when many translatologists are turning away from the truth towards the purely ideological interpretation of translation, which has its own partial truth. The Proust retranslation is important, and marks a turn to scientific method (rather than the pursuit of culture and ideology) in translation.

Theories of Translation

At last, over twenty years after the appearance of the anthology of (mainly) literary translation, *Das Problem des Übersetzens* (ed. by H. J. Storig), Rainer Schulte and John Biguenet have produced an equivalent in English. *Theories of Translation: An Anthology of Essays from Dryden to Derrida* (University of Chicago Press, 1992), an immediately indispensable work for a student of translation. It gives extracts from 21 writers: ten German, four French, two Russian, two Spanish and three English, nine of them duplicating Störig, Levy inexplicably missing though present in the useful Select Bibliography, where some non-literary translation theorists also appear. There is some fine 'new' material by Dryden, a brilliant and strange piece by Hugo Friedrich, who thinks the stuffy Malherbe created a style in opposition to that of Seneca's original. I note that Schleiermacher, the first writer who distinguishes non-literary translation, also makes a sharp distinction between interpretation and translation which would surprise the ESIT–Sorbonne school. Peter Szondi writes a subtle and disputable analysis of Celan's translation of Shakespeare's Sonnet, 'Let not my love be called idolatry' . . . I could have done without the Derrida, but then I would, wouldn't I.

The Lost Transposition

'Abstract noun plus *de/di/von* plus abstract noun becomes adjective plus abstract noun' is the one not uncommon transposition which Vinay and Darbelnet, but not W. Friederich (the excellent *Die Technik des Übersetzens*) forgot. I suspect it occasionally works for any language pair, and can be applied flexibly according to context. Examples: *Contradictions d'intérêt*, 'contradictory (conflicting) interests', 'interesting contradictions'; *die Schönheit der Natur*, 'natural beauty', 'beautiful nature' (not to mention 'the beauty of nature'!).

The Morality of Art

The classical text for the moral view of art is, I suppose, the Preface and the *premier placet* (first petition to Louis XIV) of Molière's *Tartuffe: L'emploi de la comédie est de corriger les vices des hommes . . . Le devoir de la comédie est de corriger les hommes en les divertissant.* I would translate the second sentence as 'The duty of drama is to correct men while diverting them.' The sense of *comédie, corriger* and *divertir* has not changed much since the 17th century; 'divert' could be replaced by 'amuse'. Molière being the most anti-sexist of writers, it would be pedantic to replace 'men' by 'people' etc. The 'classical' text for the opposing view is 'All art is quite useless' (Preface, *The Picture of Dorian Grey*, Oscar Wilde) by the author of . . . *The Ballad of Reading Gaol*. Coming from him, that's rich.

Authoritative Texts

Authoritative texts can be categorised as aesthetic ('literature') and non-aesthetic (official statements). All have to be closely translated, the former for sense and sound, the latter for sense only. Authoritative statements in philosophy, politics, science, history etc. come somewhere in between, and while the precise sense of the original is paramount, its sound must also claim attention; but typically, there are fewer decisions to be made.

Traduttore, Traditore

'Translators, to lay the old adage to rest once and for all [*sic*], have to be traitors, but most of the time they don't know it, and nearly all of the time they have no choice, not as long as they remain within the bounds of the culture that is theirs by birth or adoption – not, therefore as long as they try to influence the evolution of that culture, which is an extremely [*sic*] logical thing for them to want to do.' (p.13 *Translation, Rewriting and the Manipulation of Literary Fame*, André Lefevere, Routledge, 1992).

Notes: (1) Translators are not traitors when they attempt to translate accurately; when the result is substantially short of being accurate, as may be the case in poetry, it may be treacherous. (2) The 'old adage' is always valid in the case of consciously or unconsciously inaccurate translation; it will never be 'laid to rest.' (3) This adage, as well as *les belles infideles*', demonstrates that translation is, amongst other things, a moral endeavour. (4) I do not think a translator can abandon his culture, but when he translates (or retranslates the Proust title), he is concerned with the truth rather than his own or 'the other' culture.

The Translation of Irony

Irony in translation is lost unless it is perceived and understood. I suspect it is not used in languages that have had little contact with others, and/or where a religious constraint against lying precludes it. Basil Hatin has pointed out that Arabic readers normally take sentences literally, and therefore misinterpret the sophisticated irony that appears in Western writing. Adjectives like 'interesting', 'remarkable', 'curious', 'odd' are misunderstood. Sentences like 'The Israeli government can take all credit for . . .' are construed as Israeli propaganda, where in fact they are ironical. Innocence of irony is the glory of little children, who always believe what you say and possibly the handicap of speakers of languages who have little contact with other languages.

IV
MARCH 1993

German Translation Teaching Textbooks

Übersetzen lehren and lernen mit Büchern (ed. F. G. Hönigs, 1987, Groos, Heidelberg) is a useful review of German translation textbooks and the didactic principles they should embody. Unfortunately it is short on translation examples; Christine Nord frequently condemns the way that translations and variants are produced without once exemplifying them. Little reference is made to the most practical of these books, W. Friederich's *Technik des Übersetzens*. However, the bibliographies are helpful for anyone teaching from or into German.

John Desmond Gallagher, who contributes, is the remarkable *Lebende Sprachen* reviewer who writes equally well, and helpfully, if rather pedantically, in three languages; he has written over 400 articles and half a dozen translation textbooks.

Tracking Metaphors

If you can't find an equivalent metaphor in a bilingual, then try a monolingual dictionary. Thus, for *monter sur le podium* (climb on to the podium!): *devenir champion, vainqueur après une épreuve sportive* (becomes the champion, the victor after a sporting event).

Teaching or Revision Tips (continued)

Does your translation (text, sentences, clauses) make sense? Does it sound convincing? Can you visualize it all (a) in reality, that is, in real life or in your imagination? (b) on paper, in the appropriate context (periodical, advertisement, technical report, private commission, or whatever)?

A Hunch

I suspect that three times out of ten you should translate *choix* as 'decision', and *proposer* as 'recommend'. So much for literalism.

A Mismatch

In bilingual dictionaries and perhaps in the conventional wisdom, *neugierig* is equated with 'curious'. In some contexts this is right, but in others, 'curious' means 'I'd quite like to know' and *neugierig* is 'inquisitive', up to 'I can hardly wait to find out'. Note too the exceptional sound and the prolonged tenseness of *Gier* differentiates between the two words.

Environmental Rights

Human, animal and environmental or natural rights are in the background of translation, language and reality. Terms such as 'cabbage' and 'vegetable', when seriously used of incapacitated people, infringe these rights (in French and German there are thankfully no equivalent metonyms) and have to be avoided, more precisely rendered, or at least commented upon in a medical translation. But I find PVS, permanent vegetative state, acceptable.

André Lefevere

André Lefevere's entertaining and instructive *Translation, Rewriting and the Manipulation of Literary Fame* (1992, Routledge, London and New York) is the first in a series entitled *Translation Studies*, edited by Susan Bassnett and André Lefevere. The main thesis of the series is that 'Translation is, "of course" a rewriting of an original text (like editing, anthologising, adaptation and, to a lesser extent, criticism).' Rewritings are 'undertaken in the service of power'. 'All rewritings reflect a certain ideology and a certain poetics and as such manipulate literature to function in a given society in a given way.' It all sounds too mechanical and determined, and allows little scope for individuality, a fresh 'science of translating', the new development of a scientific method based on logic, facts, universal rights and other more disputable non-cultural factors. Historically, there is much truth in it (and Lefevere is mainly concerned with the past), but even then it is too sweeping.

Lefevere stands out from other members of the Manipulation School (Lambert, Hermans, Toury, Bassnett, Kittel etc.) in offering a large number of excellent translation examples and in going easy with the jargon, though five 'parameters of discourse' within three pages seems excessive. He is interesting on patronage and canonization, though apparently unaware that Marx canonized Balzac long before Lukacs; he gives fascinating examples of the retranslations of Aristophanes' *Lysistrata* in accordance with the moral 'censorship' of various periods; he shows how Homer and Catullus have been re- or mis-translated, though he does not appear to recognize the 'mis-'; he reviews the re-editing of Anne Frank's diaries, and the selective anthologizing of African poets; finally, he describes how Karl Gutzkow had to 'doctor' *Dantons Tod* in order to get Büchner any hearing at all in middle class German theatres. Lefevere's reading and range of languages is enormous, his writing lively and 'uninhibited', and whilst many instances 'function in a given society is a given way', they could sometimes be regarded simply as gross and unnecessary distortions and mistranslations.

A Truism

For literary as for non-literary texts, there is a high correlation between writing and translating ability.

Transferred Words

Transferred words denoting natural or processed products normally retain their original meaning (tomatoes, potatoes, even tangerines – oranges from Tangiers). When they are implicated in social organization, however (liaison, commissariat) they often acquire new specialized senses and may, as in the case of commissariat, i.e. office of supplies for the forces, lose all previous senses.

Literary and Non-literary Translation

The distinction between literary and non-literary translation, imagination and reality, is more clear cut than that between all other types of translation. Granted that both types of texts can be tested against their originals, literary translation is often exempt from the second type of control, which is the real world. In principle, all statements in literature are figurative; the connotations of words are likely to be more significant than their denotations; language is idiolect, and its identity has to be respected; distinctions between synonyms are important; all sounds come alive, and may even have a meaning in conflict with the sense. Finally all narrative is allegory; it has moral force, is therefore a comment on behaviour. J. B. Priestley's naturalistic 'well made' play, *An Inspector Calls*, has since its first production in 1945 been played in a naturalistic style. Now its new National Theatre director, Stephen Daldry, has suddenly and brilliantly translated its 'non-literary' naturalism into an allegorical and symbolical expressionism, often in the style of Greek tragedy. It is a powerful and moving production, and the sometimes flat, rather banal language is forcefully in contrast with the high poetic style one might expect in such a production. The play is torn wide open, every gesture and sentence have an increased symbolical charge.

Semantic Slippage or Jargon

Many media words appear to be slipping continuously towards a slough. Thus John Birt, D.-G. of the BBC (no less) in a recent message to his staff: 'We have laid out our vision of the BBC's role in this rapidly changing (new) world; we shall deliver value for money; we shall deliver an effective BBC; we shall take hold of our own destiny; an even more creative BBC; deliver our goals; a programme strategy review; as creatively as possible against a background of changes in society and in the rest of broadcasting; channel strategies against which our future achievements can be measured; a sharper sense of our own performance; against our strategic aims; creative and collaborative, highlighting achievements as well as identifying and solving problems; to deliver these aims; the overall theme is focus and involvement.' This is junk language.

Teaching Tips

Never 'commit' a faux ami without mentally adding a back-translation of the correct and the incorrect translation.

Thus: *skurril*; scurrilous; ludicrous; *gemein (niedrig, grob verletzend)*. Never explain a new word without adding its word family (pain (ob.) pain, painful, painfully), or stating that 'it is on its own'. Words are best learned through association or contrast.

Menachem Dagut

A Teacher's Grammar of the English Verb by Menachem Dagut (edited by Batia Laufer; Haifa University Press, 1992) is addressed to teachers of English to native Hebrew speakers, but any teacher of English would profit from such a clear, plain and jargon-free exposition of the uses of the modern English verb, where Hebrew is merely incidentally used as the language of illustration, and each page is rich in examples that all have the implications of speech. The chapter on verb and particle combinations, which includes phrasal verbs and nouns, is particularly enlightening. Menachem Dagut was a fine Israeli linguist who wrote two outstanding articles on the translation of metaphor. He was also a lovely man.

Translating Nonsense Verse

All nonsense verse has a resonance of sense, and the unfortunately anonymous translator of *Air du rat* ('The Rat's Song'), which like several of Léon-Paul Fargue's poems has been exquisitely set by Erik Satie, has preserved both the resonance and the semblance of sense:

Abi Abirounière	Ro Rodentian
Qui que tu n'étais dou?	Who what were you not then?
Une blanche monère	A white ratian
Un jo	A love
Un joli goulifon	A lovely goulifon
Un oeil	An eye
Un oeil à son pépère	An eye of his daddy
Un jo	A love
Un joli goulifon	A lovely goulident.

The translation is more 'sensible' (rodent, rat) than the original, but why not?

Martyn Hill, the fine singer, has pointed out that the translator of Fargue's *Ludion* has missed out by transferring the title; 'bottle-imp' that is, the genii in the bottle, might give a sufficient resonance of sense.

Minority Languages

Ann Corsellis, the Principal Consultant to the Nuffield Projects and

the sole *animatrice* of the Institute of Linguistics Bilingual Skills
Certificate and Certificate in Community Interpreting, has pointed out
that the term 'community languages' for ethnic minorities is losing
ground, since it is increasingly confused with EC languages and disliked
by those who speak them; 'minor', 'rare' and 'esoteric' for Asian and
African languages are inaccurate and pejorative. I suggest that the only
appropriate superordinate term is 'UK minority languages'.

Tangente
How to translate *tangente*, the term that is currently dominating
Italian politics? Kickback? Milan is the *tangentopoli*, the 'bribesville'
of the North.

The Vatican Museums
In the Sistine Chapel, nothing is written, let alone translated. In the
Raphael Rooms, the light is so dim that nothing can be read. In the
Museum of Contemporary Art, all titles remain in their original
languages. (There is an arresting *Crucifissione* by Ottone Rosai of a
man in working clothes being crucified.) The mass is in the vernacular,
but the Church still appears to mistrust translation.

Les Gens du Passage
Les gens du passage, edited by Christine Pagnoulle (1992), has
come out in a handsome format and can be obtained for 500 Belgian
francs from Départment d'Anglais, Université de Liège, 3 place
Cockerill, B-4000 Liège, Belgium. It includes some interesting
articles, both with and against the wind, on philosophical and literary
translation (Baudelaire, Heaney, Duras, medieval texts), translation
tools, and translation as a profession. A good buy. (There is also an
article of mine.)

Parallèles
Parallèles, the civilized and varied annual translation journal of
the Geneva School of Translation and Interpretation (ETI, 102 bd
Carl-Vogt, CH-1211 Geneva 4) is now in its fifteenth year. Its latest
number has a fascinating article by Ingrid Alksnis, *La Sentinelle
oder Le Gardien de la Porte* showing how Alexandre Vialatte
revised his translation of Kafka's short story or parable *Vor dem
Gesetz* twenty-one years after its publication in 1955. In these 'many
years', 'his attitude towards the original changed very much in
favour of a translation that was more faithful to the syntax', if I may
translate Ms Alknis as literally. Ms Alknis gives various reasons: the
story, first a sketch of *The Trial*, became autonomous, therefore
needed greater care and concision (*Geschlossenheit?*); no
concessions to agreeable presentation; the echo of the original has to

be stirred (*erweckt?* Benjamin). And I think the increasing scientific impact on literary translation.

Faded Language

A language at any stage (*tout état de langue*) appears to be 'full of', i.e. has some faded words of yesteryear, slightly literary, slightly romantic which the translator has to dust down; thus *prémices*, not 'first fruits' but 'early indications'. Much of this faded romanticism was swept away by Hemingway sixty years ago.

Italian-English Translation

The excellent manuals by Christopher Taylor and John Dodds have been quickly followed by a third, *Translating Texts: From Theory to Practice* by Margherita Ulrych (1992, Cideb, Rapallo, ISBN 88 7754 070 2).

Language International

Language International, published by Benjamins and edited by Geoffrey Kingscott (Praetorius Ltd, 5 East Circus Street, Nottingham NG1 5AH), is a bright language monthly and has a nice mixture of articles, news, interviews, reviews, calendars and reports on the latest technology. In Vol. 2, No. 6, Dec. 1990, there is an excellent article on '*The Translation of Names and Titles*' and an Endpiece on the moral responsibility of translators, both by Geoffrey Kingscott. I quote from the latter: 'I am wary about introducing the moral dimension into translation, since who knows where it should end . . . The translator is like an advocate . . . and more than likely will have to appear for a villain . . . There must be no skimping or shirking, just because we do not really approve . . . of the cigarette manufacturer wanting to promote his products in Third World countries [here I am horrified]. What translators must do is to maintain their detachment and do a professional job, which means (perhaps) putting the client's view across, however repugnant.'

I disagree with all these statements. I think that the moral factor in any job is important, and no one should hesitate to mention it. (Not to do so is as old fashioned as the taboo on mentioning God, money, particularly one's own salary, sex and one's own politics.) The translator may appear for as many villains as she likes, but she must not translate a statement that is morally repugnant to her, without making it clear (unless this is unnecessary) outside the text that she does not endorse the statement. I do not think that anyone's 'detachment' is either desirable or possible, and I think that the translator is always bound by the Human Rights declarations, which are still developing, and which will be followed by universal animal and ecological rights declarations. Further, she must never reproduce as her own a statement that she knows to be factually or morally untrue. As for 'who knows where it should end?', I am always hopeful that any discussion with action on the 'moral dimension' may lead to a little less injustice and inequality.

Recettes de Cuisine
Cookbook recipes or political recipes for dirty tricks? Only the context will tell.

V
MAY 1993

Diagrams

I am continually surprised by the number of students who translate a page with hardly a glance at the illustrations, diagrams, tables, graphs or even the little *Economist* picture insets at the top of the page. It is a kind of graphic illiteracy. A sentence like *la facture énergetique se dégrade (– 11%)* is mistranslated as 'the energy bill has decreased by 11%', when the table below makes it clear that the deficit has increased by 11%.

Professions and *Professionels*

In a report on French foreign trade in 1991, the item *biens d'équipement professionels* (lit. 'occupational capital goods') as a diagram heading appears puzzling. It includes *machines, matériel électrique, électronique professionnelle, navale et aeronautique, matériel de précision* (machinery, electrical equipment, industrial electronic equipment, shipbuilding and aeronautic plant, precision goods?). A possible translation therefore might be, selecting an appropriate superordinate term from the five hyponyms or subordinate terms: 'engineering capital goods', since all items relate to engineering. On the other hand, 'industrial' is a more general term than 'engineering', and it is close to the French. Therefore I think 'industrial capital goods', contrasting with 'intermediate goods' and 'vehicles and transport equipment' (*biens de transport*) a more suitable translation. (Acknowledgements to Richard Nice.) Note that a default translation is often arrived at by looking for opposites and contrasts. For my part, I find the word *profession*, not to mention *Beruf* and 'profession', a frequent irritation; it is permeated and stuffed with Man's (*sic*) snobberies. Where English puts 'socio-economic', French has *socio-professionnel* as well as *socio-économique*. In the socio-economic groups, the French *professions intermédiaries* is the English 'intermediate (junior and non-manual) occupations'. ('Intermediate professions' is mere translationese.) Whilst the primary meaning of *profession* is 'occupation', it rises to 'vocation' in *formation professionnelle* (vocational training) and goes down to business in *adresse professionnelle*, 'business address' and to 'trade' in *journal professionnel*, 'trade paper', *association professionnelle*, 'trade association'. As for German, it appears to flutter between the posh *Berufung* (vocation), *Beruf* (occupation) and *Gewerbe*, the oldest profession in the world. Remain the poor translators, asserting themselves as a profession, and 'the professionals', a nauseating media-word. For all

33

that, 'she'll do a professional job' is indispensable in contrast with 'amateur', and how low that word often sinks.

The Beloved Country

Fifty years ago, when I was in Cape Town for a week as a soldier, the park benches, restaurant doors, buses and the entrances of most public buildings in South Africa were besmirched and degraded by monolingual notices marked WHITES ONLY or NO BLACKS ADMITTED, though in fact then and even more now, Afrikaans ('designated' in 1925) was the majority white language. That was the time of the colour bar, the cruel reality which was 'disguised' in 1947 by the opprobrious euphemism *apartheid*, the worst of all the transferred or loan words ever to have been admitted into another language.

Now, *apartheid* is over and the country is still provisionally run by whites. The changeover will take a long time, and translation is going to be important first in the visual and semiotic aspect. It is a pity that at least in Pretoria and Johannesburg, most public notices, street and road signs, and picture titles in the respective fine art galleries[1] are still in the languages of the 'bilingual state', as five years ago a Pretoria professor magnanimously described it to me, speaking as an Afrikaaner to an Englishman. (I bawled out at him.) I am offended that in the lovely Arcadia Park, in Pretoria, where a sizeable minority of the children in the playground are black, nearly all the notices are in English and Afrikaans.

As there are nine principal African languages, the authorities are hesitant to 'promote' any individual languages(s), since this would encourage political unrest. Nevertheless one or two African languages could become symbolical national languages. Albie Sachs, the celebrated freedom fighter and academic who acts as the ANC executive member on cultural affairs, categorises the translation requirement usefully under three heads: (a) conference and international translators, (b) community translators for social affairs, (c) commercial translators, including tourism. (I have slightly adapted the designations.)

Meantime (it is a fateful interim period), the case is urgent for setting up a National Languages Council as an advisory body to the government, for language planning in education, the civil service, industry and cultural affairs, representing all significant political organisations, with a large research department attached.

Translation and Linguistics

Translating is from first to last a linguistic process, but between its beginning and its end there is much that is not related to linguistics,

[1] Ironically, in Pretoria, the 20th century pictures (unlike the conventional 19th century) in the main art gallery are exciting and mainly African, but the titles are only in Afrikaans and English

and translation theory, or whatever it is called, is far from being merely a branch of applied linguistics. Admittedly there is no aspect of the semantics and pragmatics of grammar, lexicology and sometimes of phonetics, not to mention text linguistics, that has not a valid contribution to make to translation studies. But, as has been too often pointed out, a translation is not a direct journey from Language 1 to Language 2. Whether the SL text makes sense is a matter of logic; whether it is well written or not is a question of stylistics, implicating linguistic and/or literary criticism; whether its content is comprehensible to the readership is a matter of personal research or world-knowledge or area or cultural studies; whether it is true depends on the translator's knowledge of the topic; whether it is good and beneficial may depend on its relationship to human/animal/environmental rights.

All this in criticism of a number of books on translation recently published by respected and less respected linguists propounding new and less new models theories and processes purporting to describe translation; these books are mainly large and undigested lumps of linguistics or linguistics lecture notes not once applied to translation principles let alone examples. And in criticism of vocational translation courses that offer general linguistics as a separate component of the programme, where it is only appropriate as a background liberal study.

Additional TL Text Information
The more authoritative the content and the more important the language of the original text, the stronger the case for putting any additional information (usually cultural or linguistic) outside rather than within the translation. (I refer to my *Textbook of Translation*, p.92 for an enumeration of methods of supplementing information inside or outside the text, to which should be added:

(1)(g) Add classifier, e.g. 'Speyer' becomes 'the city of Speyer' (etc. as required)

(5) In translator's preface.

(6) In translator's afterword or postscript.)

Concept
A recent Franco-German business meeting was ruined because of a 'classic mistranslation': *Konzept* was translated as *concept*. Certainly the story of the three words is unusual: *concept* (F), appearing in 1404, has remained a little used philosophical word till recently, when it developed *concept de base* (basic concept), *concept publicitaire* (advertising concept), *test de concept* (concept testing) presumably with media and English influence. *Konzept* has developed widely since the last War, taking over areas of draft, plan, programme, rough copy, concept, idea, as well as entering into current collocations where

it may mean 'train of thought' or 'balance of mind'. But the German for 'concept' is typically *Begriff*. Further it may cover the vogue French *formule* and the English 'scenario'. The English 'concept' (16th century) remains much closer to the French particularly in its primary sense as 'basic idea'.

Trials of a Translator

'I'm fed up translating verbose politico-economical jargon-riddled nonsense which I then have to inject with any meaning I can infer from the atmosphere . . . I'm increasingly being asked to revise English economic texts which Italian professors are keen to write in English (it's good practice for them, they tell me) [and more prestige and money]. Their grammatically correct English is deceptive . . . I have to truncate endless sentences of Italianised syntax. What to do? Rewrite? Re-interpret? My clients seem to think language is a garment which communicating people clothe their ideas in and which can be peeled off and replaced at a moment's notice.' (Letter from Jane Dunnett, a translator in Pisa, erotic as ever.)

The Translation of Longer Sentences (again)

Average length of sentences depends on the register as well as the language, and a little corpus-based computerised research would be useful. My impression is that English has shorter sentences than most European languages, but my non-anglophone students deny this; owing to Biblical/Hebrew influence, English may have the most co-ordinate sentences. Newspaper French seems to have an extraordinary tendency to expand its sentences with its endless relative clauses and the typical journalistic obsession with crowding in time and place:

Lundi 11 janvier après-midi, c'est un Richard Branson jubilant qui est

Monday 11 January afternoon, it's a jubilant Richard Branson who left

sorti du palais de justice de Londres, levant le pouce en signe de

left the London law court, raising his thumb as a sign of

victoire, commentant son triomphe, mais déjà magnanime, prêt, sous reserve

victory, commenting on his triumph, but already magnanimous, ready,

de la 'sincérite' de son puissant adversaire, à conclure un armistice

subject to the 'sincerity' of his powerful adversary, to conclude an armistice

avec lui: officiellement reconnu coupable de 'pratiques commerciales

with him: officially recognized as guilty of unfair commercial

déloyales', pour ne pas dire de 'coup bas' à l'égard de Virgin, British

practices, not to say 'a hit below the belt' as regards Virgin, British
*Airways devra verser 610,000 livres sterling (un peu plus de 5
millions*
Airways will have to pay £610,000
de francs) de dommages et intérêts à son concurrent et à M. Richard
damages to its rival and to Richard
Branson, tout en supportant l'intégrité des frais de justice, soit 3
Branson, whilst bearing the entirety of the legal costs, that is
millions de livres.
£3,000,000.
Suggested translation: 'Richard Branson was jubilant as he left the
Law Courts on Monday 11 January. He gave a thumbs-up sign to show
he had won (and as a reflection of his triumph – omit?); but now he
was generous and prepared to conclude an armistice with his powerful
opponent, as long as he was sincere. British Airways had been
officially found guilty of unfair commercial practices, not to say 'dirty
tricks' against Virgin. It will now have to pay £610,000 in damages to
its rival and to Richard Branson, as well as paying all the legal costs,
which amount to £3,000,000.'
  Please note again that Thomas Mann, Proust, any legal document,
any official statement should never have their punctuation, syntax or
even vocabulary treated in this way.

The Translation of Colloquial Language
  I think it is axiomatic that (after metalingual language, slang, and
puns) colloquial language, including dialect, should be, ought to be,
the least literally translated of all forms of language. Colloquial
language, which I put between informal language and slang on my
scale of formality, is a wide band of language closely related to period
and place (hence dialect), typically speech used in normal conversation reproduced in writing, and consisting variously of (a) abbreviated
words ('recce' for 'reconnaissance' or 'prep'; previously 'pub' and
'mob' once frowned upon by Swift); (b) abbreviated grammatical
words ('won't', 'shan't'); (c) 'deviant' grammatical structures (ain't);
(d) idioms consisting of cultural ('a pig in a poke') or universal ('light
at the end of the tunnel') words; (e) standard metaphors ('hotbed').
Note that conversational language merges into slang, but slang is
'ruder'. Lauren G. Leighton in her absorbing book, *Two Worlds, One
Art: On Literary Translation in Russia and America* (1991, Northern
Illinois University Press, De Kalb, Illinois), states that the problem of
colloquial language has been discussed by Russian and Soviet
translators for many years, and that some of them have given it up in
despair, while others are still struggling with it.
  Personally, I question whether it is a separate single problem, and I
think one has to suggest several translating principles:

1. If the colloquial original is natural (conforms to social usage), the translation must also be natural

2. Therefore, the translator should not make up new TL abbreviations, but can only compensate for SL abbreviations by using more colloquial language, e.g. modal particles (like *eben* or *ja*).

3. As in the case of dialect, the translator usually moderates colloquial language, since a 'full' rendering is apt to sound ridiculous.

4. Any deviant grammatical construction (e.g. 'without you have read') can only be closely translated by an equally current TL deviant construction. Otherwise it has to be normalized or compensated elsewhere, but usually by a vigorous colloquialism, not by 'blandscript' (a literal translation of the Russian *gladkopis*, coined by Leighton).

5. Unless there are neologisms or unusual metaphors or collocations in the text, they must not be created for the translation. Leighton points out that in Russian, use of dative instead of locative or genitive, confusion of aspects, mispronunciation, malapropisms and mixed tenses are often pointers to colloquial language. She concludes that any attempt to convey colloquial speech in its entirety is absurd (agreed), but unlike her, I see no reason why it should not be conveyed systematically, allowing that the translator has to miss out at certain places. I echo her emphasis on the translator's tact and moderation first and last.

VI
JULY 1993

Lauren Leighton

Lauren Leighton's wide-ranging and jargon-free book on literary translation is the most enjoyable I have read on translation for many years. She is particularly good on literal translation, colloquial language and cultural words (or *realia*), and comments intelligently on Marilyn Gaddis Rose's explication of Steiner's 'hermeneutic motion'. (She's not so good on me.) She deplores the lack of an agreed translation terminology in the West (which Soviet theorists achieved at the sacrifice of a gross distortion of 'literalism') – Kornei Chukovsky was always swearing at literal (mis)translations of English or Russian idioms – but this is not surprising given the recency and the controversial nature of the subject. (George Steiner has pooh-poohed the lack of worthwhile or original translation theory, but he has always overlooked the useful literature on translation methodology, which, with the outstanding exception of Tytler (1790), barely existed till the 1960s.

The Moral Universal

Of the five universals, the moral, the factual, the logical, the aesthetic and the linguistic (all previously explained), the moral is the most important. It is now evolving, internationally and politically, founded on the Human Rights Declarations, for the first time in history, in the slow UN action against the Serbs in Bosnia. And note the antiquated protests: 'The lives of our soldiers must not be endangered . . . No good ever came out of interfering in a civil war . . . The slaughter will drag on forever . . . There are rights and wrongs on both sides . . . We must mind our own business . . . The chetniks and the ustashi are only in their second round, you must let them fight it out.' Thus the cultures resist the universal truth.

Wie rafft ich mich auf in der Nacht

I never leave a house before daybreak without Brahms's wonderful music in Platen's words stealing slipping running in my mind. The poem's concentration of sound and language loses much (30%?) in Bird and Stokes's brave translation (in the *Fischer-Dieskau Book of Lieder*):
Wie rafft ich mich auf in der Nacht, in der Nacht,
How I sprang up (pulled myself up) in the night, in the night
Und fühlte mich fürder gezogen,
And on and on felt myself drawn! (And felt myself drawn even further)

39

Die Gassen verliess ich, vom Wächter bewacht,
I left the streets in the watch's watch (guard)
Durchwandelte sacht,
Wandering soft, (throughout)
In der Nacht, in der Nacht,
In the night, in the night,
Das Tor mit dem gotischen Bogen.
And out (through the gate) by the Gothic arch.
But Brahms's music would get all the meaning back in any language.

The Translation of Idioms

In the standard definition, an 'idiom', which is a hyponym or subordinate term of a 'phrase', is 'a group of words whose meaning cannot be elicited from the meanings of its components'; the standard example is 'It's raining cats and dogs', which like so many idioms is misleading, since as in may other accepted idioms, e.g. 'see the light' or 'see light at the end of the tunnel', 'looking for a needle in a haystack' (*eine Stecknadel im Heuhaufen suchen, chercher une aiguille dans une botte de foin*), the meanings of the components are clear. I have always preferred to define idioms as extended standard metaphors which may be universal or cultural (more often cultural); they can be translated (a) by finding another metaphor, (b) by reducing to sense (thereby losing their emotive force) or (c) occasionally literally. Examples: 'to be over the moon', *être aux anges*; at first light, *bei Tagesanbruch*; 'you are asking for the moon', *du verlangst das Unmögliche*; 'we're not out of the wood yet', *on n'est pas encore tiré d'affaire*; 'you're asking for the moon', *tu demandes la lune*; 'a pillar of society', *eine Säule der Gesellschaft*.

Note that some idioms are grammatical (*venir de . . .*, 'he's just'; *es steht schlecht um seine Gesundheit*, 'he's in bad health') and *ipso facto* can never be translated literally; most idioms usually pass all too quickly from freshness through a prolonged stage of cliché to obsolescence. Hence take care in translating them. Eleni Sella read a brilliant paper on this topic at the recent outstanding translation conference she animated at the Ionian University in Corfu, which has the only accredited translation school in Greece.

Corfu and Athens

Corfu is the Italian term internationally used for the island and town of Kerkyra (Ancient Greek: Corcyra). The exhibits in the Archaeological Museum, as indeed in the great museums in Athens and on the Acropolis, are adequately labelled in Greek and English. Shamefully, disgracefully a group of sculptures on the Parthenon are missing . . .

Poetry Translation

The great translators of poetry, George, Leyris, Campbell did not, could not, translate literally, but they gave the *illusion* of translating literally. I am surprised that poetry translators do not publish various versions of one poem; great painters have often exhibited various versions of the same subject.

Sexist Language

Christine Klein-Lataud of York University, Toronto, has shown that Canadian French has been more successful than metropolitan French in desexing the language: *les droits de l'homme* has become *les droits de la personne* (human rights).

ESIT

Whilst the Paris School still dubiously regards the theory of interpretation as the point of departure for a theory of translation, the dubious theory of deverbalisation, where all trace of the source language text disappears after the transfer, appears to have been modified; according to Danica Seleskovitch, *les mots qui frappent* in the source language text [the key-words?] remain.

The Law of Titles

The titles of authoritative texts have to be closely translated. All the more so, if they are the titles of great poems. All the more so, if they are proper names, so 'outside' language. Thus Yeats's *Byzantium* has to be translated as *Byzantium* in any language, whatever the various cultural connotations in this or that language which can be footnoted. Any other translation (like *In Search of the Infinite*) is preposterous and insulting to Yeats and the truth. This is as near to an iron law as I can devise in this fuzzy subject of translation theory.

The University of Bir Zeit

Bir Zeit University, which is in fine buildings on a magnificent site in the territories occupied by Israel by military force and some singularly hurtful and conspicuous red-roofed settlements, runs a two year Arabic and English translation course (including French and Hebrew options) which is recognized as amongst the best in the Arabic speaking world. I am proud to be the only British translation theorist to lecture there. (Chomsky had lectured on politics.) The students and staff who managed to come (there had been 'impediments' for all of us) asked me searching and well informed questions on translation. The chief interpreter and translator for the Palestinian delegation to the peace talks, Taisir Hammad, teaches there, as does Hanan Ashrawi, and talked to me about the difficulties of interpreting in a 'diplomatic' and a frank mode. (Should Israel 'abide by' or 'give in to' UN

Resolutions 242 and 338?) In many people's view, Bir Zeit is a symbol
of Palestinian freedom.

Jerusalem and Israel
Hebrew and English dominate the golden city. It seems a pity that
in a country with a sizeable Palestinian Arabic minority (1.7 million
out of a population of 4.5 million – Arabic is the second official
language), there is so little trace of printed Arabic within the pre-1967
state boundaries, and the language is not much learned. The pictures in
the magnificent art galleries in Jerusalem and Tel-Aviv have Hebrew
and English titles only, in spite of some superb Vuillard, Boudin,
Courbet and many others, that is, no French titles, let alone Arabic.
The amazing Israel Museum, the most splendidly laid out I have ever
visited, makes an effort by displaying some descriptive panels on art
movements in Arabic. The music programme from Radio Jerusalem,
the best I have ever listened to, restricts its talk to naming titles,
composers and players in Hebrew (none of that Western chat for
once), but how much better this would have been if it had also been in
English and Arabic.

Sorry
'I'm sorry' has two meanings, often seriously confused:
1. I regret I did this.
2. I regret that this has happened (through no fault of mine). *Es tut
mir leid* and the hypocritical *je suis désolé* (cf. *je suis ravi*) are equally
ambiguous.

For Tiny Tots
In principle, it is unnecessary to transfer the title of any organization that includes the term 'international', unless it only covers a few
countries and is not well known. A title like *Institut international du
fer et de l'acier* should always be translated, not transferred.

Componential Analysis Register
The register of a text can sometimes be preserved by using componential analysis. Thus for *un bond*, a 'sharp rise' rather than 'a leap'
or 'a jump'.

Anthony Pym
Anthony Pym, the author of the stimulating and erudite *Translation
and Text Transfer* (1992, Peter Lang, Frankfurt am Main) writes
innumerable sentences like 'Traditional authority mechanisms tend to
subordinate meritocratic indicators to factors like birthright and group
identification' (p.153) at such varied and lofty levels of abstraction
and often of obscurity, always without references or examples or

further details, that he is not easy to follow. This is a pity, because his is an intriguing and original book.

The basic issues discussed are 'the materiality of texts, the role of equivalence in exchange, the significance of quantity [but regrettably not the impact of concision], the er . . . dynamic forces [a tautology] setting up the er . . . translation situation, and the ethical implications of the translator's profession', the latter including a perceptive discussion of two quotations (p.172). Pym sees no future for translation theory as an aid, let alone (in my concept) as a frame of reference for translators, but he wants it to merge with social theory, and apparently he will then use it in comparing American and 'Soviet' (the book is not always up to date) machine output statistics. The book is not strong on translation examples, although two ('*Movida*', and an extract from a speech of de Gaulle's) are a thread through the book.

It is regrettable that in naming five possible sources of authority for the improvement of a translation or a text, Pym restricts himself to variations on the old SL/TL dualism (pp.163–4), and never mentions the two (of at least five) most obvious non-cultural sources, that is, the visible truth and logic. His later discussion of ethics is rather sceptical, but when he states that 'the ultimate aim of translation is to improve the intercultural relations with which translators are concerned', I applaud, though I would not put it quite like that. (Please see *About Translation*, pp.43–44. Pym, like X and Y, appears to show an obsessive ambivalence about my work, but it would be tedious to list his misunderstandings, which are not distortions.)

Technical

'Technical' is semantically one of the most slippery of all internationalisms. Beginning in classical Greek as 'craft' or 'art', it now has the available senses of 'process', 'procedure', 'industrial', 'infrastructure', 'practical', 'complex', 'difficult', 'technological', 'workmanship', 'mechanical', 'engineering' (from 'ingenious'), 'strictly interpreted', 'nominal', as well as the 'cover-up', mystery (= *métier*) sense in the collocation 'for technical reasons', *aus technischen Gründen* (. . . 'the train was cancelled'), or *incident technique*, 'technical hitch'; a 'technical point' can even stretch to *un pont de procédure*.

In some cases, one may have to resort to default translation. Thus, in a list of items of health expenditure: *consultations*, *visites* (home visits), *actes de radiologie* (radiotherapy), *soins dentaires* (dental care), *actes infirmiers* (nursing care), *actes de masso-kinésithérapie* (physiotherapy, including massage), *biologie* (NB – *laboratory analyses*), nothing appears to be left for *actes techniques* but 'use of general hospital plant', which could be discreetly disguised as 'use of technical equipment'.

Rouault

The titling in French and English of the pictures in the Royal Academy of this superb, concentrated, serious painter, so full of compassion or of rage, was good, although I don't know why *Fille* was always translated as 'Girl' rather than 'Prostitute'.

Translation Theory as a Comprehensive Frame of Reference

In my concept, translation theory consists of a small set of correlative principles (with their keywords defined), underlying a comprehensive frame of reference, which should assist the translator. The frame, which may be applied to any aspect of translations, has three columns. In the first column, an item of any length of text (from punctuation mark to the whole text), or a figure of speech, or a genre of writing, or a text-type, may be selected. The second column consists of all possible contextual factors relating to the occasion of the translation, including the linguistic and referential contexts. The third column consists of a list of all possible translation procedures, which when they are related to whole texts I call translation methods. Then the translator selects the most appropriate procedure or method that matches the relevant contextual factor. Thus Knesset could be translated as 'Israeli Parliament', but it is 'Knesset' in a formal or informal text for educated readers in the West.

Theodor Kramer

Theodor Kramer (1897–1958), the fine Austrian and Jewish poet who lived as an exile in England from 1939 to 1957 (he was the Librarian at Guildford Technical College from 1943 to 1957), is still too little known amongst English Germanists. His translator Fritz Brainin, who claimed to write *Nachdichtungen* ('poetic recreations', not 'free translations') died recently. Here is a brief taste of Kramer's bittersweet poetry: *Gemeindekind*

Welfare Child
Ich keene keinen Vaterhof
I've never known a father's farm,
ich steh auf keinen Grund.
don't stand on any ground.
Meine Mutter hat mich ausgeschüt'
My mother, a maid, has cast me out
im Strauch wie einen Hund.
like a pup in a bush to be found.

Meine Mutter ist ledig verdorben
My mother, unmarried, has turned bad
das Dorf gab mir Lumpen und Brot
from the village I got rags and bread

und gab mich auch her
and got loaned out free
in die Dachdeckerlehr;
as a roofer trainee:
ich schwing wie ein bleiernes Lot . . .
I swing like a bob of lead . . .
(Brainin's translation is uneven; I fear only the first two lines are successful.) The quotation is from the noble and rich periodical for anti-fascist literature of exile and resistance, *Mit der Ziehharmonika* (with the concertina), published by the Theodor Kramer Gesellschaft in Vienna.

Four Correlations for Technical Translation
1. The more technical the topic, the less knowledge of the source language is required.
2. The more technical and 'pure' (as opposed to 'applied') the topic, the less knowledge of the source language culture is required.
3. The worse written the text, the better the translator has to write.
4. The more technical the text, the more knowledge of the topic the translator has to have.

Some Tentative Remarks on Frames
When a typical discourse is restricted to typical situations, the language used tends to clot into a few keywords, and to have restricted senses. Thus Richard Hoggart in the third volume of his fine autobiography *An Imagined Life* collects sets of words and phrases that would now be called 'politically correct' (PC), such as unwaged, ethnic, committed, gender, alternative, caring, grass roots, supportive; coupled with their antagonistic complements, such as: paternalistic, divisive, patronising, Bourbons, emotional (making a value judgement); or the computer-flavoured PR words such as: menus, interfaces, scenario, module, on stream, in synch, infrastructure, mindset, flavour of the month. Such wordsets or frames, which represent typical attitudes, would normally be modified in translation with a judicious set of transferred and more general words.

Amour Propre
The main English dictionaries (Collins, Oxford, Longman) are misleadingly concise on *amour propre*, defining it as 'self-respect', which I think is wrong, or 'self esteem', which is inadequate. I suggest, adapting from the *Petit Laroussse*: an acute feeling of personal dignity and value, which causes one to suffer for being underrated and, often as a consequence, to want to impose oneself on the esteem of others.

Fauré and His Chansons
What right, I ask myself, has this Winifred Radford to translate, to

mistranslate, this beautiful line of Jean de la Ville de Mirmont [*sic*] *Et mes rêves légers ne se sentent plus d'aise* (from *La mer est infinie* ... in *L'horizon chimérique*, The fantastic ... not, the illusory, horizon) as 'And my light dreams are overjoyed beyond words' instead of as 'And my light dreams no longer feel happy', i.e. virtually the opposite. Could she, like so many before her, be thinking that she is translating not what's there but what she thinks the poem means ... or is this a slight oversight ... or is this a crass howler? I shall never know, and when I listen, I don't care, having little French *sprachgefühl* and being so absorbed in Fauré's universal music (but see p.55).

Another Latin Tag

'(*Par exemple Dixit Stiglitz* 1977)'. The bibliography and the source are missing, but according to me, by default translation, which I may be overdoing, no writer could be called Dixit Stiglitz, therefore this must mean 'Stiglitz (1977), for example, also held this view'.

Reduction to Prose

Chaque poste concourt en 1989 à la croissance des dépenses. Every item contributed in 1989 to the growth of expenditure.

In 1989, every item showed a growth in expenditure.

In 1989, there was an increase in expenditure in every item in the balance sheet.

Translation as Text

Translation as Text by Albrecht Neubert and Gregory M. Shreve (1992, Kent State University Press, Kent, Ohio) is the first volume in a new series of Translation Studies originally published from 1978 onwards by the 'Leipzig School' since 1978. A well-planned book, it first discusses eight translation models; then discusses the relation between translation, extralinguistic knowledge and process; then analyses the concept of a text by way of Dressler and Beaugrande's eight features of text linguistics, including acceptability via Grice's cooperative principles; and concludes with a section on Translation as Result.

The book has considerable virtues. It accepts standards of translation: 'Of great concern for serious practitioners and eager users of translation is the great amount of translation which is neither destructive nor constructive, but simply awful'. The book is rightly impatient with the weavings of several linguists and philosophers, points out that a term such as 'equivalence', however difficult to analyse precisely, is virtually indispensable operationally, and stresses that the place of linguistics in translation studies has been grossly exaggerated. The section on acceptability includes much excellent practical discussion, and there are particularly useful remarks in context on metaphors, titles, cohesion, and alliteration. Unfortunately, in a book of nearly 150 pages, translation examples are missing in the first sixty, and they get rare in the concluding section. I found definitions rather scarce, and I could not profit overmuch from the pieces on prototypes, superstructures, global propositions and philological translation. The cricket example defeated the book's stated purpose of being realistic. And the authors appear to be a little besotted with the term 'text' (as so many others are with the term 'discourse', not to mention 'discursive' and 'discoursal') not to mention texture, textness, textualize, textuality, textualisation and textonymy. However, as a mainly 'top-down' book, it is well worth reading.

The Five Direct and the Three Indirect Purposes of Translation: a Revised Version

1. To contribute to understanding and peace between nations, groups and individuals, on the basis of the truths they share, not the cultures that distinguish them.

2. To convey messages, instructions and orders.

3. To communicate useful knowledge.

4. To explain one country's culture to another.

5. To translate and retranslate the world's great books, the 'canon', the precious life-blood of master spirits (Milton, adapted); the best that has been thought and written (Arnold, adapted).

1. To offer an insight into communication, language and languages, which are understood synchronically and diachronically by contrast and comparison with other languages.

2. To enrich the grammar, idiom and lexis of the target language with those of the source language which are the reflexions of new concepts and objects.

3. To serve as a skill for learning a foreign language.

VII
SEPTEMBER 1993

Variant Spellings
   Variant spellings and transliterations, particularly in first letters of words, are sometimes a translator's trap. A few British English words tend to begin with C where American English uses K (Cinematograph). Where British English has oe and ae, American English, French and Italian have e (many medical terms). U and Y may interchange. Some transferred Arabic words may begin with j or dj (thus 'jellaba' or 'jellabah', a loose cloak with hood, in the Middle East). Beware of Russian names beginning with Ch, Tch, Tsch (Tchaikovsky). And so on. Lateral thinking required.

Golden Advice
   Extract from *How to Work Effectively with Translators and Interpreters*, an excellent piece by Ann Corsellis (*Criminal Practitioners Newsletter No. 14*): 'Give fuller clearer explanations of legal concepts and procedures than you would normally. A client and non-specialist may not know the precise meaning of such terms as: caution, bail, jury, magistrate, CPS, probation. Indeed, they may not exist in the same form in the other language.' Sometimes, the common use of a word ('officious' as 'arrogant, pompous') makes one forget its basic meaning ('obtrusively offering services, meddlesome'), which has to be reactivated after half a lifetime.

Technical Terms
   In technical language, descriptive terms gradually congeal into technical terms or collocations, particularly in their translations; when they endure, they become standardized. Thus 'global warming' does not yet appear to have settled down in French (*réchauffement de la planète, réchauffement global*) or German (*Erwärmung der Erdatmosphäre, globaler Temperaturanstieg*), but it has in Spanish (*recalimento global*).

Translating or Disentangling Zeugmas and Hendiadys
   Hendiadys (expressing an idea with two words connected with 'and', instead of modifying the other, e.g. 'nice and warm' for 'nicely warm' (*bien chaud*) and zeugmas, a verb or adjective connecting two nouns ('I lost my gloves and my temper in the taxi') both have to be translated 'normally', unless they are intended to be comic. For *forze sociali e produttive*, I suggest 'social forces and productive capacity', but I wasn't given the context (as so often, I don't need the context: often, this is simply a defence mechanism against the text linguists).

Contemporary Translation Theories

Contemporary Translation Theories by Edwin Gentzler (1993, Routledge, London) has chapter heads on the American translation workshop (Pound, I.A. Richards, Will, poetry translation); the 'science' of translation (Nida, Wilss, Kade); early Translation Studies (Holmes, Lefevere); polysystem theory and Translation Studies (Even-Zohar, Toury, Bassnett, Hermans); Deconstruction (at a time when Eagleton says it's finished, others are starting); the future of Translation Studies. After a skirmish with Reiss and Vermeer, Gentzler concentrates on Translation Studies, in particular the variety that deals with the relationship between writer and translator without reference to reality. Various theories of translation are described, but there are no translation examples (one by Walter Benjamin is discussed without reference to the original).

Translation theory, according to the Translation Students, is moving from Text to Culture, but the meaning of this cryptic remark is not explained. Both Even-Zohar and Toury are first praised and then demolished. The book has many airy and confident remarks such as: 'Some radical rethinking of certain positions is taking place, and certain surprising risks are being taken as definitions within the field get called into question' (p. 198), or 'In the nineties, those translation theorists who have worked through the contribution of deconstructionists [seems rather late, now that Eagleton has abandoned it] will not only be at the forefront of their own field, but may begin to engage in meaningful exchanges with those from other fields' (p. 192). Thus a factitious excitement is created, but the generalizations about language and translation are platitudinous and too vague to be useful. The important distinctions in this kind of writing between fiction and non-fiction are not made.

Theory

My own definition of a theory is that it is an idea that is used to explain something, and that it always requires testing; if it is not largely verified (but it can never be completely verified), or if it cannot stand, with evidence in favour and against, it is pointless, incomplete and useless. A theory, which is more powerful than a hypothesis and less secure than a theorem, requires a methodology and appropriate illustrations. (If it is obvious and completely true, like the so-called theory of relevance, it is a universal principle, not a theory.) Translation particularly lends itself to theorizing, as is shown by the literature about it. Savory alone produced twelve valid and contradictory theories of translation. But often one learns more from the evidence than from the theory.

Unfortunately, the word theory has a wide-spread negative connotation, as in the undermentioned Goethe-*Wort*, of being aca-

demic, abstract, hypothetical, remote from reality and from practice
'in theory' etc. For this reason, I have to call my courses 'Principle:
and Methods of Translation' not 'Translation Theory'.

Anti-Goethe?

Grau, teuerer Freund, ist alle Theorie,
Und grün des Lebens goldner Baum. (Faust Part 1.11.2038–9
Mephistopheles's – not Faust's – apothegm to the Student (*Schüler*)
after telling him to spend his time seducing women:
  'Grey, dear friend, is all theory,
  And green life's golden tree.'
is often regarded as the sum of Goethe's wisdom, ignoring its context.
would simply regard it as an example of this writer's less attractive
(superior and snobbish) pronouncements. He also wrote brilliantly or
translation and movingly on a huge range of experiences in life, and hi:
Faust is a tremendous affirmation of the essential togetherness o
feeling and reason, of the goodness of trusting simplicity, and o
seriousness; it is also a condemnation of book-learning.

Incidentally, I can't think why the Penguin translator (Phili｢
Wayne) had to muck up the second line of the apothegm. ('But green i:
life's glad golden tree.')

The Nord

The curious and woefully monolingual museums of the Nord ar｢
mere 'literature' compared to Georges de la Tour's *Le Vielleur a｢*
Chien ('The Hurdygurdy Player with the Dog'), which was onl｣
authenticated in 1972, at Bergues. The standard of translation (int｢
English) – Flemish is barely recognized – in chance tourist offices an｢
hotels is low. ('Do not shout fire (*au feu*). Do not lose your self-contro｢
(*sang-froid*). Warn either the floor groom (*garçon d'étage*), the mai｢
or the management.')

The Translator Intervenes

Extract from *L'intelligence artificielle distribuée* by Jean Ercea｢
and Jacques Ferber (*La Recherche*, 233, June 1991):
  La théorie des actes de langage, issue des travaux realisés par deu.
Américains Y.-L. Austin et Y.-R. Searle dans les années 1960. . .')
Possible translation:
  'Speech act theory, which originated in the works of the Oxfor｢
philosopher J.L. Austin (1911–60) and the American J.R. Searle in th｢
60s . . .'

On most occasions, there would be no need for the translator t｢
indicate the corrections of fact made, but she could ask th｢
commissioning agent to inform the authors, who should be gratefu｢
The example illustrates:

1 The translator must check all proper names not known to her.

2. The 'linguistic' red light: no Americans would have the (repeated!) initials 'Y.-R.', which could be French (Yves-Rene?)

3. Normally, the readership would have no interest in the mistakes made by the authors, so there is no need for the translator to make any type of reference to these mistakes in the translation or in a footnote.

4. In principle, a translator is responsible for the (real) truth of the translation, even if it clashes with (linguistic) accuracy.

5. Austin, but not Searle, is in the Collins and the Fontana *Biographical Companion to Modern Thought*.

6. A 'house on the hill' construction, *les travaux réalisés par . . .* is translated as 'the work of . . .' and would be in most contexts, even if de Gaulle had written it.(?)

Interlanguage

The gap between usage and translationese is often uncannily slight. Thus, from a hotel brochure in Volendam, Netherlands: 'Spaander chose for the trade of fisherman, but at the instance of his father, he went to Edam, where he acquired above all the French language . . . He introduced the various artists to Volendam with the help of photomaterial . . . Studios were erected . . . Alterations were put out to contract, among other things the present bar. Various men of consequences have had their stay at Hotel Spaander, considering the many names in our hotel registers. The tangible proof of the many artists is still hanging on the walls in all the rooms of the concern.' Note that much of the interference could be French or German as well as Dutch.

The Written Word

Translation, faxes, telexes, modems, the Web, even Derrida.. all reassert the present importance of the written as against the spoken word. The great linguist Henry Sweet would take cheer.

The Contracting Apostrophe

(Negative particle or auxiliary plus pronoun)

It appears to be becoming increasingly unnatural to write 'is not' or 'cannot' instead of 'isn't' or 'can't' in any but administrative and formal texts, unless the negative is being stressed. This is a question of house-style in the target language text. Contracting apostrophes are now used in some editorials.

VIII
NOVEMBER 1993

PC

The Official Politically Correct Dictionary and Handbook by Henry
Beard and Christopher Cerf, in conjunction with the American Hyphen
Society (1992, Grafton/HarperCollins, London) is important reading for
any translator. Implicitly based on the assertion of human, animal and
ecological rights, it recasts and/or comments on a collection of words,
collocations and institutional terms which appear to infringe these rights
(e.g.: ugly, cosmetically different; underdeveloped, overexploited; unedu
cated, alternatively schooled). The book is brilliant, thought-provoking
and often (in my own opinion, like everything else in these *Paras*) absurd.
I think that the attempt to attack and revalue the literary canon on a PC
basis, as John Carey has done in *The Intellectuals and the Masses* (which
is a kind of witch hunt) is finally unjust as well as shallow. (The
complacent Arnold Bennett becomes a great writer.) But Shakespeare
was the precursor of PC, in the sense that he anticipated the condemnation
of many popular human prejudices; and PC will not go away, least of all
from a translator, who will have to transmit it, usually unobtrusively and
tactfully. If 'it is necessary to destroy the language in order to save it' (the
Hyphen Society's motto), the translator's role is substantial.

Sarcastic

The primary sense of 'sarcastic', which is a near-internationalism (a
term is required for a grecolatinism which is current in virtually
all Romance, Germanic, Slavonic languages, as well as Greek), is bitter,
sharp, mocking, hurting – it derives from the Ancient Greek *sarkazein*,
to tear flesh. Only, I think, in English is it always associated with irony.
However, unlike irony, which may be subtle, it is usually unmistakable
and therefore the translator has no difficulty in translating it.

The Deadline

The deadline dominates professional translators, freelancers in
particular. The request to complete an assignment 'yesterday' is
symbolical for an employer who expects a translator to work into his
foreign languages and to look up the odd word she doesn't know in a
pocket bilingual dictionary. The deadline is often the distinction
between academic and real translation.

Since a translation is never finished, the only way to deal with
deadlines is to keep a sense of priorities, to make up a working time
table (if hard-pressed, for a non-literary text, to put facts before style),
and again, to remain in touch with the employer.

Translation Should (usually) be into the Modern Language

Composing and performing the amazing K.491, his finest piano concerto, I cannot imagine Mozart not making use of all the resources of the pianoforte if he could, instead of the softer earlier fortepiano version. Nevertheless Anthony Halstead and the Hanover Band's playing of Bach on early instruments is often magical. The only successful archaicizing translation I have heard of is Rudolph Borchardt's translation of Dante. It requires an extraordinary degree of empathy.

Limits of Translation

'In translation, Malraux's writing suffers a sea change. The highly-charged rhetoric, which is glorious in French, is unacceptable in English.' (*What Am I Doing Here?* Bruce Chatwin.) Nonsense. Neither *La Condition humaine* (1937), nor the superb analysis of Goya (*Saturne: essai sur Goya*, 1956) were full of 'highly charged rhetoric' (that came later), but if they had been, they would have been as 'unacceptable' in French as in English.

The London Language Show

In the detailed advertisement for this event, which includes much ALL (Association for Language Learning) jargon about language strategies and quality deliveries, the importance of translation in business is characteristically overlooked.

Norms and Standards

Translation, Poetics and the Stage: Six French Hamlets, by Romy Heylen (1993, Routledge) outlines a cultural model of translation, and discusses six French translations of Hamlet written between 1769 and 1977 by Jean-Francois Ducis, Alexandre Dumas and Paul Meurice, Marcel Schwob and Eugene Morand, André Gide, Yves Bonnefoy, and Michel Vittoz. Unfortunately, Heylen pursues the translation norms of each version without discussing their standards as works of translation, i.e. as works of art.

It is Three O'Clock

It has often been pointed out, most recently at this year's FIT (International Federation of Translators) Conference, that this type of sentence may in context have many and contradictory senses, e.g. it's late; it's early; it's time to go; you have 10 minutes; it's 3 o'clock etc.). And usually, all these senses are at hand via literal translations into other languages.

Prescriptivism

Plus normative, the current dirty word in translatory as well as translation studies. But any teacher prescribes when she is pressed for time, instead of recommending, advising, qualifying, etc.

Phrasal Adjectives

Phrasal adjectives such as 'run down' are less common than phrasal verbs or nouns. They follow the common progression whereby past participles start a life of their own as adjectives. There is no particular difficulty in translation, but the correspondence is likely to be less vivid and less physical; the translator should seek an equally concise 'equivalent' adjective (*agotado, épuisé; leer, abgebaut* etc.).

The Cave

Translation plays a significant part in Steve Reich's new multi-media opera *The Cave*. Most of the time the performance is accompanied by subtitled screens in English, French and German, the versions, mainly from the Old Testament and the Koran (not always accurate) focusing on the Abraham and Isaac story. The singing is in English throughout, but as it is characteristically blurred, the English subtitles do not come amiss. Acknowledgements are also made to ten translators, including Reich, who translated statements by West Bank and Israeli witnesses. At times Reich has benefited from Janáček.

Translation Facts

According to *Commercial Translations* by Godfrey Harris and Charles Sonnabend (Los Angeles, ISBN-0-935047-02-6), in 1984 the EC calculated that translation work was increasing at the rate of 10% per year, and that more than 150 million pages were being translated annually by some 175,000 professional translators.

Titles of Periodicals

Titles of periodicals are normally transferred, but titles of trade papers such as *Entsorga* should be transferred with a gloss, viz *Entsorga*, the German trade journal for refuse and sewage disposal.

The Poetics of Translation

The Poetics of Translation by Willis Barnstone (1993, Yale University Press, New Haven and London), a long meditation on literary and religious translation (theory rather than practice), is exceptionally erudite, aphoristic, and often rhapsodic. As an anthology of perceptive remarks about translation throughout history, it is as rich as *After Babel* (George Steiner) as an anthology of translations. It is also wordy, repetitive and name-dropping, Borges, Benjamin, Kafka and a mysterious Pierre Grange published by Sackett and Milk being mentioned and quoted rather too frequently.

Barnstone is one of the modish literary translation theorists who regard all texts as translations, since no one ever works alone, beginning with God who is 'the eternal translator', followed by the reader who is (of course!) also the translator. All this, I think, derives disastrously from Jakobson and Steiner and needs Gombrich's flat rebuttal: 'It's not a collective consciousness that creates a style. Someone has to invent it (*A Lifelong Interest*, E. H. Gombrich, Thames and Hudson, 1993). Here is Barnstone typically: 'In art no man or woman, translator or 'original' artist is . . . an island'. [I have been living with that cliché for sixty years] . . . 'Because translation involves the movement from A to B and is consummated by their commingling [*sic*], when A, the other [he means *l'autre*], is absorbed into B, one's own text, invisibly or glaringly, by silent stealth or noisy confession, that new art object, that double-headed hybrid offspring of uncertain parentage, is born and presented to the world by means of the translator's double art.' (p.88).

However, many of Barnstone's aphorisms are good: 'All art must be translated as art . . . Literalism remains the powerful frequent premise of all translation . . . The question of equivalence is central to all translation theory . . . but equivalence does not exist in rigidly literal translation that omits connotative meaning, nor in very free translation that seeks to colonize the source text as its own'. Further, Barnstone accuses early translators of the New Testament of antisemitism for translating 'rabbi' as 'master', Jacob as James, Jeshua as Jesus, and Jehuda as Judas. Unfortunately, the book concludes with an ABC of Translating Poetry which is a compendium of platitudes and 'poetic' hot air.

Howlers

Howlers are therapeutic, since hopefully they encourage humility and thoroughness. One never repeats the same howler, nor forgets it, especially if it is associated mentally with an important exam. Desirably, one reads round it, backtranslates, thinks of synonyms and variations.

Which leads to my apology to the Editor and any readers I have for my own howler in my para on Fauré and his Chansons (*The Linguist*, Vol. 32, No. 4, p.133). I now assume that a 'strict' translation of '*Et mes rêves légers ne se sentent plus d'aise*' is 'And my light dreams are beside themselves with joy'. *Je ne me sens plus* means 'I am out of my mind', which meets the case, but I did not know it.

The Evanescence of Idioms and Clichés

The idiom *noyer le poisson* (literally 'drown the fish') is translated in the *Harrap* as: 'play the fish; tire out one's opponent; pigeon-hole; discourage an author-inventor by leaving their work behind in the safe 'by mistake'; in the *Collins-Robert* by 'sidestep the question;

introduce a red herring into the discussion; in the *Petit Robert*, approximately, by 'deliberately confuse an issue by tiring whoever one is arguing with and making him/her give in'.

Now all these definitions are right, but they cover a wide range of frequency and currency, which the translator has to review for all idioms and clichés, which may either become obsolete, or, when less frequently used, gradually become useful again.

American Judiciary Interpreters and Translators

The National Association of Judiciary Interpreters and Translators of the USA issues an interesting quarterly newsletter *Proteus* from NAJIT, 531 Main Street, Suite 1603, NYC 10044. The current number has an excellent piece on the work of court interpreters, and the book reviews cover the whole translation and dictionary field; the new *Dahl's Law Dictionary* (E-Sp, Sp-E), which includes Puerto Rican terms, is reviewed by Janis Palma herself.

Translating Eponyms

'*What is Pinteresque?*', an article by David Mills in the *Sunday Times* of 5 September, comments on the changing senses of literary eponyms. (Eponyms always lie between the dictionary and the encyclopaedia, mainly within the encyclopaedia (real life), but beginning and ending in the dictionary (language).) 'Dickensian' has moved from 'observant' to 'quaintly Victorian' [has it?] and 'Chaucerian' from 'picturesque' to 'bawdy'. The *O.E.D.*'s definition of 'Pinteresque' as 'pertaining to the playwright Harold Pinter' is rightly considered unhelpful, in contrast with a *Financial Times* report: 'full of dark hints and pregnant suggestions, with the audience left uncertain what to conclude'.

In translation, there are additional considerations: the authority of the text, the knowledge and motivation of the putative readership, the different culture. The fail-safe procedure, which is also the most educative, is to translate using a couplet, viz. the sense plus the proper name (i.e. the image), but the proper name (here, Pinter) can be left out if the readership is unlikely to be interested, whilst the sense (which may be 'sinister' or 'hushed') is kept. Contrariwise, a sophisticated readership can be given the eponym without the sense.

Tytler and Nietzsche

Tytler (1790) was to my knowledge the first writer to criticize the ideological translations of the past with his brilliant condemnation of Voltaire's version of Hamlet's 'To be or not to be' monologue. The second was Nietzsche, who in *The Joyful Wisdom* (1882) claimed that owing to our superior historical sense, we would not have the 'courage' to translate in the way that the Romans pillaged the Greek authors. I take 'historical sense' to be scientific method.

Text and Meaning

Text and Meaning, edited by Gert Jäger, Klaus Gommlich and Gregory M. Shreve (1993, Kent State University), is a delayed *Festschrift* for Albrecht Neubert on his sixtieth birthday, and contains noteworthy contributions in German and English from translation scholars and linguists such as Helbig and Ružička. Mary Snell-Hornby writes an exceptionally thought-provoking piece on *Word against Text: The Role of Semantics in Translation*. She lists five graded groups of what she calls prototypes, ranging from context-free terms such as 'oxygen' and semi-internationalisms (e.g. museum), through basic level items such as 'chair' and 'cook', and proceeding to affective words ('bleak') and finally culture-bound 'elements' such as 'haggis' and 'wicket', where 'translation difficulties increase'. These are useful categories, but in my view, only the basic level items are prototypes in Rosch's sense, where 'electric chairs' do not come under the prototype 'chair', nor 'whale' under the prototype 'fish'.

After this, Snell-Hornby grandly states that it is a truism of translation theory that the translator is not concerned with words but with texts. I would have said they are concerned with both, and down with truisms anyway. The main example given is a passage from a guide to York's Castle Museum, where *wo wohlhabende Gutsbesitzer sich wärmten und gewöhnliche Heidebauern hausten* is nicely translated as 'where wealthy landowners warmed themselves and simple moorland peasants had their humble homes'. The translation rightly underlines the contrast between the two images, and what I would call the primary meaning of *hausten* (dwell, live), here called the 'prototypical' meaning, is skilfully particularized. I should add that this paper is rich in helpful suggestions for translators, and plainly written. But the prototypes here have nothing much to do with Neubert's constricting 'prototypical texts'. For the rest, there is a superb piece by Werner Bahner on Robespierre's use of political key-terms, which is an exceptionally intelligent instance of Marxist sociolinguistics; and a perceptive analysis by Rudolf Ružička of the 'pragmatic turn' in linguistics from semantics towards pragmatics. This paper however, like others which even lack any examples, is somewhat spoilt by sentence openings like: *Dem im PRO- subjekt des eingebetteten Satzes stattfindenden Zusammenstoss der thematischen Spezifierung des affizierten Patiens mit der von überreden, ugovorit' determinierten Eigenschaft 'aktiven' Handelns ist* . . . Literally, 'To the PRO-subject of the embedden sentence occurring clash of the thematic specification of the affected patiens with the 'überreden, ugovorit' determined quality of active acting,' i.e. 'The clash of the thematic specification of the affected *patiens* (object) occurring in the embedded PRO-subject – with the quality of active acting determined by 'überreden, ugovorit'. Surely it is time that even such brilliant scholars as Ružička abandoned these Germanic convolutions and observed a more natural (universal) word-order?

IX
NOVEMBER 1994

The Barber Institute

The Barber Institute of Fine Arts in Edgbaston Park Road outside Birmingham, with its outstanding Gwen John (*Mère Poussepin*), Degas, Claude, Redon (*Crucifixion*), Hals, Van Dyck, Sickert and many others, is I think the finest small picture gallery I have ever visited. But in the main it is pathetically monolingual. The university's language department is quite close, and the detailed and helpful leaflets for each bay all need translating. I do not know why Magritte's amazing *Saveur des Larmes* ('The Savour of Tears'?) has been anaesthetized into the bland 'Taste of Sorrow' (*Le Goût de la Tristesse* – yuck), given that English is said (of course!) to be the more concrete language.

La Patrie

In the Birmingham City Museum (which needs no puff) C. W. R. Nevinson's picture of the wounded and dying soldiers in the barn, to which the description, 'they are crying for their mothers' is an organic complement, is not as profound as *The Third of May*, but it as as moving. In English, the title, *La Patrie*, a grim instance of dramatic irony, stands (compare Wilfred Owen's *Pro Patria Mori*); in some other languages (*das Vaterland*), it could be translated literally with the same 'equivalent effect'.

Translation Studies at Birmingham University

A recent conference on Translation Theory and Practice run by the Department of Hispanic Studies and the School of English at Birmingham University showed that interest in this field increases steadily. The conference was dominated by papers on literary translation. Some made careful and enlightening comparisons of translations of Lope de Vega and Joyce, which enhanced appreciation of these authors. Others went far down the way of cultural relativism ('the shift in literary criticism is away from the writer and his text'); one speaker examined five translations from *Coriolanus* without a single reference to the original text, which was not reproduced, and felt guilty about Harold Bloom. Another proposed that equivalence and fidelity are pseudo-problems in translation theory, but this idea was generally dismissed, as translators spend most of the time seeking equivalences at some level or length, and fidelity is a concept inseparable from interpretation and translation.

Translating Metalanguage

Ambiguities and standard metaphors in the source language normally have to be rethought rather than translated into the target language, but always as closely and concisely as possible. Thus: *trouver le sens de 'pièce' dans 'le porte-monnaie est dans la pièce' ou dans 'la pièce est dans le porte-monnaie'* (literal or nonsensical translation: 'find the meaning of piece in 'the wallet is in the piece' or in 'the piece is in the wallet') could become 'find the meaning of "room" ' in 'the book is in the room' or 'there is room for the book', thus retaining the two nouns. Secondly: *un mot comme 'la' appartient aux trois catégories article* (the), *pronom* (it) *et nom* (the musical note A) could be translated as 'A word such as "level" belongs to three categories: verb, adjective and noun', since I doubt whether any English word is at once an article, noun and pronoun. Thirdly, for *Il rend le livre illisible* (i.e. he makes the book illegible/he returns the illegible book), a reasonable punning English verb is required: he runs the race (i.e. he directs the race/he takes part in the race). This sentence does not account for the two syntactic functions of *illisible*, which can be done with 'He met the man with the book', where 'with the book' can qualify 'he' or 'man'. Lastly, *Cet homme est un lion* (= *il est courageux*), *un agneau* (= *il est doux*) *un tigre* (= *il est féroce*), *ses cheveux d'or* (= *blonds et lumineux*) should normally be translated literally as 'This man is a lion (= brave), a lamb (= gentle), a tiger (= fierce), his/her golden hair (= fair/blond and luminous (bright, resplendent?). The French quotations are all taken from *Intelligence artificielle et Langage naturel (La Recherche 245*, July–August 1992, Vol. 23), and I thank my gifted student Helen Dimitriou for drawing the article to my attention and for solving some of its translation puzzles.

Translation Material

The ideal translation material is challenging linguistically and technically. *The Economist* is an outstanding resource.

Reception Theory and Hype

The claim has recently been made that because William Morris received ecstatic reviews for his 'translations' of the Norse sagas (in fact he reshaped them, after reading them in the original), these translations were generally popular at the time. In fact sales statistics are a better indication of popularity than the small tight band of contemporary hype (academic or media) and even then, the latter can artificially jack up the former. I am not questioning that the investigation of translation reception, including its attendant gossip, and its gushing style ('quite simply, a marvellous piece of editing') is an essential part of cultural history and sociology; I am maintaining that a sensitive and intelligent comparison of a translation with its original, in Leavis's undogmatic sense, is the essence of translation theory and criticism, and is useful.

Galician Symposium

Galician is often considered to be a dialect of Spanish or Portuguese, but in Vigo, the largest city in Galicia (the more attractive Santiago de Compostela is the capital), it is one of the four languages of Spain, with Castilian, Catalan and Basque. Vigo University held two exciting and crowded translation conferences run by Carmela Noia Campos and Esther Sanchez, and is about to set up its own translation degree. One day, perhaps, a nation such as Spain will designate a *lingua franca* for administrative matters, diplomacy and foreign relations, will exercise subsidiarity domestically, particularly in regional government, and will give translators free play to translate cultural and literary texts from one of its languages to another. Now, such a move would be seen as imperialistic, and enormous funds, time and effort are consumed, accompanied by deadening boredom, in the translation of administrative texts three ways between Galician, Castilian and Catalan. (N.B. Don't confuse Galicia in NW Spain with Galicia in Poland and the Ukraine.)

The Key to Technical Translation

The Key to Technical Translation, Vol. 1 (Concept Specification) and Vol. 2 (Terminology/Lexicography) by Michael Hann (John Benjamins, Amsterdam, 1993) for German-English or English-German scientific translators is, I think, innovative and comprehensive in design.

The first volume carefully explains key concepts in a dozen technologies and includes basic E to G glossaries, paying particular attention to synonyms and 'polysemes'. The second volume has a superb German polyseme dictionary, an English thesaurus with German translation of headwords, a German collocation dictionary with English translations of citations, a 'global' dictionary (it's explained!) and gender rules. The book is a good and attractive read, not just a reference book. The slighting reference to literary translators, foreign correspondents and interpreters (p.7 – they only need 'a few general dictionaries') is regrettable, but I suspect that this book is a magnificent achievement.

Evil

It is not surprising that Cardinal Hume protested against the apparently official translation of the common little Latin word *malum*, relating to contraceptive practices, in the new encyclical *veritatis splendor*, as 'evil', a uniquely powerful and animate word, when it might also have been translated as 'bad', 'wrong' or even 'wicked'.

Even *übel* pales beside 'evil'. No text linguistics can solve this translation indeterminacy, but the fact that a dead or extinct language is being used as an original text for presently evolving languages does not help.

An Israeli Translation Theory of Peace
'You have to translate through negotiation into reality.' Yitzhak Rabin, October 6, 1993.

Greco-Latin Semi-Neologisms
I take it that as a general rule, neologisms in fiction are 'reinvented' when translated (thus Joyce's 'Chuffy was a nangel' becomes *Chuffy war/êtait ein/un nengel/nange*), whilst in non-fiction they are normalized or reduced to sense unless they are likely to affect the target language culture (thus jargoneers' might be *parleurs de jargon* or *die Jargonsprecher*).

What however is to be made of the Greco-Latin 'neologisms' so common in Romance languages, which sound so pretentious in English or German? Thus *l'incapacité des voyageurs européens à sortir des cadres sociocentristes* (Lit. 'The incapacity of the European travellers to leave sociocentrist frames'). In a sociological text, the 'jargoneers' would want 'sociocentric', on the analogy of 'Eurocentric' and this might be advisable if the term were frequently repeated. Otherwise, I would prefer 'the inability of European travellers to abandon the cultural conventions of/centred on/their own society'. The difficulty is quite common, and each one usually has to be considered on its contextual merits, where each translation is a fresh beginning. (Shades of T. S. Eliot.)

Geographical Features
Rivers (water spirits) and mountain-ranges are normally preceded by definite articles; towns, rarely in Romance languages, but always for the Hague; but la Terre-Ferme may be the NE coast of South America (the Spanish Main) or Terra Firma, the Venetian mainland territories. I assume that Peter Foulkes's le Canigou is animate because 'it' is a massif, not a mountain.

Etymology in Translation Again
Les caraibs sont de faux prophètes qui courent les villages comme les porteurs de rogatons en papauté. Since the passage was written in 1578, *rogatons* can only mean 'humble requests' (during the period of papal government), as its other meanings (tittle-tattle, scraps of stale food, delicacies, rejected scribblings) came after 1666.

The Musée d'Orsay
The *Musée d'Orsay* in Paris is mainly French-bound (that is, titling,

notices and brochures are in French), and the mainly French paintings
in the amazing Barnes Collection are entirely English bound; but for
the Barnes's special exhibition at the d'Orsay, there are informative
brochures in English, French, German, Spanish and Italian as closely
translated and gracefully written as anyone could wish. That's
progress.

Teaching Translation and Detecting Allusions

Teaching Translation and Interpreting, edited by Cay Dollerup and
Anne Loddegaard (Benjamins, Amsterdam, 1992) is a large (pp. 343)
and handsome book, but I looked in vain (outside a brief useful piece
by Maria Julia Sainz) in it for any description of the methods and
process of teaching translation; of the qualities and qualifications of a
good teacher of translation, and how to appraise one; of the mechanics
of a class and a course; of student participation in the various types of
classes; of a desirable curriculum and syllabuses. I have attempted all
these tasks but I would expect a conference to do it better. The only
thing approaching it is a small and useful passage on entrance- and
end-of-term tests by Mary Snell-Hornby; but final examinations and
the relevance of the world-wide Institute of Linguists' Diploma in
Translation are not discussed.

There is an outstanding paper by Anne-Marie Beukes on the
complicated language situation in South Africa, where Afrikaans has
been 'equally the language of the oppressor and the oppressed'. Sergio
Viaggio in a breezy paper with no examples says the translator should
be versed in the poetics (a controversial topic) and rhetoric of his
languages, and be able to 'detect and reproduce literary allusions', but
he does not mention any relevant reference book for these allusions,
nor mention the signs such as alliteration, displaced word-order,
rhymes, assonance, inverted commas, capital letters (with examples)
for detecting them. Christiane Nord is similarly general and is under
the mistaken impression that neither the SLT author nor the TLT
reader nor the initiator can check whether the translation comes up to
their expectations. However, Brian Mossop contributes a superbly
practical and searching piece on 'The Translator as Terminologist',
including brief glossaries of structured terms for terminology.
Remains an appallingly large quantity of papers without translation
examples.

Apostrophes

There are two kinds of apostrophes, contracting and possessive.
Contracting apostrophes (e.g. isn't, don't) are usually inappropriate in
the written language, except for dialogue, although the *Economist* is
now sometimes using them. Possessive apostrophes are normally used
for the possessive or genitive case, but 'of' plus its object emphasises

the object. Thus 'the works of Mozart' is more dignified, and old-fashioned, than 'Mozart's works'.

Literary and Non-Literary Translation

Normally, all translations should be accurate, economical and agreeably written; these are the factors that bring literary and non-literary together, and it is as important to recognize this essential unity as to recognize the essential unity of the 'two cultures' (the arts and the sciences) which are in parallel with them. Nevertheless the differences between the two kinds of texts and their translations are significant, and they are often blurred in the literature, beginning with the book-titles, which give no indication of the type of translation (from Tytler to Toury) that is being discussed. Traditionally, all such books were about literary translation, but with the rise of linguistics, the antagonism of some linguistics to literature was carried over to linguistics-influenced translation theory which ignores literary translation.

One can make broad distinctions: non-fiction ('informative texts') are concerned with reality and denotations, fiction with the imagination and connotations. Literary texts are ultimately allegorical and, more or less indirectly, a moral comment or criticism of life, in my opinion. Non-literary texts are concerned with facts, events and ideas, without connotations. Literary texts are full of sound; non-literary texts are not.

The desirable 'accuracy' of a literary text is not the same as that of a non-literary text. The accuracy of a literary text is likely to be more complex, with connotations as well as denotations, than that of a literary text. Metaphor straddles across both genres. In the sentence *Der Weg war lang, Le chemin était long,* The way was long, *La via era lunga,* the translations are likely to 'stand' in both types of texts, but in a literary text, the meaning of 'way' and 'long' may be varied. Further, literary language (the collocation is significant) that has to be translated is likely to be of any period, and the translator has to be particularly sensitive to slightly faded language. (Example: 'esconced' in Henry James.)

Paraphrase as a Translation Procedure

Paraphrase, which I think is a better word for Jakobson's 'intralingual translation' i.e. the expression of a statement or stretch of text in different words, particularly in order to clarify, is the translator's last resort, but it has to be used often enough. What is one to do with: *Puisque rien n'est parfait, il est naturel que tout système de pouvoir génère sa contestation* (Lit. As nothing is perfect, it is natural that every system of power should generate its disputation). Here one has to go for the (likely) meaning: 'As nothing is perfect, it is natural that any power systems should give rise to its opposing school of thought'.

And again: *Pour autant qu'il prenne en compte et organise sa remise en question* . . . (Lit. In as far as it takes into account and organizes its own putting into question), perhaps 'In as far as it takes into account and fashions the manner in which it is disputed'.

The European School of Literary Translation

This original and enterprising institution, which was founded and is run by Magda Olivetti in an enormous exhibition hall designed by Luigi Nervi, is now in its second year in the Unione Industriale, Via Fanti 17, Turin. The teachers and students, instead of waiting in vain for publishers' contracts or submitting proposals, are preparing books of short novels, essays and stories from German, English, French, Russian and Spanish for Einaudi and other important publishers. They have also arranged a series of evening seminars on translation for film, theatre and literature to educate the public. The students' enthusiasm is boundless. Why not a sister organisation in the UK?

The Meaning and Translation of Dashes

The punctuation mark '–' may replace the abbreviation 'viz.' or a colon in the middle of a sentence ('It goes to the heart of British life – to the meaning of family'), or it may signify a rather unexpected contrast. ('A fifth of British mothers are single – against a tenth for the rest of Europe'), or, in pairs, as an alternative to brackets, it may enclose a sentence or phrase in parenthesis. It sometimes indicates an anacoluthon, that is, a sudden break in the grammar. ('You really ought – well, do it your way.') In French it appears to have a similar function, as well as replacing inverted commas for dialogue. Writers of long sentences such as Proust and Thomas Mann made extensive use of it. Usually it has greater force than any of the signs it can alternate with.

Translation for Drama

1. *Pace* Brecht and the *Verfremdungseffekt*, emotionally distancing the audience, the essence of a successful performance of a play is dramatic illusion, where the spectators are participating in the action (*Handlung*) emotionally and intellectually.

2. One basic task for a translator is to ensure that in a tragedy which is concerned with death or parting, which are universal experiences, the spectator of the translation is as moved as the spectator of the original; in a comedy, where the humour is broadly universal when characters are suddenly deflated, but cultural where local objects and customs play an essential role, the translation fails if the spectators do not laugh, and the method may range from close to free translation or to adaptation.

3. One can divide theatre into four genres: tragedy, drama,

comedy, farce. Typically, tragedy is least and farce most culture-bound.

4. Dramatic translation stands between translation and interpretation: translation is written to written; interpretation is spoken to spoken; dramatic translation is written to written to spoken.

5. The spectator/receptor's role is more important in drama than in any other form of art. The task of serious drama is essentially didactic and educative, as dramatists from Euripides to Molière to Schiller (*Die Schaubühne als moralische Anstalt*, the Theatre as a moral institution, a fine essay) to Brecht to Priestley (particularly in the staggering *An Inspector Calls*) to David Mamet (in *Oleanna*) have eloquently demonstrated.

6. Where a play is strongly culture bound, I think there is a case for an acting and a reading version of the translation; this particularly for comedies, where the acting version incorporates cultural equivalents, and the reading translation is at the author's level and keeps cultural explanations for the notes.

7. A translator of farces and comedies has to calculate time for stage 'business', but this is not usually necessary in (classical) tragedy.

The German *Sog*

Sogenannt (often, like 'so-called', ironical) is sometimes used for emphasis prefacing a technical or institutional term, and need not be translated. In the phrase *das sogenannte Konzertieurungsverfahren* referring to EC institutions, which appeared in the *Frankfurter Allgemeine Zeitung* some years ago, the term appears to be a direct translation of *processus de concertation*, for which there is as yet no established English translation. Therefore if the descriptive term 'consultative process' is used, any modifier such as 'so-called' would be out of place. If however the term is a translation of *procédure de concertation*, an established term for 'conciliation procedure' (between Council of Ministers and European Parliament), or 'consultation procedure' (staff/authority relations at Council Secretariat), then the modifier 'so-called' would be appropriate.

Figaro's Wedding by Jeremy Sams

The new translation at the English National Opera follows Da Ponte (*Le Nozze di Figaro*) rather than Beaumarchais (*Le Mariage de Figaro*), and this is right, this is the truth, this is the way good translation (but not translation theory) is going. But for me it'll always be *Figaro*.

Translation Theory

'At the end of the day', if I may coin a phrase, all translation theory turns on the enumeration, discussion and recommendation of the relevant translation options, choices, alternatives, and variations of methods and procedures. This process of sensitisation is the primary service the theorist performs for the translator.

La Serenissima

La Serenissima may be a familiar alternative for 'Venice', but it may also denote the fifth and last movement of Britten's third quartet, written in Venice, an intense, still and wonderful work, the last movement of which is the finest chamber music of this half-century that I have heard. Having recently been criticized in the translation journal *Target* for making such 'aesthetic judgements', I should again explain that I only make them, wrapped up in some translation point, in the hope that I can introduce perhaps one reader to such tragic joy. (For the first half-century, try the *Listy duverné* ('Intimate Letters'), Janáček Quartet No 2.)

In Praise of Trieste

Trieste, city of Svevo, Umberto Saba, and Joyce (Stendhal didn't like it), beautiful, majestic and cosmopolitan, Trieste the Italian city in Austrian buildings . . . Trieste, Triest, Třst, at the head of the Adriatic, the city round the corner, with Rilke's Duino Castle, where he wrote the great Elegies only about twenty miles away, Trieste houses Italy's senior university translation school. For the third time in four years the *Scuola* recently organised an international translation conference, this year on *La Traduzione in Scena*, having producers, theatre translators, actors and critics discuss some Italian (Goldoni), Spanish (Lope, Calderon, Lorca), French (Molière and Racine), Russian (Chekhov) and British (Shakespeare and Beckett) dramatists in translation. The *Scuola* generates enthusiasm, due to the versatility and variety of its staff, the ready articulacy of its students, and its exceptionally easy and democratic organisation.

Some (additional) Translation Exam-Day Hints

1. Bring latest edition dictionaries (as you may be faced with slang as well as neologisms) and encyclopaedias or reference books.

2. Bring the largest SL to TL dictionaries (since they have more technical words), as well as what you consider the best ones. (Therefore Langenscheidt Muret-Sanders for German, and Harraps for French and (with Sansoni) Italian; all three are in two volumes). The three volume Oxford-Harrap German, the greatest lexicography scandal since Sherlock Holmes, remains at the letter R.

3. Notes are only justified (a) to write 'Not found' for a lexical item, possibly with a brief justification of your translation, (b) if there's a mistake in the text, (c) to give an alternative version if there's a serious ambiguity in the text.

4. Do a separate check for spellings, statistics (commas, fullstops, billions, 'milliards' etc.), diagrams, and concision (pare down).

5. Look up all words that resemble English words and words you've not met or used for some time.

X
MARCH 1994

Translation Traduced

The many school and university teachers of translation, and particularly of literary translation, who are still insisting that students who translate from French into English should not use the 'same' or a cognate English word to translate a French one are doing them a deep and damaging disservice. Thus, in a recent international professional translation examination, *ambitions* was often translated as 'aspirations' or 'aims'; *organiser* as 'rearrange'; *sans nom* as 'anonymous'; *désordre* as 'chaos' and *chaos* as 'disorder', the latter couple in the same script; *répétitif* as 'monotonous'; *sans corps* as 'disembodied' or 'disincarnate'; *indivis* as 'indistinct' or 'indivisible'; *traité* (i.e. 'treatise') as 'dissertation'; *dialogue* as 'conversation'; *symétriques* as 'uniform'; *querelles* as 'arguments'; *acrimonie* as 'bitterness'; *poétique* as 'lyrical', *angélique* as 'dazzling'; *bouquet* as 'scent'. Most of these mistakes, I believe, were made not out of ignorance, but under the influence of what I think is misguided teaching. Any examiner marking such papers would have to charitably take into account the perversity of the teaching that influenced these translations as well as their obvious inaccuracy. In these cases, it appeared that accurate translations were being deliberately avoided, since they would almost certainly have consisted of words identical or cognate with the French originals. The French words quoted are virtually monosemous, and therefore context-free. If one accepts say the definition of translating in the *Petit Robert*, 'to cause what was stated in one language to be stated in another, aiming at the semantic and expressive equivalence of both statements' (*faire que ce qui était énoncé dans une langue le soit dans une autre, en tendant à l'équivalence sémantique et expressive des deux énoncés*) – incidentally, a much more satisfying definition than the brief ones in the *Collins*, the *Longmans* and the *Oxford* (*C.O.D.*) then it appears evident that the old precept of using synonyms rather than identical or cognate words violates the definition, and serves only to increase one's TL vocabulary and to avoid possible false friends.

This exam text was neither literary nor non-literary; it was a book review, a non-literary text about a literary text.

In fact my own principle of maximum accuracy would typically apply to the expressions quoted whatever the context, literary or non-literary, since they are monosemous, but I bear in mind that a literary translation cannot be as accurate as a non-literary translation, since in every segment of the text, the connotative as well as the denotative factors have to be taken into account, viz.: symbols, associations, sound and even the echoes of figurative language.

My last point is that the present wave of post-modernist post-structuralist translation studies (most of whose practitioners are university teachers and scholars) with its rejection of values, its utilitarianism ('the translation is just doing a job at a certain time and at a certain place') and its cultural relativism is misleading student-translators.

Book Reviews of Translations

Is it not time that book reviewers (e.g. in *The Guardian*) always included the names of the translator in the headings of their reviews, even if they are too lazy, unqualified or incompetent to discuss the quality of the translation?

The Disproved Familiar Alternatives

Depuis l'arrivée des Grecs de Vitylo (en 1676) . . . *et un bout de coeur a Itilo* . . .

Strict translation: 'Since the arrival of the Greeks from Vitylo . . . and a bit of heart at Itilo' . . . Close translation: 'Since the arrival of the Greeks from Vitylo . . . and a little bit of their hearts at Itilo . . .'

These are two scrap examples from an article about Corsica in a French news weekly magazine. At first I thought that Itilo and Vitylo were two neologisms, therefore familiar alternatives, denoting (by default) 'Italy' and 'Greece', since:

1. Itilo and Vitylo could not be found in any atlas; all other geographical features in the text, except for *Clochemerle*, connoting a strife-ridden village, are real.

2. The text is substantially about contrasts between Italian and Greek culture and the Roman Catholic and the Greek orthodox religions.

3. '*-ilo*' is a common suffix in modern French slang.

4. 'Viti-' or 'vines' may connote Greece.

5. 'Itilo' and 'Vitylo' contrast phonetically and appear to be made up. My 'neologisms' were merely conjectures . . . ('Ities' is a Second World War neologism for 'Italians'.) However, I soon realised that these guesses were 'ingenious but idiotic', as K.A.R. Sugden, my best classics teacher used to say. Vitylo and Itilo are unlikely nicknames for the two countries, and would have been put in inverted commas. When I found Itilo in a motorists' tourist guide (these, like road maps, are often more detailed than the best atlases or gazetteers), as a village in Greece, my theory was disproved; but I still cannot find Vitylo, even in historical atlases.

The TL as Language of Habitual Use

Normally and where possible, the target language is the translator's language of habitual use, but this precept is in danger of becoming a fetish or a mystique (or chauvinism, in the old sense). Sometimes a foreign translator writes better (English) than a native one, in spite of occasional errors of usage, and is therefore to be preferred. If the foreign translator has a native partner as reviser, the latter can usually make the necessary amendments satisfactorily. For informative texts, many countries have to do without native TL translators, but this is inadvisable for publicity, manuals and other persuasive texts.

Emphasis and Word Order

I suspect that emphasis and word order are the most neglected factors in translation and in translation theory. Thus a sentence like *On ne peut le faire qu'en l'élaborant*, the subject being an author's writing and the object being the 'trivial stuff' (*la matière triviale*) of his writing, can be wildly translated as 'It can only be done by elaboration', 'Only by elaborating on it can it be done', 'Only elaboration can ensure its achievement', 'Nothing but elaboration will do it', etc. etc., as though there were no difference between any of these versions and the strict 'It can only do it by elaborating on such trivial stuff.' In principle, there is always a strong case for retaining the same subject of a sentence in a translation, though there may be other semantic (lexical or grammatical) factors that make this difficult.

Britannicus

At the recent translation conference in Trieste, I was programmed to give a 'presentation' on four translations (English: John Cairncross (1967) and Samuel Solomon (1967); Italian: Maria Luisa Spaziani (1986); German: Wilhelm Willige (1956)) of Racine's wonderful play *Britannicus*. (Unfortunately, I missed the C. H. Sisson OUP translation.) Before starting, I asked those of my audience (perhaps 200 people) to put their hands up if they knew the play; two or three did. I therefore spent my hour in trying to explain to and persuade my audience why this is a great play today (and for ever), and incidentally, how important it is (with examples) to translate its greatness 'straight', cleanly and barely, with the concision of the original. The unit of translation here is normally the line ...

Britannicus is about world political power and its relation to power within the family:

Ce n'est plus votre fils, c'est le maître du monde. (180)
He's not your son. He's master of the world. (C)
He's no more your son, he's master of the world. (S)
Non è piu vostro figlio. È il padrone del mondo.
Er ist nicht Euer Sohn mehr, ist Herrscher der Welt.

The corruption of this power-mad world, which is the civilisation, the entire universe of the time, is exposed by a young girl, a creation of

Racine, not of Tacitus, therefore remote from intertextuality and inter-translation, a woman of shining and piercing intelligence as well as thin-skinned sensitivity and vulnerable strength, in my experience the most moving person in all drama, though I have never seen the play that I have read a hundred times (I was lucky enough to have to teach it with responsive students for several years), more moving to me even than Cordelia, on the same level as Lear and Hamlet, the play's main tragic character, Junie:

> *Combien tout ce qu'on dit est loin de ce qu'on pense.*
> *Que la bouche et le coeur sont peu d'intelligence.* (1523–4)
> How distant thought is from the spoken word!
> How little do the lips and heart agree! (C)
> How far is what one says from what one thinks!
> Between the mouth and heart how few the links. (S)
>   *quanto lontani*
> *sono i loro discorsi da ciò che hanno in mente.*
> *La bocca e il cuore parlano, ma separatamente.*
> *Was man sagt, gibt hier vom Gedanken nicht Kunde,*
> *Und der Mund steht kaum mit dem Herzen im Kunde.*

(Note the niceness of Cairncross's 'lips', of Spaziani's *ma separatamente* and of Willige's *kaum . . . im Bunde*.)

This hypocrisy, the toadying insincerity of this world is vividly illustrated:

> *Mais ceux qui de la cour ont un plus long usage*
> *Sur les yeux de César composent leur visage.* (1635–6)
> But those with longer knowledge of the court
> Compose their face in line with Caesar's eyes. (C)
> But those with greater knowledge of the court
> Stayed in their seats, eyes fixed in Caesar's eyes. (S)
> *Ma chi ha della corte più antica cognizione*
> *Sullo sguardo di Cesare modella l'espressione.*
> *Während die, die den Hof seit langem schon kannten*
> *Mit fragenden Blicken zum Kaiser sich wandten.* (W)

(Only Cairncross preserves the suggestive 'compose'.)

Racine's acute sense of 'psycholocation', of the importance of a person's position in a room, in relation to other persons, enlightens the setting:

> *Il m'écarta du trône où j'allais me placer* (110)
> (steered) Me from the throne I was about to mount. (C)
> Barred me the throne I was about to mount. (S)
> *e mi scostò dal trono che stavo per sfiorare.*
> *Und hält mich beflissen vom Throne getrennt.*

Junie is continuously aware of Nero's physical presence:

> *Vous êtes en des lieux tout pleins de sa puissance* (712–3)
> *Ces murs même, Seigneur, peuvent avoir des yeux,*

Et jamais l'Empereur n'est absent de ces lieux.
You are in places echoing with his power,
These very walls, my Lord, they may have eyes,
And never is the Emperor far from here. (C)
You're in a place full of his mighty presence,
These very walls, my Lord, perhaps have eyes,
And never is the Emperor without spies. (S)
Tutto esprime e rispecchia il potere sovrano.
Anche questa parete, Signore, guarda e sente,
e mai l'Imperatore potremo dire assente.
Sein Wille gebietet in all diesen Räumen
Diese Wände selbst sehen mit Augen nach mir,
Und entfernt ist der Kaiser niemals von hier.
(The last two lines are best and closest in the German, unusually).
Racine's portrait of Nero the voyeur (*derrière un voile*) and sadist is
psychologically precise:
J'aimais jusqu' à ses yeux que je faisais couler. (402)
I loved even the tears I made her shed. (C)
I love the very tears I caused to flow. (S)
amavo anche il suo pianto che per me scaturiva.
Die Tränen noch liebt ich, die sie geweint.
(Je me fais de sa peine une image charmante.)
Racine's political perception is extraordinary, anticipating many
later situations:
Nos ennemis communs ne sont pas invincibles . . . (895)
Notre salut dépend de notre intelligence . . . (916)
Our common foes are not invincible . . .
Our safety hangs on working hand in glove. (C)
The image is of two previous enemies brought together by their
present enemies, which anticipates Rabin and Arafat, Mandela and De
Klerk, not to mention Churchill and the devil. *Nos ennemis communs
combinent de nous réanir.* No Racinian characters can conceal their
feelings to which their eyes are an unerring guide.
What remains strongest is Junie's voice (as though now) calling out
to her lover rushing to his destruction:
Mais du moins attendez qu'on vous vienne avertir. (1562)
But wait at least till you are summoned hence. (C)
But wait at least until they tell you so. (S)
Aspettate qui almeno che vengano a avvertirvi.
Verweilt, bis man kommt und ruft Euch hinein. (W)
(Solomon seizes the essential simplicity of the line.)
The tight economy of the language (formal and restricted by rule)
the delicacy of the sound, occasionally lengthened by the threatening
r's and s's:
(Que veut-il? Est-ce l'amour qui l'inspire?

Cherche-t-il seulement le plaisir de leur nuire (55–56) – only the Italian can approach this), the quietness of all the characters deafened by the great *monstre* Agrippine – these are enormous tasks for any translator, and these four have produced eloquent introductions to this astounding play.

Notes on Psychiatric Translation and the Diogenes Syndrome

For any translator, the medical vocabulary is confusing enough; the psychiatric vocabulary is often chaotic, given the perennial divide between behaviourism and mentalism, as well as the various degrees of eclecticism between them, not to mention the renewed efforts, now exaggerated by PC, to sanitize terms that arouse prejudice. However, translating a 1985 article on *Das Diogenes–Syndrom* in the *Fortschritt-liche Neurologische Psychiatrie* I found the language sober, *sauber* and restrained. A few lexical points:

Entmündigung; 'sectioning' is the tactful British cultural equivalent; I preferred 'certification', as the German context perhaps removed it from prejudice.

Sammeltrieb. The jargon terms are *'collectionism'* and *'syllogomania'*, but I preferred 'the urge to hoard'.

Lebensraum. 'Personal environment' or (of course) 'personal space'. (The political sense is hopefully a fossil.) *Der Tod des Lebensgefährten hat eine neurotische Störung im Selbstwerterleben zur Dekompensation gebracht.* 'The death of her life-partner had been offset by a neurotic disturbance in (the experience of?) her self-esteem.' ('Decompensation' is usually a medical term, but not here.)

Bezugsperson. 'The person one relates to'. An English coinage is desirable.

Asozialität. (yuck). 'Unsociable behaviour.'

. . . *Sie lässt sich aus der Wohnung des Bruders herausklagen, um auf diese Weise leichter an einen eigenen Besitz zu kommen.* 'She had herself evicted by court order from her brother's house, and in order to obtain a new property (more easily).

(*Ausklagen* for *Einklagen*, 'sue, prosecute'. Thanks to Sabine Nice.)

Thymoleptisch. Obsolete word. 'Psychotropic'.

Versteinerung. Petrifaction, 'state of rigidity'. (Diogenes the philosopher in the latter part of his life abandoned all normal social habits and lived happily (?) in a tub. As the average life span increases, so does the syndrome.) The subject of the syndrome lives in a state of rigidity.

Idioms

Idioms, whether used by Thomas Mann or in ephemera, cannot be translated literally, whether they are up to date, passing or obsolete, unless they have a perfect literal equivalent in the TL. Thus *durch mehrerer Herren Länder*, in the second paragraph of *The Magic Mountain*, is simply 'through several countries' or 'through several types of countryside' or some such expression.

XI
MAY 1994

Collocations Again

The typical translation difficulty with collocations in non-innovative texts is when one meets a smooth collocation like *technische Konsumgüter* and asks oneself abruptly: what are 'technical' consumer goods? Have I ever seen that? If not, one plays safe with 'consumer durables', 'high tech consumer goods' or even 'industrial consumer goods'. But often, *technisch* or 'technical' is only used to make an impression.

Note that there are two types of collocations: (a) two or more words that are frequently juxtaposed ('deliver a letter'; *einen Brief zustellen*; *distribuer une lettre*; green memories, *souvenirs vivants*, *frische Erinnerungen*); (b) the items of a particular lexical frame or field (e.g. letter, alphabet, graphic, postman, pillar-box). The first is of more direct interest and use to the translator than the second, which is also useful when restricted to a particular 'discourse', e.g. 'subvert, space, deconstruct, signifieds' for structuralism. Perhaps it would be less confusing if the two types were distinguished as 'syntactic collocations' and 'discoursal collocates'.

Los Fusilamientos

The title on the picture, which is another crucifixion, in the Prado is *Los Fusilamientos de Moncloa* but it is often referred to as *Los Fusilamientos del Tres de Mayo*. I think the appropriate translation is 'The 3rd of May Shootings'.

Translation

'Look after the sense, and the words will look after themselves.' This has a point, but it is too casual; if the piece is difficult, you often have to look into the names and the words before you can look for the sense. And after you have the sense, if the passage is packed with meaning, you have to go back to the words.

Book Reviews

When an extensive review of Georges Duby's *Love and Marriage in the Middle Ages* appeared in *The Guardian* of 11th January without mentioning the name of the translator, Jane Dunnett, I protested, and received no reply. Jane Dunnett also protested, and had a reply from Richard Gott, the Literary Editor, stating . . . 'the fact is that we do make efforts to mention translators when we remember to . . . However, it is not the task of a newspaper to provide free publicity for translators (*sic*). I can well understand your need to improve the statu: of your honourable craft, but I'm not sure why it should be the job o literary editors to assist. As I say, we do our best.' Coming from *Th(Guardian*, which makes such wide use of translations, this is patron ising, too plausible ('I can well understand') and duplicitous. (I coul(use a harsher word.)

Jeremy Sams

Jeremy Sams, the latest translator of *Figaro's Wedding*, *La Bohème* and other operas as well as Anouilh's plays, gave a fascinating insigh into his views on his work to the IOL Translating Division. He see. translation as a hybrid, but always finally as his own English work written primarily for actors or singers, yet true to the author. Metapho is the heart of a theatrical work, a continuous 'handhold' for the trans lator; a play with few metaphors is 'hard to translate', he believes Admittedly literal language is always easier to translate than meta phorical language, but it is less dramatic and flatter and insipid to suc) a translator. On the other hand, Jeremy Sams was told by his father a an early age never to translate say *organization* (F) or *organizzazion(* (I) as 'organization', thus leading the way to an exceptionall inaccurate translation method. He was under the mistaken impressio) that thesauruses only exist for English, but he rightly emphasised th(*Roget's* unique advantages for English translators. He thinks play should only be translated for the stage, and is scornful of the *Pengui. play* translations. For him, a play is only a play when it is staged; thi is a point of view, but for me there are at least four plays of Racine tha I can only enact properly in my mind when I read them, and I do nc want to see them on the stage, whether in French or in English. Am the only one?

Not Alone

'I am surprised and disappointed . . . that the absence of love in th) spirit of the Schumann's writing elicits no comment in the translator' preface.' Thus Hugo Canning in his fine review of *The Marriag Diaries of Robert and Clara Schumann* edited by Gerd Neuhaus an(translated by Peter Ostwald (Robson Books) in the *Sunday Times* of 2 March 1994. Robert had written of a pianist 'whose Jewis) physiognomy disgusts me', and 'Jews remain Jews: first they take seat for themselves, then comes the turn of the Christians.' 'Indu) gence for the Schumanns,' Hugo Canning writes, 'evaporates at thei abuse of Mendelssohn, a man who did his all to promote Schumann' music.'

I quote this review to show that Hugh Canning, who love Schumann's music, is looking in vain to the translator to make the kin of external comment from the translator that I have been asking for i) similar cases. Remains the strange paradox that Schumann was *par excellence* the inspired setter of the poems of the great Jewish and German poet Heinrich Heine. *Ich grolle nicht?*

The Literary Register

When literature is close to life, there should be no such thing as a literary register, since literature, like vocal music, makes its own use of speech rhythms, as well as all kinds of technical and professional registers which demonstrate the infinite relish for facts and words of a good writer. Yet 19th century Romantic writers seem to have acquired a register of their own, partly taken from previous centuries, which now has the faded flavour of a literary register. To translate them is a pain, since (scrap examples), for 'lissom' one can only find the current *souple* or *agile*, for 'fleet' *rapide*, for 'woe', *misère*, for 'blushful' *rougeâtre*. Translations of Hugo or Wagner should produce a more antiquated vocabulary.

Titles and Christiane Nord

These Paragraphs have frequently been concerned with the translation of titles. I have suggested that they can be categorised as (a) 'descriptive' (describing the topic of the text) or (b) 'allusive' (symbolising the topic of the text or referring to one of its main features), and that whilst a descriptive title should normally be closely translated, an allusive title is often replaced by a descriptive title or a different allusion in a non-authoritative text (where the alien culture, concision and sound effects should be borne in mind), but is usually closely translated in an authoritative text. I have also noted the tendency for literary retranslations of titles to prefer a literal rendering of the original.

Such observations would be regarded rather askance by Christiane Nord, whose curiously titled book *Einführung in das funktionale Übersetzen: Am Beispiel von Titeln und Überschriften* (UTB Francke, Tübingen and Basle, 1993, pp. 315) contains much interesting and useful information. Her 'corpus' consists of 12,500 titles (German, English, French, Italian and Spanish) in literary, technical, informational and children's literature, and the most useful part of the book is the detailed discussion of a few of the translations. Her list of typical semantic and grammatical structures of titles also serves as a reference rather than as a guide to translation, and she curiously regards her titles as text-types (*Textsorten*), thereby devaluing the so-called 'cotexts', i.e. the texts themselves. Like her functionalist colleagues, she seems to think that most texts run on tramlines, and she converts translation into the terms of a commercial transaction or a PR exercise. The book has numerous painstaking and pointless statistics, and is distinguished by an exceptional number of platitudes (*Werbung braucht Adressaten* – publicity requires addressees/target groups; *Der Schein trügt oft* – appearances are often deceptive) as well as a series of so-called 'theses' of a mind-boggling banality (e.g. 'In order that the title can fulfil its representative function, the information delivered in the title must be comprehensible and acceptable – that of the target title for the target receptors (Functional adequacy)'. There are sixteen more theses at this level.

The Quality of a Dictionary

All dictionaries, good or bad, have their uses. The monstrous definition of *contestation* in the Harrap's Bilingual French and English, 'contestation, on the part of a minority of fourth-rate, left-wing, students' should not divert from the fact that this is the largest most comprehensive dictionary of its kind, particularly in the colloquial and technical field. In any event, words in bilingual must always be checked with words in monolingual dictionaries.

Beverly Adab

I warmly recommend *Annotated Texts for Translation: French–English* by Beverly Adab (Multilingual Matters Ltd, Clevedon, 1993, pp. 292) to students preparing for the Diploma in Translation, for any professional translation examinations or for final degree examinations. The book contains an Introduction to Key Concepts, where opposites like Neubert and me are neatly reconciled, a Preface to the texts which proposes a practical (hands on!) methodology, thirty contemporary non-literary French texts, covering a wide range of topics mainly from newspapers but with De Gaulle and a medical text for contrast, their suggested translations, and detailed and sympathetically written annotations which are also a useful reference for any writer of translation criticism or extended commentary.

Lisbon and Evora

Lisbon's fine Guggenheim Museum is doggedly monolingual; not even the leaflets in the rooms are translated. Evora, on the other hand, a historical jewel, has its tourist publicity co-written into English by an excellent but anonymous journalist – 'It is a place to go to, not through.' Evora University recently held an absorbing conference on Anglo-American studies, but even now, twenty years after the carnation revolution, a professional translation course does not exist in Portugal.

Political Refugees

By courtesy of Edda Ostarhild, the Institute's Director, I have read an absorbing article, *Uber die sprachlichen und kulturellen Ursachen von Missverständnissen und Widersprüchen in Asilverfahren aus der*

Sicht des Dolmetschers (On the linguistic and cultural reasons for misunderstandings and contradictions in immigration proceedings for political refugees from an interpreter's point of view) by Petra Wurzel (*Zeitschrift fur Türkeistudien*, 4/93, pp. 101–125). The article is packed with arguments and translation examples, and a translation should surely be in the hands of all British community interpreters and translators.

Here I have only space to summarise some main points:

1. These legal proceedings are usually instances of the vital importance to the interpreter of a knowledge of both languages and cultures, as well as of the background and educational level of the asylum-seeker, of whom s/he has to be frequently asking further questions for clarification.

2. There is inherent ambiguity in all languages; 'How often?' may mean 'How many times?' or 'How frequently?' (cf., 'Why?' which has four meanings.)

3. The applicant's language, if it is non-Indo-European, say Turkish, is likely to be much more restricted than the court's. Thus *arkadas* (Turkish) has five common German equivalents, and many more in the spoken language.

4. Since (say) Turkish is so restricted, it is hard to tell whether *yalamak* means caught, arrested, detained, surprised or called to account. Technical legal and descriptive words are often covered by synonyms, and therefore the interpreter has to pursue their distinction. Two Turkish words, *baski* and *baskin* have about a dozen German meanings, three or four of which would make equally good sense in the situation.

5. The poorer the education of the applicant, the greater the danger of legal proceedings being misunderstood. (The first of three 'correlations' in the article.)

6. Most Turkish political refugees are Kurds, who themselves have an inadequate knowledge of Turkish.

7. Turkish interpreters often ignore the distinctions in German prefixes, e.g. the difference between 'shoot' (*erschiessen*) and 'shoot at' (*schiessen auf*).

8. Typically, applicants for political asylum use only 'we' and 'they' as subject pronouns, leading to confusion. Objects of verbs are often omitted, and attempts and acts of rape or suicide confused in statements.

9. Geographical administrative units are frequently confused.

The article highlights situations that could occur in many countries.

The Victoria Sandwich Cake

The new M and S cake only has the information (description and ingredients) and some instruction (when to store) components of its packaging translated into French, Dutch and Spanish, presumably the most common but rather surprisingly chosen languages of those residents of at least the south-east of this country who (a) eat cake, (b) don't speak English. Persuasive words like homestyle, classic and traditional are not translated, and 'foreigners' (shades of the Aliens Department), an ugly word now, to be avoided by translators, are told nothing about whether or when to freeze the cake.

The translations of the ingredients are beautifully literal, but the colon instead of the three dots after *avant le/houdbaar tot/antes de* to introduce the sell-by date on the front of the package seems confusing to me. The Spanish is immediately followed by: *Ver frente del envase*. Goods for cooking have, additionally, cooking instructions (*cuisson*, *cocción*, *toebereiding*) in the three languages, which give the translators more licence in the syntax. For fish products, German is added.

World English

American English continues to 'jolt' the language and words of the industrialized countries, so that one 'hears' it in the translation: *der gut eingeführte* (introduced) *Markenname*, 'the established brand name'; *personalpolitische* (political) *Ziele*, 'policy aims for our personnel'; *die Aufgabenstellung* (formulation) '*task allocation*'; *Weiterbildung* (education), 'further training'; *exzellente englishe Sprachkenntnisse*, 'excellent knowledge of English'; *ein fachlich überzeugendes* (convincing) *Niveau*, 'a technically persuasive level', *ein bestehendes* (existing) *Team*, 'a team that is in place'; *die Position ist reizvoll* (enticing), 'the position is attractive'; *der von uns beauftragte* (commissioned) *Berater*, 'our appointed adviser'.

The Order of Things!

Michel Foucault's *Les Mots et les Choses* (Gallimard, 1966) was retitled *The Order of Things* (Vintage Books, Random House, 1973) by exclusive arrangement between the publisher and the author. The translator of the book is not even mentioned or referred to.

XII
JULY 1994

Proust Again
Given *Le Temps Retrouvé* (the last book in the series), which eliminates the other senses of *perdu*, I think the only suitable translations of *A la Recherche du temps perdu* are '*In Search of Time Lost*' or '*In Search of Lost Time*'.

New York
New York appears to be the only place with two familiar alternatives – Gotham (old fashioned) and the Big Apple.

T. S. Eliot on Translation
'When I read a terza rima translation of the Divine Comedy and come to a passage where I remember the original pretty closely, I am always worried in anticipation by the inevitable shifts and twists which I know the translator will be obliged to make, in order to fit Dante's words into English rhyme. And no verse seems to demand greater literalness than Dante's, because no poet convinces one more completely that the word he has used is the word he wanted, and that no other will do.' ('What Dante means to me' in *To Criticize the Critic and Other Writings*, T. S. Eliot, Faber and Faber, London, 1965. Quoted by José Manuel Mora Fandos in a Research Paper, University of Valencia, 1993). I do not think that the place of literal translation in approaching the work of Dante, whom Eliot called the most universal of all poets, or of any great poet, has been better stated.

Organisation and Ambition
I think that 'organisation' and 'ambition', like their Romance analogues (e.g. *ambition* (F), *organisation* (F)) are two grecolatinisms which normally translate into their Romance language cognates.

However, the place of grecolatinisms outside Greek and the Romance languages (Romanian, Italian, Romansch, French, Catalan, Castilian, Galician, Portuguese) is not so well established. 'Ambition' and 'organisation' would now frequently be translated into German as *Ambition* and *Organisation*, but fifty years ago, 'ambition' would more commonly have been translated as *Ehrgeiz*, which is now, being both physical and 'transparent' (craving for honour), a stronger word than *Ambition*. (Perhaps *Ehrgeiz* is the concept word, whilst *Ambition* is more appropriate for concrete instances of ambition.)

At that time, grecolatinisms were frowned on by the conservative, purist and right-wing German hegemony (as they were a century

earlier in England by some 'folksy' writers like the fine poet William
Barnes), but not by Hitler, who had some sound ideas about language
though he wrote atrociously. In fact in Karl Breul's *Cassells German
Dictionary* of 1940, 'ambition' does not appear as a German word, and
is translated as *Ehrsucht* (now obsolescent?) *Ehrgeiz* and *da.
ehrigeizige Streben*; 'organisation' is translated as *der Bau, die
Körperbildung* and lastly (somewhat reluctantly?) as *die Organisation*
The massive incursion of English into German came after the War
with military occupation and Allied control of the media, including the
setting up of English periodicals and radio stations and American and
English films; soon afterwards, TV completed this unique, irresistible
and virtually unresisted linguistic invasion. Note that in German the
deliberate and unnecessary substitution of grecolatinisms for
Germanic words (e.g. *Translatologie* for *Übersetzungswissenschaft*
carries on the tradition of inkhorn pretentiousness.

I think that most, not all, English grecolatinisms should be trans
lated into their corresponding grecolatinisms in Romance languages
unless they are evidently false friends, as are some common words and
some technical terms. In the EC, now the EU French-English
Glossary, *organisation* has about 75 collocated entries, and is trans
lated as 'organization' in all but two cases, where it is translated a
'body' (*organisation européenne*, 'European body'; *organisation de
vente*, 'sales body'). Standard collocations or those in natural social
use are the most powerful factor in sometimes forcing an unexpected
variation on to a word, and 'body' hovers rather capriciously
arbitrarily over *organe, organisme, organisation, corps, ensemble* and
even *masse* in some contexts and collocations.

In most other cases, I think it is perverse and a perversion of the
truth to avoid translating a word by its cognate in the target language
always provided that both words have the same meaning and are
roughly equally frequent within the register and the discourse.

National Languages for Export Week
The President of the Board of Trade, Michael Heseltine, recently
made an eloquent speech to launch the overdue conversion of British
industry to foreign languages, putting a welcome stress on the cultural
as well as the linguistic barriers to be broken, but he barely mentioned
translation, which is what makes exports stick. The Languages Lead
Body has set up new national language standards and there will b
Business Culture Training and Developing Business Language
Strategies (this Body was never short on cliché) before attention i
turned to Translation 'and Interpreting'.

(Conference interpreting and community interpreting are difficult
and important skills, but business (liaison) interpreting is usually a
adjunct to the four language skills.)

Hopefully the Languages Lead Body will bear in mind that in the tasks relating to exports – publicity, manuals, correspondence with clients, contracts, etc. – the translating has to be done by personnel completely at home in the foreign language and culture. For translating into English, writing well, particularly in summaries and note taking, will be as important as knowledge of foreign languages. It is high time that in this context, 'languages' and 'translation' are recognized as two separate skills.

Bilingual
'Add "bilingual" to your CV – in two months!' says a current advert. The technical discussion about 'compound' and 'co-ordinate' bilingualism continues, but the term is deteriorating to 'person with an elementary knowledge of one foreign language'.

Modern Quotations
A dictionary of modern, as well as one of standard quotations (Penguins or the new Oxford) is an essential component in a translator's reference library. Such quotations are not always identified by inverted commas – unusual word-order, capitalized words, odd use of language, casual misquotations, may all signal quotations ... Example: 'why go to war because of a quarrel in a distant country of which we know nothing' ... (not the former Yugoslavia, but the Munich betrayal of Czechoslovakia by Neville Chamberlain).

Standard Institutional Terms
The most common method of translating the names of important institutions, provided they are transparent, is to translate their components literally and retain the FL acronym: thus for *Agence Nationale de recherches sur le sida (ANRS)*: National Agency for AIDS Research (ANRS), referring to it later as ANRS. In a technical paper, the French title should be added in brackets.

Equivalent Effect Again
The principle of equivalent effect or (Nida's) dynamic now functional equivalence is usually defined as producing virtually the same effect on the target readership in translation as was produced by the original text on the source language readership. The effect is assumed to be mainly emotive, rather than cognitive, since the effect of acquiring new information is not particularly emotionally important. It is usually agreed that national cultures are the biggest barriers to equivalent effect. However, the nature of this effect has to be further examined. For persuasive texts, one assumes the effect has to be strong and lasting, otherwise the translation (like the original) fails, and the translator should as far as possible remove the source language cultural barriers. For translated poetry and serious drama,

the immediate effect may be different, but with repeated readings and
increased understanding, particularly of serious poetry, where it is
usually essential to read the poem 'a hundred' (*trente-six*) times before
it informs one's 'structure of feeling' (Raymond Williams). . . . for
translated poetry and drama, the reader should eventually feel the
same impact as the original reader, even where the human content of
the text is 'clothed' in cultural language. Thus, in Siegfried Sassoon's
poem *Does it matter? / Ist das so schlimm?* (Wolfgang G. Deppe),
Qu'est-ce que ça peut faire? (Jacques E David):

> Does it matter? – losing your legs? . . .
> For people will always be kind,
> And you need not show that you mind
> When the others come in after hunting
> To gobble their muffins and eggs . . .

> *Ist das so schlimm – die Beine verlieren?* . . .
> *Die Leute sind stets zu dir gut,*
> *Und du brauchst nicht zu zeigen, wie's tut,*
> *Wenn die andern vom Jagen heimkehren*
> *Und Semmeln and Eier soupieren* . . .

> *Qu'est-ce ça peut faire? – perdre une jambe ou deux?*
> *Tout le monde sera constamment si aimable,*
> *Et pas la peine de prendre un air lamentable*
> *Quand vous verrez les autres, après la chasse, revenir,*
> *Pour dévorer leurs toasts, leur bacons et leurs oeufs* . . .

Here the German substitutes its own culture (*Semmeln*), the French
writes in a more typical English culture (bacon, eggs and toast); when
the poems are finally 'possessed', equivalent effect, which, here again
is emotional rather than cognitive, is achieved in spite of the diverging
cultures. And in this superb universal poem, that is only right.

A Counter-example

You can renovate (or refurbish) a building or furniture or a café
but not an exam. You can renew your subscription or your strength, but
not an exam. So when you get: *La rénovation des DEUG*, the title of
an article in *Le Monde de l'Education* (September 1993), courtesy
Janet Fraser, it has to be The Reform of the . . . Reforming the . .
Reshaping the . . . the verb-noun emphasises the state, the gerund the
process. Unlike many of my previous examples, the transference of
the verb-noun '*rénovation*' i.e. the use of the same cognate in this
translation would be inappropriate. Note also that *rénover* is a false
friend for a literary genre, which you can revive; for morals (*le
moeurs*) which you can restore, and for a title (*un titre*), which you can
renew!

(As for the DEUG, which is in the *Collins Robert* (note the general tendency for dictionaries also to be encyclopaedias) the translation depends on the TL setting and the readership. For a peer readership, the French acronym, which recurs in the article, should be retained, and the full title of the exam translated and explained (Diploma in general university studies, ordinary degree equivalent). For a broadsheet, the title 'A university examination reform' might be sufficient.

But in spite of this counter-example, I think that half the misunderstanding about the nature of translation in Britain is due to the fact that so many teachers tell their students to avoid translating an SL word by a similar looking TL word whether it's a cognate or not. Thus the students expand their vocabulary and distort and murder their translations.

Reference Books

At the recent ITI annual conference, which was notable for its keenness and its enthusiasm, Janet Fraser read a splendid paper on 'Translating Practice into Theory: A Practical Study of Quality in Translator Training': this was a dense report on a thinking aloud survey, which she conducted on 21 professional translators confronted with a text. However, these translators all appear to think that dictionaries are not for establishing meaning, but for 'refining it' and dictionaries are therefore generally to be mistrusted. I think they are wrong. Reference books are a translators' main tool, and they are increasing in number and improving in quality, as they pay more attention to contexts and frequency. Certainly it is important to assess their reliability and to take their range and date of composition into account, but the idea of weaning apprentice translators away from dictionaries, as though they can do without them, encourages many translators' extraordinary arrogance. What is important is to show people how to use reference books, and to relate bilingual dictionaries first to monolingual dictionaries and then outside language to reality, i.e. to encyclopaedias and textbooks, and where possible to the relevant work sites and informants.

At the conference, when I made my protest, and pointed out that good dictionaries embraced colloquialisms and technical terms, I was accused of living in academia, being an ivory tower (Surrey?) professor, etc. etc. But I translate too.

The further argument, which is whether databases, CD-ROMs electronic form etc., are always better than books, is still to come. First shot: I always myself write and tell my students to immediately write additions and corrections into their reference books. Perhaps this is an argument not about efficiency but about taste between book-maniacs and technofreaks, between lovers of printed words and lovers of screened images, or just, but I do not believe this, between generations.)

La Biodiversité en Panne

As soon as a neologism like *biodiversité* is accepted by a standard monolingual dictionary, the translator can use it, explaining it (the existence of a wide variety of plant and animal species in their natural environments, the aim of conservationists concerned about the destruction of rain forests and other habits) according to context and readership.

Brackets

Note the increasing (?) use in French and English of brackets as a concise alternative to 'such as/for example/ etc.':

Giscard faisait passer dans la loi une évolution des moeurs (le droit de vote à 18 ans, l'interruption volontaire de grossesse) admise par une majorite sociologique. (Le Monde, Dossiers et documents, 1988)

'Giscard introduced into law a development (changes) in social customs (such as the right to vote for 18 year olds and the intentional interruption of a pregnancy) which were accepted by a majority of the country'.

(Acknowledgements for the example and comment from David Oldfield.) Note the characteristic misuse of *sociologique* (not 'a majority of sociologists' – joke) and its confusion with *social*; also that in this context the most accurate translation of *moeurs* is 'mores' a mainly American English sociological term which was, however, a favourite expression of the brilliant American dramatic critic George Jean Nathan (1882–1958).

Note also the 'hold-all' word *évolution* (cf. *élément, phénomènes affaire* etc.) which is often 'reduced' in translation not because the genius of English is more concrete but because the translator has to write well!

The Translation of Irony

During a discussion provoked by Gunilla Anderman's rich and varied lecture 'Linguist into Translator' at the Translation Divison's AGM it was suggested that irony, which, like metaphor, is always a lie, is not appreciated in Arabic speaking countries because it is regarded as insincere and dishonest; metaphor, being more imaginative and fanciful, is not regarded thus, it is the language of children Hungarians, on the other hand, being the most sophisticated nation in the world (oh yes), appreciate exaggerated irony. The relative linguistic isolation of Arabic compared with English and Hungarian may have something to do with a Palestinian's mistrust of irony. In any event, there are cases where irony has to be 'reduced to sense', i.e reversed by the translator to ensure the text is not misunderstood.

Gunilla Anderman also pointed out the need for further research

into transcultural communication, which Juliane House and S. Blum-
Kukla have been conducting for some years: to what extent does
American English: 'That's great!' translate British English: 'That's
not bad!' and when is 'Have you had your soup yet?' a polite way of
saying 'Please pass the soup?' All this is interesting, but the medial
non-cultural factors, which appear here through the tone of voice,
have to be borne in mind.

De Gaulle

I cannot give a better example of an authoritative statement, where
every word is important and almost every word has to be translated
literally, often with cognates, than the following:

A tous les Français
La France a perdu une bataille!
Mais la France n'a pas perdu la guerre!
Des gouvernants de rencontre ont pu capituler, cédant à la panique,
oubliant l'honneur, livrant le pays à la servitude.
Cependant, rien n'est perdu!
Rien n'est perdu, parce que cette guerre est une guerre mondiale.
Dans l'univers libre, des forces immenses n'ont pas encore donné. Un
jour, ces forces écraseront l'ennemi. Il faut que la France, ce jour-là,
soit présente à la victoire. Alors, elle retrouvera sa liberté et sa
grandeur. Tel est mon but, mon seul but!
Voilà pourquoi je convie tous les Français, où qu'ils se trouvent, à
s'unir a moi dans l'action, dans le sacrifice et l'espérance.
Notre patrie est en péril de mort.
Luttons tous pour la sauver. Vive la France!

Official translation: To all Frenchmen!
France has lost a battle!
But France has not lost the war!
A makeshift Government may have capitulated, giving way to
panic, forgetting honour, delivering their country into slavery. Yet
nothing is lost!
Nothing is lost, because this war is a world war. In the free universe,
immense forces have not yet been brought into play. Some day these
forces will crush the enemy. On that day, France must be present at the
Victory. She will then regain her liberty and her greatness.
That is my goal, my only goal!
That is why I ask all Frenchmen, wherever they may be, to unite
with me in action, in sacrifice and in hope.
Our country is in danger of death. Let us fight to save it.
Long live France!
Note that the English cannot reproduce the full irony of *des*
gouvernants de rencontre ('some chance people in power'), nor the
concision and force of *ont donné* ('have not yet struck'?); '*servitude*'

does go beyond *esclavage* (slavery'); 'ask' (*convie*) is perhaps a compromise between 'invite' and 'urge'.

This and That in Discourse

Demnach . . . darüber hinaus . . . pour cela . . . Dies . . . that . . . For
many years I have been suggesting that these deictics, whether used as
simple pronouns or as conjunctions (connectives), should nine times
out of ten in non-literary texts, be complemented by the relevant nouns,
thus 'according to this model' . . . 'in addition to cutting expenditure
. . . for that reason . . . the government can attain this object.'

Verbal Nouns

It is often difficult to distinguish 'state' from 'process' verbal
nouns, and John Desmond Gallagher has shown that they may be
clarified by transferring them to a conceptual level ('the idea that');
where verb nouns are used, their 'process' sense can be isolated and
their 'state' sense eliminated by translating them into gerunds:

Die Variation von Staatsausgaben und -einnahmen zur Inflations-
bekämpfung geht von dem Nachfragesoginflationsmodell aus.

'The idea of combating inflation by varying government expenditure and government revenue is based on the demand-pull model of
inflation!' (Thus a variation is too concrete to be based on a model; cf.
'The (idea of the) road came into my mind'.)

Proteus and Phrasal Words

Proteus, edited by Nancy Festinger and D. Orantia, is the nicely
named quarterly journal of the National Association of Judiciary
Interpreters and Translators (531 Main Street, Suite 1603, New York,
NY 10044). The current issue has a useful piece, with many examples,
on Bipartite (i.e. phrasal) Nouns and Adjectives by George K. Green,
pointing out how soon such vernacular words as 'pullout' or 'pullback'
insert themselves into more formal contexts. He even suggests, given
that they are 'untranslatable', that in many cases they should be
italicised as loan words and explained at first mention when transferred
in a translation (the French would certainly protest, and I hope this
procedure would be rare). Concrete objects, he suggests, could be more
easily translated: 'turnover' as *empanada, pâte, pasticcio, empada,*
Blätterteigpastete. He could have stressed that phrasal words illustrate
the monosyllabic strength of English (as opposed to the stuffy and
highbrow Grecolatin tendency in German and English), and are concise,
simple, vivid, physical and clear, though polysemous out of context.
According to the fine American writer on English, Bill Bryson, phrasal
words originated in American English, which would account for the
disapproval with which the British educational establishment viewed
them till perhaps the start of the Second World War.

Of Sources and Contrasts

Any translator is entitled to know the source and the destination of her text; the theme of the text and the quality of its writing she must decide for herself.

The source includes the name of the author (his other works may have to be consulted), the publisher or publication (for the house style) and the date of writing, in order to put register, colloquialisms, obsolescent words, technical terms etc. in their context. A writer on economics may use a peculiar word like *salvieren* (save, salvage) found in this sense only in the *Wahrig*, which (the word and the *Wahrig*) my Austrian students don't seem to have heard of, though words in *-ieren* (derived from the French salons) which smell of Viennese society ought to be familiar enough to them.

The destination (setting and readership) helps the translator to decide whether to expand the text with explanations or to simplify it.

The theme of a complicated text should, in the translator's mind, become the gist, and often this is mainly a matter of determining strong contrasts. Thus in the last paragraph (not to be translated!) of a passage from Artur Woll (*Soziale Markwirtschaft im Wandel* – the Social Free Market Economy in a process of change – Verlag Rombach, Freiburg), there is an opposition between *Humanin-vestitionen and Sachinvestitionen* – investments in human beings and investments in material objects – which excludes any technical/financial sense of *Sachen*; and again in the clumsy sentence: *Wenn deutlich geworden sein sollte, daß in der Hochschulbildung die ineffiziente Faktorverwendung einzelwirtschaftlich nicht zu salvieren ist, bleibt die Frage nach der gesamtwirtschaftlichen Faktorallokation*, perhaps: 'If it should become clear (evident, transpire) that in university training, the inefficient use of inputs cannot be salvaged (avoided?) in certain individual (particular, single) economic categories (aggregates, aspects), the question of determining the overall distribution (allocation) of economic inputs remains to be settled' – here the opposition between *gesamt* and *einzeln* (throughout the passage) at least excludes any technical interpretation of *Einzelwirtschaft*. Lastly, the theme of the piece is university education as a business process ('students out, customers in', in the Guildford Tech 1994 version), and therefore the contrast between *Bildung* (education) and *Ausbildung* (training) is valid.

As for the quality of the writing, even those scrap examples hint that, unless the text is authoritative or 'expressive', usually, inten-tionally or *unbeabsichtigt*, i.e. intuitively, it has to be improved.

Proper Names

Whenever a proper name is not known in its context it has to be searched. For a translator, an encyclopaedia item is as much a part of a language as a dictionary item, and normally, if target language readers are unlikely to be familiar with it, it has to be glossed, inside or outside the translation, depending on its occasion. It should not be left as it is simply because it is unglossed in the source text, this being irrelevant.

The traps are (a) mistakes (it wasn't Göring who wanted to take out his revolver when he heard the word culture), (b) misprints (Wurms), (c) variant spellings, (d) transliterations, (e) familiar alternatives (Boney), (f) unusual collocations especially in medicine, inventions etc. (*oscillation, rythmée de la luette*; Müller's sign), (e) geographical features (*Magonza, Mainz*), (f) bilingual surnames (Kopernik), (g) unusual or surprising looking names (Caron as Beaumarchais). So *au sortir de la quatrième glaciation de Wurms* becomes 'after the fourth and last Würm (Würm is a river in Bavaria; the French form is Wurm). (I should explain here that whilst I have many sometimes bizarre theories of translation, views on behaviour and politics, obsessions with places, works of art and people, my main job always is to help students and sometimes translators to translate, and if I can't be liked, I want to be appreciated therefore.)

Literal Translation and Auden

'To read is to translate, for no two persons' experiences are the same. A bad reader is like a bad translator: he interprets literally when he ought to paraphrase and paraphrases when he ought to interpret literally' (*The Dyer's Hand and Other Essays,* W. H. Auden, 1963, Faber and Faber, p.3). In the case of the translator, I think this is right, when literal translation results in the closest possible semantic and pragmatic equivalence (which is not often, but more often than most people think), whilst in other cases, 'paraphrase', which must always be as concentrated and as concise as possible, has to be resorted to, when literal translation makes no sense; this is quite common, but not as common as most people think. (For me, Auden has always been one of the most exciting poets and most thought-provoking writers.)

Translating the Metalingual

As I have stated elsewhere, translating the metalingual (i.e. SL puns, SL linguistic terms and references to the source of other languages), always offers the translator a number of choices, depending on the importance of the linguistic reference. In the following quote from a popular sociological work a compromise can be made by distancing the reference:

Il suffit de comparer la définition du mot 'connaissance' à 25 années d'intervalle pour constater combien la maîtrise du 'fait' est à la fois récente et humiliante.

– la connaisssance est l'ensemble des notions conformes à la vérité (Quillet, 1968)

 – *la connaissance est l'ensemble des spéculations ayant pour but de déterminer l'origine et la valeur de la connaissance philosophique ou scientifique. (Hachette, 1993).*
 Nuances? Non! Mais évolution de la pensée objective.
 I suggest: 'We have only to compare how knowledge was defined 25 years ago with now to realise how recently (and humiliatingly) we have learned its true meaning. Knowledge then was regarded as the totality of ideas that conformed to the truth; now it is the totality of speculations intended to determine the origin and the value of scientific or philosophical knowledge. This is not a modification of the earlier definition; it simply shows how thinking develops objectively.' Thus I have stripped the original of its local French references, since I think the author is trying to make a general, not a French point. In any event, the original French quotations and dictionary references could be added in footnotes or at the end of the book.

Of Proust and Punctuation (Ironical Inverted Commas)
 The use of inverted commas to ironically quote typical discourse is beautifully illustrated in Proust, and can be translated neat: *Elle adorait passer toute une journée a 'bibeloter', à chercher du 'bric-à-brac', des choses 'du temps'* (*Un amour de Swann*, p. 79). She loved spending a whole day 'looking round for little things in antique shops', searching for 'bric-à-brac', things 'of the period'. (Note that *bibeloter*, now obsolescent, was current in the 19th century, so cannot now be translated by a neologism; my translation is sadly inadequate, but . . . please improve.)

Case Grammar, Phrasal Nouns and Discourse Analysis
 German and English phrasal nouns like *Durchbruch*/break through and *Durchsetzung*/carrying through may have missing case partners, or they may have their own independent life. Thus a sentence such as '*Der Durchbruch erfolgte mit der Währungsreform*' may mean 'Success came with the currency reform' or, if *Durchbruch* refers to the *neue Wirtschaftsordnung* in the previous sentence, it will be 'It (the new economic system) came with the currency reform'. With the continuous increase and upgrading of phrasal nouns in Germanic and Slavonic languages and the hyping of verbal and phrasal nouns in the media, there must be many parallel translation pairs. Note that phrasal adjectives, originating as 'process' and becoming 'state' past participles of phrasal verbs, may have quite different forms or morphologies in translation – thus, 'broken down', *kaputt*; 'run down', *baufällig, schäbig*.

The Emphatic Power of Verbal Nouns
 Much as I jib at turning English verbs into nouns, when they are

passivized, this seems the most effective procedure. Thus: *Der Beitrag Franz Etzels muß hier besonders genannt werden.* 'Special mention must be made of Franz Etzel's contribution', rather than close translation: 'Franz Etzel's contribution must here be specially mentioned'.

The Singularly Emphatic Tongue

Is English the only language that distinguishes 'one' from 'a': (except for Turkish), leading to common mistakes or ambiguities among translators, and that has emphatic present and past tenses (*do* love, *did* love), all three features often neglected by translators?

XIII
SEPTEMBER 1994

Connotation

It would be helpful if lexicographers marked off the connotations of words separately, under the appropriate subheading in mono and bilingual dictionaries. For example, out of context, in *teuere Turkentarife*, what is the connotation of *Turke*? Beating down prices, wild, irregular, subject to haggling? According to the Webster, the connotations of 'Turk' used to be cruel, hard-hearted, tyrannical – but that's over now, though 'Young Turk' remains as a 'young revolutionary'. Perhaps translate as 'wildly expensive charges'?

However, in this piece on insurance policies, it became clear, since *ein Diskriminationsverbot* ('a ban on discrimination') was in the previous sentence and *ein besserer Gesetzschutz der Ausländer* ('better legal protection for foreigners') came three sentences later, that Turks as symbols/tokens of foreigners rather than their connotation were intended, and that the translation here might be 'expensive charges for foreigners' (such as Turkish workers), since 'Anglo-Saxon' readers would not be aware that in Germany, Turks (a word to be avoided anyway – 'foreign' and 'foreigners' are also often avoided) stand for *Gastarbeiter*/foreign workers. (Warm thanks to René Haas, one of the awful 30% brighter than the teacher.)

Note that a connotation is as subject to cultural context as a denotation, but the rarer or more technical a word, the fewer connotations it is likely to have; a common but monosemous word denotatively (e.g. 'gold') may have multiple connotations (virtue, excellence, scarcity, brightness, etc.). It is a pity there is no general English Dictionary of common Connotations, Tokens and Symbols, which would be invaluable for translators, if their currency and periods of use were indicated in each instance. Note the grisly German euphemism: 'guest workers'.

Accessing Acronyms

I suspect non-literary translators waste more time chasing acronyms than any other chunks of text. Hints:
1. The acronym may be within the text, or in the bibliography.
2. It may be an internationalism, probably English.
3. It may be made up of first letters, or first syllables, or a combination of both.
4. An increasing number of dictionaries and encyclopaedias include acronyms as normal head-words.
5. Test for misprints/misspellings/variant spellings/transliterations/ historical acronyms or referents.

6. Some acronyms are invented, and can only be cleared up by appropriate informants.

7. Translators should join the campaign against any unnecessary, obscurantist, obfuscating or elitist uses of acronyms, which I lead.

8. Beware of confusing acronyms and neologisms.

9. The names of private firms are often acronyms, which translators need not decypher. 'Translate' IKEA as 'IKEA, the Swedish takeaway furniture superstore'.

Anti-Circumlocution (*Umschreibung*)

In one sentence you get *Gesetzentwurf*, in the next, *das Paragraphenwerk*, referring to it. Translate 'the bill' in both cases.

Quotations Again

Quotations have to be checked by translators, particularly the old trick of inverting the sense of a quotation with the multi-purpose three dots to indicate an omission. Thus, recently: 'Newmark says: 'A content word . . . has to be translated by its primary, most common sense'. The essential qualification was: 'whose meaning is not affected by its linguistic context', which, in ordinary language, is rarely, and this was craftily omitted and the sense of my sentence was therefore turned upside down.

Natural Translation

Derek McCulloch, in a telling article in the *Sunday Times* (5.6.94) has claimed that the standard of first year students in written German is deplorable. He quoted 'The train she arrived on was late' as a test sentence. As I see it, there is a choice here. The closest natural translation is perhaps *Ihr Zug war spät*, but this might also refer to a train she owned, or had money on, or was due to meet. An unambiguous translation would be: *Der Zug, mit dem sie ankam/fuhr, hatte Verspätung* but this sounds like a 19th century novel, therefore unnatural now. The only way to translate the full sense naturally is to split the sentence into two, but this produces different emphases: *Sie ist mit diesem Zug angekommen, aber er hatte Verspätung*. In fact there is no difficulty in translating the sentence, but the translator has to know what kind of translation she is to aim at, not to mention the dear old context (see p.111).

Past Participles as Nouns

In contrast to English, the Romance and the Germanic languages frequently use past participles and adjectives as nouns referring to people, whilst adjectives and occasionally present participles can refer to qualities. English usually adds the noun e.g. *Versicherte*, 'insured persons'; *die Beiträge der Jüngeren*, 'premiums for younger customers'; *Senioren*, 'senior citizens' (the standard term, however dislikeable).

The Shock of Art and Music

Housman in *The Name and Nature of Poetry*, famously wrote: 'If a line of poetry strays into my memory, my skin bristles so that the razor ceases to act'. Me, sometimes if I hear Schumann's *Widmung* ('dedication', with its concentrated adoration – the beloved becomes twelve objects, including a grave – by Rückert) or Strauss's *Zueignung* ('Dedication' again, but more personal, closer to devotion – the words an extraordinary jumble of Romantic rubbish by a Hermann von Gilm zu Rosenegg, who also wrote the poem of Strauss's *Allerseelen* 'All Souls Day', another excruciating excoriating miracle, the title not to be confused with the refrain, *Alle Seelen ruhn in Frieden* – 'all souls rest in peace' – from Schubert's supreme and tragic *Litanei*, 'Litany', words by Johann Georg Jacobi), all once sung by Fischer-Dieskau, cherished for so long, or by Peter Schreier, and now by Olaf Bär (rather than Wolfgang Holzmair or Andreas Schmidt?) . . . sometimes when I listen to these songs, I abruptly burst into shuddering, overwhelming sobbing, everything is transfigured or *verklärt*, this is joy, suddenly life is worth living. This my 'breakdown' (what a word) also occurs in anticipation before the beginning of the last scene in *Jeji Pastorkyna* – 'Her foster-daughter' – commonly known as *Jenufa*, Janáček's masterpiece, and inexplicably but invariably, during the Susanna-Marcellina duet in *Figaro's Wedding* (the correct translation) . . . and at other blessed places and moments.

This shock of music is deeper than the notorious 'tingle factor', which is often protracted and exploited by John Adams and other minimalists, but was recently beautifully discussed by Yehudi Menuhin, a political as well as musical hero, who gave the Heine-Schubert *Doppelgänger* sung by F.D. as a main example. Furthermore, the shock of art is recursive and cumulative, more acute at every recurrence (*senti questo*! 'feel/hear this' in *Figaro* again), an amazing reunion and nth meeting again with the composer, provided it is judiciously spaced. (Note the translation points carefully, if there are any.)

German Noun-Compounds and Case Grammar

Any occurrence of an unfamiliar German double noun compound, however convincing it sounds, should be tested for a missing case partner. Thus: *Regelung der Informationspflichten*: 'regulating the obligation to provide full information to users', since 'information duties' is obscure; *Binnenmarkt für Risikopolicen startet*: 'opening of internal market for insurance policies with (variable) risk premiums'.

4567890

The Translation of Geographical Terms

Geographical terms should normally be translated by their standard modern target language equivalents: thus Den Haag/The Hague; Nürnberg/Nuremberg; Sevilla/Seville; Livorno/Livorno/Livourgne (F) (Leghorn is now absurd? a joke rather than a pronunciation solution); Praha/Prague; Bodensee/Lake Constance. Belgian features, if not anglicised (Antwerp not Anvers or Antwerpen, Ghent, not Gent or Gand) are usually given their Walloon names, but in an official document, Flemish and Walloon names should be given.

Kundera and Janáček

The well-known Brno novelist Milan Kundera has often written sensitively about Janáček, but I think he exaggerates when he writes: 'There is something poignant, even tragic, in the fact that Janáček spent most of his creative forces precisely in opera, thereby putting himself at the mercy of the most conservative bourgeois public imaginable. His innovation lies in a new reassertion of the value of the sung word – the Czech word, which 99% of the world's theatres cannot understand. It would be hard to imagine a greater accumulation of self-afflicted obstacles. . . . The difficulty lies in the psychological meaning that the melody confers on the singing of each phrase, each word, rather than on the scene as a whole. If the words are sung in Czech, the listener in Berlin or Paris hears only syllables devoid of meaning. If they are translated, French cannot place the tonal stress on the first syllable as Czech does, and the same intonation would have a different psychological meaning.' (*Les testaments trahis*, Gallimard, 1993.) In theory, this is undeniable, but Janáček now has world-wide audiences, so there is no 'tragic' situation; surtitles can compensate for the intonation differences; and given the overwhelming music, unless one is in the first three rows, it is hard to pay attention to or hear the words anyway.

Some Austrian Institutional Terms

Austria has a bicameral parliament, the *Bundesversammlung*, the Federal Assembly, which has a *Nationalrat*, the National Council, and a *Bundesrat*, the Federal Council. Strange as it is to refer to a chamber as a *Rat*/council, it is perverse to translate it as 'assembly' (Collins Dictionary and some older textbooks). The *Rechnungshof* ('audit department' rather than the too 'British' National Audit Office?) has a *Präsidium*, which in academic texts might be translated by the couplet: 'executive committee' (*Präsidium*). Perhaps the most authoritative reference book for national and international institutional terms is the annual *Europa World Year Book* (Europa Publications which also produce the *World of Learning* for higher educational institutions). The Austrian *Länder* are translated as 'provinces (contrast German *Länder* or 'states'). The less important an institutional term, the more licence to produce an informal translation. (Note that the Austrian Socialist Party has been renamed the Austrian Social Democratic Party, but is still SPÖ or SÖ.)

Emphasis

The English equivalent of *c'est . . . qui* is often 'there is'. Thus: '*Ein wesentlicher Punkt über den man sich geeinigt hat*': 'There was one essential point they agreed on'. And again, functional sentence perspective is more important than grammatical 'accuracy': *Dem Rechnungshof soll gesetzlich ein Stellungsnahmerecht zum Entwurf des Bundesfinanzgesetzes samt Anlagen eingeräumt werden, heisst es in einem aktuellen Zwischenbericht an die Präsidiale* (=*Präsidialkanzlei?*): 'the audit office is to be granted the legal right to take a view of the federal finance bill together with its schedules, according to a current intermediate report to its executive committee.' (Contrast with the literal translation: 'to the audit office a right to take up a position on the draft federal finance act together with supplements should legally be conceded, it is stated in . . .')

Keywords and the Thread of a Text

A translator can sometimes thread her way through the text by mentally simplifying its keywords. Thus '*Fiskalismus*' (a coinage) = tax policy; *Finanzpolitik* = financial policy; *Monetaristen* = protagonists of basic rates control; *Geldpolitik* = bank rate control.

The French Obituary Future

French obituaries have a habit of beginning with a perfect tense (*nous a quitté . . . est disparu*) to describe a death, following with a perfect to describe a birth, and then pursuing the life in future tenses. English begins with a perfect or a past, and continues with the past till the end.

Creating Metaphors in Translation

I see nothing wrong in adding a dead or standard metaphor to a translation to make it more graphic, provided the SL text is non-authoritative, informal and the sentence fairly trivial. Thus *annehmbarer* may become 'a more acceptable face'.

Jean Delisle

Jean Delisle's latest book, *La Traduction raisonnée*, an introductory manual for professional English to French translation (Ottawa University Press, 1993, 484pp.) is also most helpful for any French to English translator, though it is a pity that in such a large work he never discusses the translation of literary or authoritative texts and gives the impression that every text has to be 'naturally' translated, thus leaving the reader unprepared for translating Burke, Bagehot, Churchill, Enoch Powell, let alone Greene, Peake, Joyce. For him, texts and translations run on tramlines; his piece on metaphors, recommending Pisárska and ignoring her unspeakable 'model' (who could that be?) is sadly incomplete.

That said, the book is an exceptionally efficient, well-organised guide to the theoretical and practical analysis and translation of sixty modern French journalistic texts. Delisle's categorisations are admirably Cartesian: his division of translation procedures into *report* (transference, including monosemous words), *remémoration* (translation routines, e.g. transpositions) and *créations discursives* ('recreations' or paraphrases, often on the basis of *compléments cognitifs* (extralinguistic knowledge of 'cultural baggage') is pedagogically useful, as is the brilliant and comprehensive glossary. Everything is explained, and therefore this is a book for the lonely student as well as the teacher. There is a plethora of examples and exercises, and how good to get away from the sickening jargon, literary (post-modernist) as well as linguistic. As in the works of many text and discourse buffs, I miss any thorough treatment of connectives, particularly conjunctions, and the vast range of '-ing' forms. The examples of gobbledegook, however, are super. Any translator would benefit from reading, consulting and referring to this book, particularly when disagreeing with it.

Proactive

'Proactive', which I assume to be an internationalism, is an admirable grecolatinism, originating in psychology, that connotes initiation, intiative, resistance to standard reactions, making things happen, preventing predictable and unpredictable disasters.

Legal French

F.H.S. Bridge's *Council of Europe French-English Legal Dictionary* (C. of E. Press, Strasbourg, 1944) has just appeared, and is to be warmly welcomed. It can be obtained from HMSO, Agency Section, 51 Nine Elms Lane, London SW8 5DR. Most entries are extensively glossed as well as translated. It is a pity the book has no introduction, but it should be studied in conjunction with Martin Weston's excellent *English Reader's Guide to the French Legal System* (Berg/Oxford).

The New Eagleton

Terry Eagleton (*TLS*, 15.7.94), after dismissing Derrida a few months ago, now says structuralism (plus post-structuralism and post-modernism?) is as dead as the Pre-Raphaelites; cultural relativism is patronising; culturalism reduces everything to culture as ruthlessly as biologism hacks everything down to biology and ignores an astonishing amount about the material composition of human beings; real freedom will only arrive when people are able to attack their own cultures as well as celebrate them . . . Will the literary translatologists now go into reverse as well? No sign yet [February 1998].

Wilss

Wolfram Wilss's latest book (*Übersetzungsfertigkeit; Annäherungen an einen komplexen übersetzungspraktischen Begriff* – Translation skill; approaches to a complex and practical translation concept – Narr, Tübingen, 1992) is his best. The grand panjandrum of translation theory is always sound and sensible, if occasionally rather obvious; has a rich and prolix rhetoric; is dazzlingly polymath – there are nearly 400 titles in the impeccable and useful bibliography – philosophy, psychology, pedagogy, sociology, translation theory, the natural sciences, computer science . . . you name it, it's there. There are particularly useful sections on interference and routine translating, but perhaps too much psychology, with plenty of English translation examples. '*Die ÜW*' is personified like some goddess, but Wilss is nicely ironical about the other fads.

The Paradoxes of Translation

Like my master F. R. Leavis, I am always trying to find areas of agreement about my subject with my colleagues and my students; but this is often a vain task, since translation reflects politics, morality, aesthetics. Most people would agree that one purpose of translating is to make the original text comprehensible to the putative reader. I would add, normally outside the text, if the text is authoritative and needs explanation. Many would disagree. I would add, even if the text is culturally or linguistically obscure to the first readership. Many would disagree. And then, in other moods, I say why not make the second readership do its own homework, which the first readership had to do? Why hand out everything on a plate?

Reference Books

As well as the standard dictionaries of ('canonical') quotations translators have to have dictionaries of modern (Penguins or Oxford) and international (Penguins) quotations on their desks.

XIV
NOVEMBER 1994

Reference Books Again

1. The 1993 *New Shorter Oxford English Dictionary*, edited by Lesley Brown (two volumes £60) has a claim to be the most useful large dictionary available to the translator into English, including both technical and colloquial vocabularies. Its citations and etymologies are superb. Its only rival is the now dated American English Webster's Third International.

2. The 1994 large one-volume *Oxford-Hachette French-English English-French Dictionary* (£20, pp. 1036) the first bilingual dictionary to be partly based on corpora, has a claim to be the most useful for the translator between the two languages. Note also the new Larousse French-English dictionary published last year.

3. Further to my *Paragraphs – 33* on Acronyms, there are a large number of dictionaries of acronyms: among the most useful, I recommend the *Oxford Dictionary of Abbreviations*. Apart from political terms and international organizations, I think medicine is the most important and frustrating harbinger of acronyms (TIA, 'transitory ischaemic accident, i.e. ministroke; MRI, magnetic resonance imaging; CT scanner, computerized tomography scanner). Note that acronyms are becoming increasingly English in many fields, but many, like slang, are the subjects of fads and fashions.

4. For famous modern and contemporary personalities, I now recommend the *International Who's Who* rather than *Keesings Contemporary Archives*, which is best for modern national and international events.

5. For one-word translations of basic words in English, Portuguese, Russian, German, Italian, Spanish and French, there is *The New College Multilingual Dictionary* by E. B. Williams and A. Senn (1967, Bantam Books, New York.)

6. There is a mysterious new series of Wordsworth Editions reprints, at £1.99 (*sic*) each, including a *Dictionary of Proverbs* and of (genuinely modern) *Idioms* (1993) ed. by E. M. Kirkwood and C. M. Schwarz.

Concision and Brevity

A translation has to be economical, not necessarily brief. *Hamlet*, with its brilliant satire on the prolixity of the 'self' besotted monologger Polonius – what a typical modern committee member he would be! – is one of the longest and most concise of all plays. So are several of Dickens's works, as Maugham failed to discover when he abridged them so unsuccessfully. Note the dramatic irony of Polonius's 'Brevity is the soul of wit' – which has to be translated 'straight', though it is perhaps a more pertinent criticism of Mediterranean than of Northern cultures – and Gertrude's sharp rejoinder, 'More matter with less art.' And Polonius' excellent sense in spite of his numbing loquacity.

Communicative and Semantic

About twenty years ago I distinguished two broad, sometimes overlapping bands representing methods of translation which I termed 'communicative' and 'semantic'. I use the terms less now, since my correlative approach largely supersedes them, and they have sometimes been reproduced too rigidly. Recently Gerd Wotjak of Leipzig University appropriated the terms without acknowledgement, whilst Brian Mott, in his otherwise most useful book, *A Course in Semantics and Translation for Spanish Learners of English* (PPU, Barcelona, 1993) has adopted, acknowledged and seriously misinterpreted them.

The Reine Sprache?

Jetzt hat er sich ausgeschlafen, 'now he's slept himself out.' Since there is no linguistic or cultural barrier here, I think the translated German expression usefully supplements the English stock of idioms.

The Paradox of Translation

Inter- or extratextually, a translation has to be understood even if the original isn't, or if the original can only be guessed. The translator has to work out an interpretation (even if it is a guess) of the original as a basis for his version.

Platform Papers

Platform Papers: 1. Translation (1992, National Theatre Book-shops, £22.95) is an engrossing booklet (but with all too few translation examples) comprising discussions with the drama translators Jeremy Sams and Ranjit Bolt and the dramatist-translators Christopher Hampton, Michael Frayn and Timberlake Wertenbaker. MF stresses the need for the translator to know the language and culture of the original, rather than, like Stoppard, using a 'literal'. TW seeks the same 'weight of word and power of phrase' and says that both translations and adaptations must become transformations. All agree that drama (I think all translations) should be in the moder language, but should exclude anachronistic slang ('chicken-shit') and idioms. CH criticises the French translator who insists on changing his play to suit French audiences) ('I know the French theatre-goer better than you'). Translators have to empathise with their plays, and plays bear the hall-marks of their translators. MF notes that translations have a shorter shelf-life than originals (particularly for comedy and farce). JS, a brilliant writer, points out that to talk of 'updating a play' is a nonsense. Genista McIntosh believes that 'playing music on authentic instruments' will kill the play. The avarice as well as the miserliness in *L'Avare* is emphasized. Both JS and RB translate lighter and more trivial plays more freely. A free version of say *Le Misanthrope* may be due to the translator being unaware of its importance and seriousness. RB's concept of 'translation as completion' comes close to Benjamin's *reine Sprache*. The booklet is a sign of the National Theatre's interest in foreign plays. It has still to discover Hebbel, Grillparzer, Hauptmann and Bernhardt.

The Farce and the Truth of Literal Translation

From seemingly time immemorial, literal translation has been the source of misunderstandings, and humour from hilarious jokes to subtle irony. Most issues, it appears to keep *The Linguist* going; see 'Towards Universal Understanding', *TL* 33/3, p. 100, 'Take one of our horse-driven city-tours; we guarantee no miscarriages', or 'we love harmonious music' (*Harmoniemusik*, music for wind instruments). On the other hand, literal translation tells the truth and exposes prejudices when words like *matador*, *Verbindungen* (bull-murders, duels) etc. are related to reality. And literal translation may enrich a language with non-cultural words, 'language-feeling' for *Sprachgefühl*, 'time spirit' for *Zeitgeist*, 'world outlook' for *Weltanschauung*.

The Ill Assorted Trio?

I have spoken often on Language Teaching and Translation Theory, and on Linguistics and Translation Theory, but not on the three together. The relation between Language Teaching and Translation had always been delicate; previously translation occupied too much of language teaching syllabuses; now it occupies too little, but it cannot replace the graft of written and spoken language learning, where it serves as an introduction and a later control.

Translation begins and ends with language, but draws on many topics outside language. Linguists frequently inject their undigested and unrelated linguistics notes into their essays on translation theory. The study of language is as objective and value-free as possible; translation theory is value laden, but it is based on universal values.

Translating Literary Language

The five main features of well written literary language are (a) that it is virtually figurative and allegorical, (b) that its sound is as important as its meaning – it is in the deepest sense, onomatopoeic, (c) it follows the 'quick' rhythms of speech, which have to be rendered by the translator, (d) it is concentrated, each word is indispensable, (e) it is likely to have more polysemous words and collocations than denotative language.

It is sometimes confused with the language of fantasy and nature which follows an outworn and faded poetic tradition (or a 'worn-out poetical fashion', see *East Coker*, T. S. Eliot).

Literary language is often indistinguishable from non-literary language, except in as far as it deals with imaginary people and places which have more or less symbolical names. *War and Peace* is notable for transferring occasionally and 'seamlessly' from literary to non-literary language, for example in the second Epilogue.

However, literary language and its translation has a greater licence than non-literary language to go beyond normal conventions of style, 'ignoring' the reader. Non-literary language and its translation, however bold and innovative in its vocabulary, must at least in its syntax be within the range of the reader.

The translator is more obliged to reproduce the full denotative and abstract meaning of non-literary language than of literary language, since he has additionally to do justice to sound in the latter. In the course of history, literature has sometimes built up a rhetoric (Augustan Classicism, Pre-Raphaelitism, Georgian verse) which succeeding poets using 'non-literary' language have then eliminated (Edward Thomas, a great writer, try the tragic and delicate *Lights Out*, Robert Frost, the Movement).

Well written literary language has to be closely translated, and the reader is normally catered for in a preface and notes outside the text. Particular care has to be taken to bring out the connotations of polysemous words and expressions, and to preserve repeated words, which are often keywords. There is sometimes a case for adapting cultural metaphors and for transforming fictional proper names so that their meaning is translated and their source language morphology retained. Thus (Howard Jacobson's) 'Wrottesley' would perhaps translate as *Pourriton* in French, *Pudrisley* in Spanish, *Apodriston* in Portuguese, *Putridsley* in Italian, *Foulchester* in German, and *Gneelston* in Russian.

In Mörike's sensitive poem, beautiful set or realised by Hugo Wolf, *In der Frühe*, describing mental confusion and torment at night contrasted with the relief and release of the morning, special care has to be taken in translating the affective 'unique' words *wühlen* (burrow, root, dig), *verstört* (distraught, disturbed), *geht herfür* (emerge, proceed). The fused music and poem seizes a universal human experience.

The fact that literary language must remain aesthetically pleasing in translation means there is a constant tension between the informative/semantic and the aesthetic function. Typically, the literary translator should have a command of an exceptionally wide affective vocabulary.

Multilingual Periodicals

The *UNESCO Courier* (32 languages), the Council of Europe's *Forum*, the *Reader's Digest*, and the *Scientific American*, the four of which contain many educative and humanistic articles, are good material for language comparison and translation criticism.

A Better Matched Trio?

Linguistics, Literary Analysis and Literary Translation by Henry G. Schogt (1988, University of Toronto Press, Toronto) is I think an instance of a book skating intelligently and abstractly with too few examples over the surface of its subject. 'There is no general linguistic theory of translation', declares Schogt, though he earlier mentions four. 'I hope that contacts between linguists, literary analysts (critics) and translators continue to grow', he concludes his book, without giving any conclusive justification for his hope. He frequently asserts that neither linguistics nor translation theory can give translators the answer they are looking for, and he does not explain the uses of the two disciplines to them. Nevertheless this is an interesting and allusive book, and the discussion of Weinreich's concept of hypersemanticization, i.e. the layers of meaning within a segment of text, is useful.

Financial Translation

The *Actes 1993* of the conference in Paris (pp. 130), obtainable from Christine Durban at 70 rue de Rome, 75008 Paris for FF 250+30, are a 'mine' of information on British, American, French, and to a lesser extent EU and German financial terms; hopefully a second edition will include a comprehensive index. The diagram of translations of corporate titles (p. 33) is enlightening, and it is a pity that cross-references are not made to the originating *Aufsichtsrat/Vorstand* (supervisory board/board of directors).

The Music Deepens the Translation

Nowadays composers set originals rather than translations: after the Bible and Songs from the Chinese (Arthur Waley), Britten set Rimbaud, Hölderlin and Michelangelo direct. In the 19th century, Hugo Wolf made notable settings of Spanish and Italian translations. The supreme and haunting song in the *Italienisches Liederbuch Benedeit die selige Mutter* (Blessed your mother, now with God) has its original:

E nel petto mi sentii
And in my breast I felt
Una fiamma si vivace
Such a powerful flame
Che disturba la mia pace
Which troubles my peace
Mi fa sempre delirar

Continuously maddening me
intensified into:
Und in meiner Brust gewaltsam
And powerfully within my breast
Fühl ich Flammen sich empören
I feel flames rage
Die den Frieden mir zerstören
which destroy my peace,
Ach, der Wahnsinn fasst mich an!
Ah, madness grips me!
The translations show that the anonymous Italian and the Paul Heyse texts are sheer cliché, though, as R. A. Stokes has pointed out, the German with its *empören/zerstören* and its alliterative *Flammen/fassen/Frieden* is much more powerful. Wolf's music transfigures the words.

The Translation of Traditional and Historical Idioms

Whilst an idiom is conventionally defined as a word-group whose meaning cannot be deduced from its parts, traditional and historical idioms, which depend on world-knowledge, should be researched by translators not familiar with them. Thus, *on en parlera à Landerneau,* meaning 'this is a complete triviality', can only be feelingly understood if one has been in (passed through) that God-forsaken Breton town. Such idioms (*idiotismes*), e.g. 'it's raining cats and dogs', 'kicking the bucket', are senseless when translated literally (for the translator, that is their mark of identification), are best understood and memorised through their history and have to be handled sensitively, since they are often clichéd, stilted, affected or obsolescent. The standard advice 'translate an idiom with another idiom' is all right if one exists which is current; more often, one has to reduce it to (colloquial) sense, since by definition, an idiom is peculiar to one language (a Landerneenne protested wittily).

Quality in Translation

Is a good translation (a) one that satisfies the customer (BS – British Standard – 5750), (b) one that fits its purpose (Steve Dyson, Hugh Keith), (c) typically, accurate – as long as the original is accurate – and elegant (me)? Note that (a) and (b), though they are important and unexceptionable, could apply to any product, and they ignore the original text, whilst (c) humdrum as it is, attempts to be specific to translation. As I see it, customer satisfaction is the proof of a translation's 'success', but it is not a measure of its quality. (Customers, like readers/receptors, can be idiots.)

At the recent ITI Conference, of which there is an admirable report (*Quality – Assurance, Management and Control*, ed. Catriona Picken, 1994, ITI, 377 City Road, London EC1V 1NA) which should be in the hands of all translators, the talk was more of (a) and (b) than of (c).

Both Paul Danaher and J. D. Graham struggled interestingly with the concept of quality, and confessed themselves defeated by it, without producing a single translation example. Kirsten Malmkjaer sagely pointed out that BS 5750 was not a measure of quality of product but of quality of management and administration, and indeed many speakers, including Christine Durban in a brilliant paper, were mainly (overly) concerned with these. There was a startlingly upbeat paper on MT by Terence Lewis, claiming that 300m words were MT'd annually – his source was not stated – but his argument was well reasoned and he produced good examples. Whilst the device of putting large simple well spaced capitalized and exceptionally platitudinous keywords or commands on a screen was over-exploited at the conference, these papers give a detailed and useful picture of the trials and frustrations of a non-literary translator's life.

The Theory of Translation

Any theory of translation must provide an answer to the central issue of translation: when to translate literally and when to translate freely. (This is and always has been the issue, though I think it is modified and moderated – virtually, that is when the occasion arises – by the five medial factors of moral, factual, logical, aesthetic and linguistic truth.)

However, in the literature today, this issue is mainly ignored. Neither the so-called relevance nor the *skopos* theories – useful, important and self-evident as the principles, not the theories, are, provided that they are not respectively blown up into brutalism (end justifies means) or to the exclusion of pertinent excursuses – address themselves to the issue; they are in no way specific to translation. (The theory of a process (or of anything) must be specific to that process (or that thing). If the process is a human activity, the theory must entail a methodology and therefore include examples.) Furthermore, national cultures, discourse, text, and linguistic uniqueness, important as they are, do not constitute theories of translation.

My double correlative proposition – the more important the language of the original, the more closely it should be translated; the less important the language of the original, the less closely it need be translated – which requires explanations for the keywords 'important', 'language', and 'closely' (which I have given previously, in addition to several corollaries), is one of many attempts to answer the central issue. (See p. 54 of T. H. Savory's *The Art of Translation* (Cape, 1968) for twelve more theories.) The first one was Cicero's, which favoured 'free' (*ut orator*) translation.

Mine is a prospective and a radical theory and a methodology of translation, which covers both literary and non-literary translation, though in each of these genres somewhat differently and not to the same degree; retrospectively, I think that the finest translations of texts whose language is important have been close translations, but historically, the greater number of translations have followed the literary fashions and sometimes the ideologies of the time, and this has to be borne in mind when they are evaluated; some of these translations are 'classics', but many (those that are morally and universally significant?), now need closer retranslation. I think that in the future it will be regarded as arrogant not to translate a great literary work (forget: 'text') closely. *A la recherche du temps perdu* translated as *Remembrance of Things Past* was 'poetic' in 1922; translated thus now, it would be an impertinent and conceited translation of the title.

My double correlation applies both to literary and non-literary texts, but since literary language includes so many additional factors (particularly in poetry), literary translation (particularly of poetry into poetry, which is the only kind of translation which is never revised, since it is a text in its own right, and is succeeded by other independent attempts), is not likely to be as close as translation of authoritative statements such as legal texts. Literary translation, however, is closer and more concise than that of all other kinds of texts, that is informative and persuasive texts. (Many authors do not make it clear whether they are dealing with literary or non-literary texts. Sometimes there is a mutual contempt which reflects the 'two cultures (science v. arts)' hostility described rather one-sidedly, but accurately by C. P. Snow. Philistinism and intellectual élitist snobbery can confront each other even in arguments about translation.)

A or the theory of translation, which is a method and an aim of translating, should not be confused with translation theory, translation studies, 'translatology', *Übersetzungswissenschaft* etc., which is all you want to know about translation but never think of asking.

The Ripple Theory?

If you can't translate the words, translate the sense.

Language and Translation from Cicero to Tytler

Language and Translation from Cicero to Tytler by Frederick M. Rener (1989, Rodopi, Amsterdam, pp. 367) is a rich discursive book on the history of Western European translation theory up to the late 18th century, amply illustrated with untranslated quotations from Latin, French, German, Dutch, Italian and Spanish texts. Most topics that are now being discussed appear during this historical period, including that of the learned and the simple readership of the same text, and there is much discussion of idioms, keywords and text-categories. Tytler's role in distinguishing *res* (the encyclopaedia),

verba (the dictionary) and style or rhetoric, is stressed, but his place
as the first translation critic of ideology is ignored. This is a
satisfying book.

Pragmatics and Translation

The concept of pragmatics, together with syntactics and
semantics, is usually attributed through C. W. Morris to C. S. Peirce
the philosopher of pragmatism, as a component of semiotics, the
science of signs. It can be defined as the general relationship
between language and its user, or the use of sentences in actual
situations. Speech act theory distinguishes the performative from the
descriptive and the expressive functions of language, and is one
aspect of pragmatism. (Grice's maxims are another.) A translator has
to distinguish between standardized (e.g. 'IOU', *Schuldschein
reconnaissance de dette*) and non-standardized or 'free' (e.g. 'I owe
you . . .') speech acts. Where there is no corresponding standard
speech act formula in the target language, it may have to be indicated
by the use of a comment phrase such as 'officially', 'formally'
'authoritatively' or 'an advisory opinion' (*dictamen*). (Note that
'pragmatic' is sometimes confusingly assigned either to pragmatism
pragmatics, praxis or practice.) Pragmatics was used fruitfully by the
Leipzig translation school, but has lain rather fallow since 198:
when Geoffrey Leech and Stephen Levinson produced thei
comprehensive textbooks. It threatens to become a buzz-word in
'translatology' again.

Translation Theory in the Former East

*Translation as Social Action: Russian and Bulgarian Perspec
tives* (edited and translated by Palma Zlateva; chapter introduction
by André Lefevere; 1993, Routledge) is a collection of essays by
well and less well known ex-Soviet and Bulgarian writers, each
preceded by some lively paragraphs from André Lefevere: Zlateva
herself thinks the debate on translatability paralyzed translation
studies in the West for two decades after 1945! The essays are
uneven in quality, some being banal, others showing insight into
translation dilemmas. The claim that the critical vocabulary i
stabilized in this discourse, which is barely Marxist, is hardly borne
out in these essays; but Soviet writers were pioneers in studying
translation seriously.

A Thought Squib

For the translator, language is on co-ordinates: function words ('who'
'for') are latitudinal (linear, lateral), syntagmatic and context-bound
keywords, technical terms and repeated words are longitudinal (vertical
paradigmatic), deep-rooted and may be context-free.

The Focus of Translation

The focus of translation was for long on the past: the cyclical trends that appeared to follow literary fashions; now it is on the present, the process of translating, and how translators translate, as though anything that is translated professionally must be right. I prefer to look at the future of translation, beyond cycles (after 1692 (Salem) witches were not and will not be hanged in America again), based on the five medial truths.

XV

JANUARY 1995

Translating Difficult Sentences

There are broadly two ways of translating syntactically/lexically difficult sentences: (a) read them carefully, get the sense, and edge it towards the full meaning; (b) in particular for long and syntactically complex sentences, and when you can scarcely make head or tail of them, first translate them literally ('plough through them', I say), get the sense, and then edge it in stages towards your final (intermediately positioned) version. Which method you use may depend on the occasion and your temperament, and you may use both methods, ending up in the middle and amending them for the appropriate register or discourse. Personally, I prefer the second method, and I think most people and most translators would prefer the first. So here is an example.

Plus généralement, les processus écologiques, qui se caractérisent par le long terme, sont soupçonnés d'être réduits par le langage économique comme par le prisme temporel du mode de régulation marchande (from *Une Justification écologique?* by C. Lafaye and L. Thevenot, *Revue française de sociologie*, XXIV, 1993, p. 511).

Literal translation: More generally, the ecological processes, which are characterised by being long term, are suspected of being reduced by economic language as by the temporal prism of trade regulation.

Sense: Normally, according to the jargon of the economists and the analysis of the watchdogs who look at market values, improving the environment is short work; in fact, it takes a long time.

A version: Usually, it is considered that the process of environmental improvement is characteristically long-term, but it is likely to be made light of in economic parlance, as it is in the measures taken by market-driven regulatory bodies.

I would normally add in a note, after reproducing the French sentence and its literal translation, that I do not understand the original, but I have interpreted it in a way that hopefully makes sense. I think the 'clue' to the sentence is the contrast between *long terme* and *réduits*: the metaphor *prisme temporel* suggests that regulatory bodies analyse and therefore reduce the time taken by environmental improvement, just as a prism separates out and clarifies light; but this metaphor is obscure and does not add much to the sense. (I thank my gifted student Christopher Jones who has contributed perceptively to this interpretation.)

An Amendment on Metaphor

Though these Paragraphs may sometimes read like failed textbooks on art, morals or politics, they are substantially intended as an extension or amendment of my *Textbook of Translation*. Thus I think the first purpose of metaphor is to describe something more comprehensively, economically and usually more *forcefully* than is possible in literal language: thus 'ditch' (*badengehenlassen, im Bach landen, plaquer, laisser tomber*) for 'abandon'. Again, it appears that English has more abundant metaphorical as well as lexical/grammatical/phonological resources than other languages?

Punctuation Marks as Translation Procedures

Piertti Hietaranta, in an interesting paper in the *Kouvola Papers in Translation Studies* (Prague, Kouvola, 1989) discusses the (im)possibility of translating some Finnish clitics into English. But the clitic *-kin*, included in a question, can surely be translated by an exclamation mark, since its sense is exclamatory rather than interrogative, whilst the clitic *-han*, expressing certainty and insistence, could be expressed by putting the whole sentence in italics or bold, rather than Hietaranta's charmingly quaint 'by golly'.

Prescriptivism

It is I think a truism that it is easier to point out what is wrong than what is right or 'correct' in any segment of a translation. Hence the attraction of 'negative marking' in translation exams. Normally, precise equivalences between two languages only occur when the SL and TL words refer to the same object or (more rarely) concept; when SL and TL terms are standardized to cover the same institutions; in much scientific and technical language; in the naming of natural and human universal objects and activities; in geographical terms. And then one must assume readerships with similar educational backgrounds, and no lexical gaps, such as disconcertingly exist for universals in many languages (leg/arm, hand/foot (R), privacy (E)). Apart from these cases, there are usually options, choices, variations and personal taste. Yet so many translation teachers are still insisting on the unique correctness of their own versions (according to translation students in Prague).

Natural Translation Again

Reading this para again I shuddered, and wondered if I had made a howler with *auf dem Zug* (19th century version) or just a slip (I tell my students I never make mistakes, only slips – joke), when a few days later came a friendly and understanding letter from Mr George Baurley in Dessau, suggesting *Der Zug, mit dem sie kam, hatte Verspätung*, which I gratefully accept. But I never explained my main point, which is that it is often difficult to produce in other languages neat equivalent translations of common colloquialisms, particularly from or into English, with its numerous and exceptionally varied informal '-ing' forms, phrasal words (verbs, nouns, adjectives) and conjunctionless relative/adjectival clauses (see p. 94).

Another Paradox of (Literal) Translation
What one person calls servility, parasitism, copying, the other calls the truth, fidelity, accuracy.

The Importance of the Source Text Language
In my opinion, in the future, the degree of closeness both of a literary and a non-literary translation should depend on the importance of the source text language. (By 'language', I mean 'the words on the page' (Leavis), as opposed to the thought-content, the facts or the hidden agenda of the original.)

The importance of the language depends on the following factors:

1. The authority of the text. I take it that in serious poetry (the densest and most expressive of all forms of language), short stories, plays to a lesser extent, novels, works by experts with pretensions to style, statutes, patents, treaties, and many official statements, the language is as important as the content.

2. The make-up of the language. Technical and institutional terms and standardized language have to be translated by their accepted equivalents, if these exist, and, additionally, explained in couplets, if the readership is unlikely to understand them. Cohesive markers are always important. Translationally, concrete nouns are more important than verbs, concept-nouns, adjectives and adverbs (in that order) since the four latter are more affected by ideology, and are likely to have more synonyms in the source and target languages. Thus in a headline, 'A nasty odour in Parliament', only 'Parliament' is likely to be invariant in translation.

3. In art for art's sake writing and in nonsense literature, as well as strongly alliterative, sonorous and figurative passages, the sense where necessary gives way to the rhetoric.

4. In strongly reader-oriented texts, the source language where appropriate gives way to cultural or technical explanations.

Translation Theories
Übersetzungstheorien; eine Einführung by Radegundis Stolze (Narr, Tübingen, 1994) is to my knowledge the first course textbook of translation theories in German specifically for students, and it is a nicely produced volume. (Werner Koller's masterly *Einführung in die Übersetzungswissenschaft*, 4th revised edition 1992, is the only scholarly review in German?)

Stolze surveys the field from Schleiermacher to herself, giving herself more space than any other writer, though she produces 'categories', not theories. Goethe and Nietzsche are left out, and so are George Steiner (tut tut!), Levy, Gutt, Dagut and Louis Kelly. The main features of skopos theory, descriptive translation studies, dynamic equivalence and FSP (Functional Sentence Perspective) are efficiently described, and some criticisms are hinted at, but the quality and the value of a translation are not considered. The boxed translation examples, including an excellent translation of Stolze's, are intrusive, but I can't quite trust a writer who uses so many *freilich's* and *ja's* and *nun's*, i.e. phaticisms.

Semi-Neologisms

I usually assume that translators are not allowed to create neologisms unless they are translating them in literature (when they must do so) or if they are members of an authoritative team of translators for say urban planning or forensic law. However, there are many semi-independent, often detachable, grecolatin affixes such as mega- macro- and -ism whose use by translator may be left to their taste (*mégacité*/megacity; *productivisme*/productivism, i.e. belief in productivity, growth mania).

The Interminable Mental Journey

From the literal translation, to the meaning in the mind, to its expression, to its formulation in the context of the translation.

Translation

The only occupation where the search for the truth is pursued by way of never ending changes of mind?

A Translation Class

Sometimes a translation class becomes simply a class about the target language and its culture until it is pulled back and reduced to cover a small fraction of the original.

Contrastive Business Language

Another illustration of the contrastive nature of economic texts from a somewhat convoluted account of VW in the '70s:
'*Ein Unternehmen, das seinen Beschäftigten nachhaltige Wechselbäder auferlegte. Phasen von Kurzarbeit, Einstellstopp und Aufhebungsverträgen auf der einen Seite und forcierte Einstellungen, Sonderschichten und Mehrarbeit auf der andern Seite kennzeichneten eine sprunghafte Unternehmenspolitik, die in diesen Jahren das Wirtschaftwunderimage verspielte.*'
My difficulty (unlike the millions, I never have 'problems') was *Aufhebungsverträge*, with its missing case-partner for *Aufhebung*, which only (?) appears in the compendious (1700 pages) *Dictionary of*

Business German (German to English by Dieter Hamblock and Dieter
Wessels, Pitman, 1991) as 'agreement to revoke a debt; agreement to
terminate a contract'. (It is also explained in the Gabler *Wirtschafts-
lexikon*, Vol. 1, 1988, Wiesbaden). As the six contrasted nouns refer to
working conditions, and this one is negative, I favour 'agreements to
terminate employment contracts' and suggest: '. . . a company that
imposed alternating good and bad conditions on its employees
Periods of short time working, suspension of recruitment, and agreements to terminate employment contracts' – better, 'low pay-offs' or
'settlements' (see *Sunday Times*, 13.11.94, p. 1) – were succeeded by
accelerated recruitment, extra shifts and overtime; this erratic
corporate policy frittered (gambled) away the image of the economic
miracle.'

As often, the contextual translation ('pay-offs', G. *Abfindungen*
'reduces' or particularizes the meaning ('termination contracts'), but
adds the useful pragmatic supplement ('low').

The Perfect Translator

Listening to the great Brendel discussing his teacher Edwin
Fischer's faithful and true renderings of the great classics and
deploring all the *fioriture* (ornamentations, embellishments) and free
'improvements' of past generations of pianists, I thought I was
listening to the perfect translator. Admittedly, there is no absolute
fidelity, all Brendel's interpretations are stamped with his own genius
(pardon, ideology), there is no definitive translation any more than
there is definitive musical interpretation, but what a difference
between this and the cultural relativism that puts (lately) Raymond
Chandler on the same level as Shakespeare.

The Translation of Literary Language

A sixth feature of literary language is that it has a wide range of
vocabulary relating to sensations, feelings, emotions and all personal
qualities, on which it is likely to centre more than most non-literary
(except psychology) texts. It is in this area particularly that English is
richer in synonyms than other languages, thus making the translator'
work more complex.

A seventh feature of literary language is that it is aesthetic
entertaining and didactic whilst non-literary language is informative
and/or directive.

An eighth feature is that it is concerned with a universe which is
more or less imaginary; historical or contemporary narrative accen
tuates connotations, however factual or prosaic the style (of a Stendhal
or a Camus) may be.

Further, within literary language, poetry has the additional primary
feature of a prescribed form, which is normally translated as a priority

often comprising metre, rhythm, stress and rhyme, all of which force importance onto each single word; signally, poetry is cognitively and linguistically more dense than literary prose, and therefore the most difficult and rewarding of all text-types to translate. It is the most meaning-packed of all forms of language. (Prose translation of poetry is more useful as a pale introduction to the original, as in the Penguin series, than as translation in its own right. Nevertheless, E. V. Rieu's prose translations exceptionally drew attention to the vigour and richness of the *Iliad* and the *Odyssey*.)

(See also the interesting attempts to distinguish literary language in *Essays on Translation* by Viggo Hjornager Pedersen (Copenhagen, 1988) which I warmly recommend.)

To Translate

To translate is to choose. Choice depends on criteria. Criteria are subordinate to a theory. A translator consciously or unconsciously follows a theory of translation, just as a language or a grammar teacher follows a theory of language. Therefore, *pace* Gutt, Douglas Robinson, Anthony Pym and other distinguished translation 'theorists' who think that translation can dispense with a theory, a theory of translation (which has to give some kind of answer to the 'free or literal' question) is indispensable. (I withdraw my statement in *Approaches* that no general theory of translation is possible, but, to cover all texts, it has to be on a high level of abstraction.) Further, elegance and neatness, in their 17th century mathematical senses, should normally be the stylistic criteria of a translation.

The Paramountcy of Content Words in Translation

'If you are given a translation of the content words in parents' speech to children in some language whose grammar you do not know, it is quite easy to infer what the parents meant.' Thus Steven Pinker in *The Language Instinct* (p. 278, Morrow, New York, 1994), one of the best and most attractively written books on language that I know, a generativist's book which incidentally triumphantly restores etymology and philology (the diachronic element) to linguistics. I infer that for grasping meaning, and therefore translation, content-words plus word-order are more important than function words or grammar, which can normally be transposed in translation. The main content word is the noun, which potentially carries the main emphasis or quantity of communicative dynamism in the sentence, provided it incorporates the new information (rheme). Thus, in the Czech question: *Kde je hlávni obchodni centrum?*, if one is told that *hlávni obchodni centrum* means 'the main shopping area', one may be able to infer that *Kde je* means 'Where is?'

Heights
The height of an outstanding teacher to raise student and research cash; the height of a translator to be computer-literate? (Irony.)

Truisms and Jargon
Truisms, platitudes, tautologies, pleonasms, redundancies, the totally explicit, the infinitely varied statement of the torturingly obvious, the launching of innumerable illusory aunt sallies simply for the purpose of masterfully knocking them down . . . these the features of so much of the discourse literature . . . thank goodness one does not have to translate it.

Translation is into the Translator's (Modern) Language
I take it as axiomatic that the translator translates into the language of hers and the putative readership's time, unless she has a special feeling and the readership is likely to have a special interest in the contemporary language of the original. Normally the translator can only emphasise in her own contemporary language and dynamic equivalence can barely be attempted without it.

However, 'modern' language must not be confused with modern idioms, slang and cultural *realia*. The linguistic levels (styles and registers) of the original have to be preserved in the translation and this requires a dignified language for serious or tragic works whilst modern colloquialisms and anachronisms may be appropriate in adaptations of the classical farces of, say, Molière and Aristophanes.

Faded Metaphors
In reporting style, English tends to be more matter of fact than French *l'aube de ce siècle*: 'the beginning of the century' (not 'dawn'); *les fidèles du parti*: the party's supporters ('party faithful' is a gushier style).

Names and Words
In any original, words and proper nouns are equally important. A translator has to know the meaning and function of each word. She has to know the function and the 'referential coverage' of each proper name, and to reproduce as much of it, inter- or extratextually, as will assist the likely TL reader to understand the translation properly. Thus depending on the readership's knowledge and the relevance of the additional information to the topic, 'Tito' may be translated as 'Tito' 'Tito the president of Yugoslavia, 1953–80' 'Tito (Josip Broz) 1892-1980, Yugoslav partisan leader in the 2nd World War who became President of the country', etc.

The Principle of Increasing Familiarity
In weighing up the translation of a collocation (*types de parti*

politiques), one often starts with a too brash sounding literal translation ('types of parties), which one varies unsatisfactorily (forms,
sorts, kinds, categories, classes). The more often one repeats the brash
translation, the more natural it begins to sound. Nevertheless, this can
be misguided. In the country of the blind . . .

Three Conflicts
    For the non literary translator, the usually successful resolution of
the conflict between accuracy and naturalness; for the literary translator, the only partially successful resolution of the conflict between
accuracy (truth) and elegance (beauty), and weighing up the linguistic
individuality of the source language author against the particular
features of normal usage in the target language.

French-English Dictionaries
    I think there are now four large French-English dictionaries: the
Harrap (two volumes, 1971, £60 approx. 1105 pages); the Oxford-
Hachette (half a volume, 1994, £20, 950 pages); the Collins-Robert
half a volume, 1993, £22, 950 pages); the Larousse (one volume,
1993, £25, 980 pages). The Collins-Robert has two-column pages, the
other three-column pages. I suspect that the Harrap has the largest
number of head-words (lemmas), particularly technical terms; I think
it essential to have all four (as well as the Collins Robert *Business
French Dictionary* and the EU *French-English Glossary*) at hand in
any professional French translation exam centre.

The Source in the First Stage of Translating
    The first of the three stages of translating (approach, process,
revision) is either the immediate approach, which most translation
teachers condemn and most translators practice, or the analytical
approach, or a compromise between the two.
    Identifying the source of the original is the first step in translation
analysis: the author (themes and literary style); the publication
content and house-style); and the year of writing. The year of writing
is essential, since idioms and colloquialisms fade so quickly, the
media which live by rapid change (called innovation) dominate
language, and language can even make progress. Two months ago,
'spastic', the linguistic deposit of schoolchildren's prejudice was
thankfully 'replaced by' by 'cerebral palsy'. (The rest is in *A Textbook
of Translation*, the second chapter.)

Dynamic Equivalence
    As (*à measure que*) translated 'great' literature (*Kohlhaas, Faust,
Britannicus*) is read and reread, as it should be, the human-universal
becomes more dominant and the cultural-customary-social recedes in

the mind, so that dynamic equivalence (in principle) is achieved
sooner or later. The great Shylock speech achieves and always will
achieve dynamic equivalence in any language.

A Cry
   Why paraphrase, when you can translate?

Absolute and Relative
   No topic lends itself less to sweeping and absolute statements
('quite simply', 'it's as simple as that') as does translation. Two
examples: 'Translation is initiated by the very choice of foreign text,
always an exclusion of other foreign texts and literatures which
answers to particular domestic interests' (Lawrence Venuti). 'Always'
is absurd; the 'exclusion' may or may not be deliberate, the sentence,
like much of Venuti's work, suggests a conspiracy theory. '*Une langue
est un instrument de communication selon lequel l'expérience
humaine s'analyse différemment dans chaque communauté*' (Georges
Mounin). Mounin fails to determine or discuss the (greatly varying)
degree of difference.

XVI
MARCH 1995

Translation and Language Teaching

My impression is that most of the foreign language teachers in the schools still have the feeling that translation is only a useful exercise if it expands one's knowledge of the words and grammar of L2. For this reason, they think one should avoid any 'repetition' of the words, grammar and word order of the home language; so translation becomes an exercise in paraphrase, which should only be its last resource.

A Concise Definition of Translation

The accurate and elegant transfer of the meaning of the text of one language to the text of another for a new readership with a different culture.

Try the Negative

If one searches in vain for a suitable equivalent for a word of quality (which may be an adjective, adverb or adjectival noun), say in *techniques d'identification fragiles*: flimsy, fragile, shaky, thin, tenuous, weak, and so on, one can always try modulating it with a negative: unreliable. 'Unreliable' is not 'in' the word (*fragile*), it's more general, but at least it's safe. If de Gaulle had written the text, I would have translated it as 'fragile' (in view of the 'authorial authority'), although *fragile* has a considerably wider semantic range than 'fragile': *estomac fragile*, weak stomach; *bonheur fragile*, precarious happiness; *fortune fragile*, unstable fortune, etc.

Fashions and Dates

An editorial board member of a refereed academic journal recently stated that *A Textbook of Translation* (1988) was 'out of date'. Personally I think any work about translation may be bad or good or out of fashion, but it cannot be out of date. A scientific work can be out of date, but translation theory is not a science, although it has a scientific component. There are so many different approaches to this relatively new study that qualifiers like 'out of date' or 'traditional' are inappropriate.

T/V

Perspectives: Studies in Translatology 1: 1993 (edited by Cay Dollerup, Henrik Gottlieb, Viggo Hjornage Pedersen; Museum Tusculanum Press; University of Copenhagen, 1993) is an attractive journal notable for a fascinating article by David Pollard on Body Language, that is, the difficulties of 'translating' Chinese gestures and facial expressions into English, and for Gunilla Anderman's 'Untranslatability: The Case of Pronouns of Address in Literature'.

I pointed out in an article entitled 'Translation and the Vocative Function of Language' in the *Incorporated Linguist* (Vol. 21, No. 1, Winter 1982, pp. 30–1), when discussing the T/V issue (i.e. translating to and from *tu/vous, Du/Sie, Lei/voi,tu*) that no direct equivalent translations were possible, but that there are always more-or-less adequate compensation procedures; further that they invalidated John Lyons's statement that the issue substantiated the 'impossibility of translation', since the semantic difference could always be explained to the reader in notes or a preface, which are both translation procedures, although they could never have the same impact as the original.

One can always alternate first names and surnames. Nowadays in English the use of the bare surname (without the Mr), which used to be an 'advance' in friendship amongst gentlemen, is the nearest equivalent to '*du* ' as an insult. Before the last war, *tu/du* was common (but now impossible) from officers addressing 'the men' or from mistresses addressing their maids.

Gunilla Anderman is mainly concerned with drama, where sometimes a change in the tone of voice is the main, but not the only translation resource, as in Racine's supreme play *Britannicus*, when Agrippine, after showing her respect for her emperor son Néron with the *vous* mode of address in her tremendous diatribe in the fourth act, suddenly, in the middle of the last act heaps one *tutoiement* after another, nearly thirty in all, on him to show her superiority and her contempt.

In Hebbel's *Maria Magdalena*, Act 2, Scene 6 (1835) some kind of equivalent effect has to be attempted:

Leonhard: *Herr Sekretär? Was verschafft mir die Ehre?*
Sekretär: *Du wirst es gleich sehen.*
Leonhard: *Du? Wir sind freilich Schulkameraden gewesen!*
Leonhard: Hello, sir. I wasn't expecting to see you.
The Secretary: You scum. You'll soon see why I'm here.
Leonhard: Scum? I don't understand. (my translation)
(For the insult, I have to use a general word like 'scum'. 'You bastard, cunt etc.' is I think too close to today and would raise an inappropriate laugh. (The 'mates at school' becomes irrelevant.)

The One-Off

Once in a hundred lines, even in a 'sacred' text, you may have to translate, not just what the writer means rather than what he writes, but even what you think he means. Thus, *Au cours de brefs passages à Paris, je reçois des visiteurs dont les propos me revèlent quel est le cheminement des âmes (Mémoires de Guerre. Le Salut.* Vol III. Charles de Gaulle). 'In the course of brief journeys to Paris, I receive visitors whose words disclose to me the slow progression of men's minds'. The translation would not normally 'translate' into the original, but it is an attempt to produce a close and dignified version, where single French words (*propos, cheminement, âmes*) all leave, in spite of the abundance of the English language, considerable lexical gaps.

Standards of German

My colleague Derek McCulloch has been pursuing his research into standards of written German of first-year undergraduates, and has again reported appalling results (see *Sunday Times*, 16.1.95) e.g. the misspellings of 'tea', 'coffee' and 'bad'. However, three points have to be made: first, he gives written translation tests only, but his test sentences are all colloquial. His students have had no experience in translation, as it is largely avoided, in a prejudiced and misguided fashion, by the schools and the examination boards. So why should he expect better results?

Secondly, some of his examples again illustrate the flexibility of English and the clumsiness of German, which, for instance has no neat way of rendering '-ing' forms. Thus 'stop crying', according to the Oxford/Duden, has to become *aufhören zu weinen*; 'stop saying that' *Sag das nicht mehr (!)*; 'Stop being silly', *Hör mit diesem Quatsch auf.* So what of McCulloch's 'Children stop talking!'? As in so many cases, you can say this in German, but usually you don't, and students should be aware of this difference between spoken and written language, as well as the extra dimension of slang. *Kinder, hört mit dem Tratschen auf!* is perhaps the nearest equivalent, though *tratschen* goes beyond 'talk' to 'gossip'. Further the verb-noun (*das Tratschen*) would come rather late in any grammar course. *Ruhe!*, a more powerful word than 'Silence!' or 'Quiet' would do the trick.

Thirdly, the widest syntactic differences between languages are often in colloquial language, which makes translation difficult. The fact remains that the standards of vocabulary as well as of grammar in German are generally appalling among school-leavers, that foreign languages are started too late, and that the well-provisioned private schools appear to be better taught and have smaller classes.

(I hasten to add, in answer to a critic, that I don't teach German or any foreign language, but only translation, about translation, and English language and culture.)

Tale of a Quotation Hunt

I was recently asked for the meaning of a Dante quotation:
Quanto sa di sale
lo scendere

e il salire per l'altrui scale

It sounded wrong. As the large *Oxford Dictionary of Quotations* has a copious portion of classical European quotations, with their translations, I found the correct version there:

Tu proverai si come sa di sale
lo pane altrui, e com' è duro calle
lo scendere e il salir per l'altrui scale

'You will find out how salt is the taste of another man's bread, and how hard is the way up and down another man's stairs'.

Il Paradiso (Canto 17,11.58–60). Note: *sapere di* . . . 'to taste of'.

Werner Koller

The fourth completely revised edition of Werner Koller's *Einführung in die Übersetzungswissenschaft* contains much interesting new material, and is notable for a long discussion of various types of translation equivalences (denotative, connotative, textual – as in contracts and instruction manuals – aesthetic) and a detailed comparison of literary and non-literary texts under the aspect of translation. His attitude is refreshingly and unfashionably didactic: the literary translator must not adapt the SL text to the TL cultural reality, nor correct factual mistakes in the text, and grammatical and lexical deviations in the SL text should be preserved; thus social, fictional and aesthetic criteria have to be respected. (Numerous and pertinent translation examples are given.)

Koller is comprehensively critical of the influential 'manipulation' and 'skopos' theories, pointing out that it is absurd to confine or restrict a translation to the target language culture, and singling out (as I have done) the mistaken functionalist credo: 'The translator (as translator) is interested neither in objective reality nor in truth values' (K. Reiss and J. H. Vermeer) of which I believe the exact opposite to be true. I think Koller has a tendency to fussiness and detailed pedantry (he is not German speaking, though Swiss German speaking, for nothing – joke) but I applaud an author who, with a juicy example, complains about the bowdlerization of erotic literature, and emphasises the priority of connotation over denotation in literary translation.

One of the Uses of Inverted Commas

Normally, in non-literary translation, any neologism or literally translated unusual collocation should be put in inverted commas, which are a kind of translator's excuse. I would prefer to translate *l'entreprise citoyenne* (Michel Godet) as 'the company as an expression of citizenship' or 'the company with a civic sense', since these expressions convey some meaning to me. However, the author wrote 'citizen company', and if I want to be faithful to him, and disclaim responsibility that is how I translate it.

XVII
MAY 1995

Impressionism in Britain

This is an impressive exhibition at the Barbican, but it is pathetic that of the titles of the French pictures, only Sisley's 'The Evening, Low Tide' (*Le soir, marée basse*) and 'The Cliff at Penarth (*La Falaise à Penarth*) are also given in French.

General Words: a Warning

General words (element, spirit, case, essence, essential, make etc.) normally have both general and technical meanings, the latter only detectable in a collocation or outside the sentence. Thus Jack Lang's *La France officielle patauge dans les affaires* might mean anything, but when it is followed by: '*Les affaires sont le symptome d'une maladie . . . qui mine notre République*', *affaires* is reduced to one of two senses: 'France in its official capacity is floundering/bogged down in crises/scandals. Crises are the symptom of a disease which is undermining our Republic'. Similarly, note that *gros oeuvre* is not 'a large work' but the 'shell' or 'external skeleton' of a building.

Raquel Merino Alvarez

In her comprehensive and fascinating study, *Traducción, tradición y manipulación; teatre ingles en Espana* 1950 – 1990 (Universidad de Leon, 1994), Raquel Merino concludes by contrasting two views of dramatic translation, that of T. Hermans: 'The art of translating is a matter of adjusting and [yes] manipulating a source text so as to bring the target text into line with a particular model and hence a particular correctness notion [*sic*], and in so doing secure a social acceptance, even acclaim', and that of the Brno novelist, Milan Kundera, protesting against 'the army of rewriters': 'Translations are only truly beautiful when they are faithful'. Of these Raquel patiently prefers the latter.

Ms Merino, who identifies the *réplique* as the unit of dramatic translation, makes a statistical comparison of additions, suppressions and appropriate translation of *répliques* in a large number of modern British and American plays and their Spanish translations; she also offers a detailed analysis of Miller's *View from the Bridge* and its translations (plus three other plays), maintains that British/American play translations are largely *un teatro manipulado*, and, unlike Hermans and Co., with their pretentions to 'social acclaim,' she is using 'manipulate' in its most common pejorative sense. That apart, this is an exceptionally intelligent discussion of the issues in drama

123

translation, particularly the extraordinary semantic differences between the original published plays and their stage adaptations and versions. It is rich in original and parallel translated extracts, beautiful and widely selected quotations, and 50 page long bibliographies (English and Spanish).

Abstract Nouns

Intuitively, I think that there are more unaccountable abstract nouns in English than in French or German, and that a text segment such as *trotz vieler Krisen, Risiken und Unstabilitäten* is conveniently translated as 'in spite of many crises, risks and unstable situations/periods of instability, viz. the foreign countable abstract noun in the plural is translated by a plural collective noun/noun of duration + of + uncountable adjectival noun or by the adjective of the adjectival noun + countable abstract noun in the plurals.

The Theory of Translation

'If you are a translator, a theory of translation relates to how you should translate – how best to achieve a good and effective translation. It tends to be normative and evaluative; whereas what is referred to in linguistics as 'theory of translation' is not about how you should translate, but about what happens when you do translate . . . It is explanatory and descriptive . . . It is our understanding, as linguists, of the relationships that are set up between languages in translation, and of the processes that are involved when those relationships come to be established.' (M.A.K. Halliday, 'Language Theory and Transition Practice' p. 15, *Rivista internazionale di technica della traduzione*, 1992, Trieste).

I am happy about the first section of this valuable statement; Halliday accepts values and quality in translation. I am rather sceptical about the second part. If one is to explain the relationships between 'languages' (texts?) in translation, I think one is likely to discuss variations, that is, close and less close relationships, and so the element of evaluation will inevitably come in. Ironically, Halliday's own two diagrammed examples of translation from Chinese and Russian concern simple sentences where translation is virtually literal and there are therefore few choices, and so they are appropriate examples of his linguistic theory of translation; if he had chosen more complex sentences, it would have been another story. The linguist has, I think, to indicate the better and the inferior degrees of equivalence, not simply analyse one version. Personally, I don't think that linguistics is any more scientific, objective, simply descriptive etc. etc. blah blah blah than say history or psychology or any human science – all are value-laden. (For me, economics, also heavily value-laden, has no other purpose than the balanced welfare of humans, animals, and the earth.) Note that Mona Baker takes Halliday's linguistic rather than his translational definition of a theory of translation: 'Theory attempts to account for what happens, not tell you how it should happen' (*Language International* 6/4, 1994, p.16). In her book, *In Other Words*, she accepts and discusses published translations uncritically, shows no interest in their improvement, and ignores questions of quality and value.

False Friends or *Faux Amis*

'False friends' are words with the same or similar (e.g. *virtuel*, 'virtual') form which have different meanings in two or more languages. The degree of difference may vary from complete to slight. Such words may have anything up to thirty meanings (e.g. *affaire*, *assurer*, *Anlage*) in the second language, and normally also include the literally translated meaning (e.g. liberal).

True friends are such words when they have precisely or approximately the same meanings in one or more other languages. Usually, both true and false friends are grecolatinisms which are found in large numbers both in cognate and non-cognate languages, and they are proliferating (not in Chinese whilst they are restricted in Arabic, Finnish, Icelandic and French) all the time, in most languages since they occur predominantly in American scientific and technical vocabulary.

I have written many times that true friends are more numerous than false friends, particularly in the sci-tech vocabulary, where however there is an important minority of key false friends, carefully listed by my dear colleague Jean Maillot (he has died) in his invaluable *La Traduction scientifique et technique* (Paris, 1981).

However, a translator has to be wary of false friends, particularly of Romance words denoting human qualities (some are listed in my *Approaches to Translation* p. 162, under '103. Interference') and in administrative and legal terms, many of which are listed and wittily explained in the brilliant *Faux Amis and Key Words* by Philip Thody and Howard Evans (1985, Athlone Press). (Another standard work is C.W.E. Kirk-Green's *French False Friends* (Routledge, 1981).)

Nevertheless there are hundreds of thousands of Romance words, including sci-tech words and words ending in -ion, -ty, -ism etc. (where there are traps too) which translate similarly in English and many other languages, and it is childish and dishonest to avoid these true translations. Jeremy Sams, a brilliant translator, says he never uses the 'same' word out of piety to his father (Eric Sams, who has written lovely books on *lieder*). How mistaken! I have recently read a fine paper on Italian *faux amis* warning direly against the use of bilingual dictionaries with respect to *corretto*. I do not know what the author is on about. My Sansoni bilingual tells me that *corretto* means (1) correct, without a mistake, (2) honest, fair, straightforward, (3) Polite, (4) Flavoured, and there are plenty of citations. Isn't that good enough?

Désordre, tensions, confusion, majesté, polluer, simplicité, qualité . . . (I quote a recent exam): usually, there is no other word but the cognate to use appropriately.

Poetry

The more important the words and their order in the original, the more closely the original should be translated. Since the genre where words and their order are most important is poetry, you would expect the translation of poetry to be the closest form of translation. Far from it. This is not possible since the language of poetry includes so many additional important factors – the kind of poem, poetic form, metre, connotations, rhythm, sound, including rhyme, alliteration, assonance, onomatopoeia, word-play – which are missing or not so important in other types of writing. Nevertheless, poetry translation is always worth attempting, and I think the best poetry translations are miracles of closeness. (Stefan George, Roy Campbell, Pierre Leyris.)

Language and Reality

For the translator, the encyclopaedia is as important as the dictionary, the proper name as the word, the reality as the language, if not more so. Leaving aside the German capitalized nouns, no proper nouns, no capitalized or italicized words (in particular, personal names, geographical terms, for example, 'take a jump off Beachy Head' to be translated normally as 'commit suicide'), acronyms, title, names of buildings and organisations, should be translated without the translator assessing whether the word or its object is familiar to the putative TL readership, and either supplying the 'missing' information intra- or extra-textually (the latter in the case of an authoritative text), leaving it as it is, or exceptionally, in the case of a non-authoritative text, leaving it out as of no interest to the readership. Proper names may be purely denotative (*la Cisjordanie*, the West Bank; *der heilige Hieronymus*, St Jerome), or connotative as well as denotative, and a connotation which is clear to the SL readership may have to be explained to the TL readership. The more common or familiar a proper noun, the more it is likely to have connotations. Thus if, in a text, *la Tarentaise* is paralleled in an unfavourable context with *confusion* and *tensions*, it should not be confused with the tarentula spider (joke) and could be translated as 'the Tarentaise, an unsuitable region in the French Savoy'.

XVIII
JULY 1995

Biblical Translation

'He who translates a verse literally is a liar and he who paraphrases is a blasphemer!' Thus Moises Silva in *God, Language and Scripture* (1990, Grand Rapids Michigan, Zondervan/Harper-Collins), which includes a fruitful section on biblical translation, putting a radical view: 'Translators who view their work as pure renderings rather than interpretations only deceive themselves; indeed, if they could achieve some kind of non-interpretative rendering, their work would be completely useless.'

Alliteration Again

The purpose of alliteration has strange parallels with Gombrich's Shadows in Art (see the fine exhibition at the National Gallery). They are: (1) to emphasize the alliterated content-words, (2) to partly imitate the sound(s) of the content-words, as in onomatopoeia, (3) to produce a rhythmic effect. Note that alliteration is often supported by rhyme or assonance, and is out of place in normal informative texts, unless they are also rhetorical. In literary texts, prose as well as poetry, alliteration is important: *la forêt veloutait d'un vert sombre la pente d'une colline* (Proust *Du côté de chez Swann*) 'the forest dyed dark-green the slope of a convenient hill' (*Swann's Way*, Vol. 1, C. K. Scott Moncrieff, p. 10, Chatto and Windus, 1923).

Zipf's Law and so on

G. F. Zipf's book, *Human Behaviour and the Principle of Least Effort* (Cambridge, Mass., 1949), written long before the age of computers, is forgotten now, but the main principles (not rules): (a) the more frequently a word is used, the more senses it has, (b) the words used most frequently in a language are also the shortest ones, are, I think valid, and, as often, it requires common sense rather than computer statistics to confirm them. I would like to propose additions: (1) The more frequent a word, the more connotations it will have, and vice versa, i.e. a highly technical word has no connotations, (2) the more frequent a (non-technical) word, the less force it has, and vice versa, so that, for instance, a translator sometimes prefers a Grecolatinism (liberty, feeble) to its more common Germanic 'synonym'' (freedom, weak) to give it greater force. The words with the greatest force are, I think, monosyllabic verb-nouns like *Schluck* (in the sense of 'a mouthful') and *Sprung* (in the sense of 'a short détour').

A Clerisy Theory of Written Languages

Primitive (early) languages were complex in their grammars because these were devised by intellectually brilliant clerisies who wanted to impose them on the common people, particularly in their writing and their scripts, thus exploiting the uneducated whilst, in parallel, 'the rich' exploited the poor. Thus, in each language region, the clerisy invented a large set of cases, matching inflections and above all an unnatural and complicated word-order for their tiny numbers of literate adepts, partly at least to impress the illiterate common people with their learning. The common people with their grammatically simple and natural dialects knew nothing of these niceties. Irrespective of its educational value, which I appreciate more now, Latin (and perhaps that grisly, 'waly waly' medieval music so cherished by Nicholas Kenyon's Radio 3) had a similar function in many European countries or religious fiefs, excluding the masses (always with the exception of a few exceptionally gifted peasant or working class males, who were assimilated) from the 'good things of life'. All the above is conjecture, but too often clumsy and synthetic languages are admired as a valuable product of popular culture which they are not.

The Unfindable Word

Deshalb gab es im Leipziger Südraum kein Bischoferode is an extract from a recent report on the grisly pollution in the brown coal mines outside Leipzig. Clearly Bischoferode is not a 'bishop's ode', (joke) which would be *eine Ode eines Bischofs*, so a proper noun (a common catch when translating from German) must be considered; there is nothing in the atlases, but a road map (often a useful last resource) shows Bischoferode as a mine outside Leipzig. The context shows desolation among these mines. A likely translation is 'For this reason, the potash miners in the Southern Leipzig area did not take strike action, as they did in Bischoferode in Thuringia.' In 1993, the latter had stood for six months. I thank George Baurley and Christina Schäffner for this information.

Note that most German towns and some other geographical features form adjectives in *-er (die Leipzigerstrasse*; *das Kohrener Land*, the Kohren area). When a little known feature ends in *-er*, this may be confusing (*das Emscher Land*, the Emscher district). Some regions form adjectives in *-inische*: thus *das Anhaltinische*, the Anhalt district.

The German Compounds

As a spectator translator, how is one to view the ever pullulating German compounds: *sinnhaft, Sinnhaftigkeit*, or the suffixes *-technisch* and *-politisch* (often not to be found in dictionaries), which frequently appear to have a low semantic content: *ordnungspolitisch, wirtschafts-technisch* ('in the context of law and order'; 'from a business/economic point of view').

The Rivista

There is no coup like Halliday on translation in the second issue of the Trieste University *Rivista internazionale della technica della traduzione* (2/95), but there are some fine contributions. I particularly recommend 'The Quest for the Perfect Translation' by Gerald Parks and 'Rethinking the Task of the Translator' by the novelist Tim Parks. Personally I don't think anyone is seeking the perfect translation (mainly they are trying to improve on their last one) any more than the great writer R. H. Tawney was looking for perfect equality, as he frequently stressed, when he wrote his masterpiece, *Equality*; most translators and translation theorists are merely looking for the most accurate translation possible. G. Parks maintains that there are no universally valid guide-lines in translation and regards any description of a method as prescriptive. He does not substantiate his statement that a bad translation is better than no translation at all, which is normally true but may not be so if it is untruthful or misleading. He puzzlingly states that if one argues that a given translation is wrong, one must produce a better one. Does he apply this criterion to a gourmet or a wine-taster? Tim Parks produces a refreshing and pertinent critique of L. Venuti's rather lop-sided views on translation, to which he (Parks) rightly relates Derrida and Paul de Man, but it is a pity that he has to link these with Walter Benjamin, who died in 1940, and who he appears to think is their contemporary. Benjamin is a difficult writer, but he never regarded a translation as superior to its original. After a brilliant comparison of his own close with a loose version of an Italian literary text, Parks states: 'Faithfulness is by no means a dull thing, but a dynamic process that requires infinite sensibility and resourcefulness'. Nothing about translation has ever needed saying so much as that.

Amongst a large number of finely particular research papers and reviews, I single out Federica Scarpa's 'Cultural Adaptation in Italian of Shakespeare's Imagery of Food and Cooking', which is erudite and subtle, as is Scarpa. She gives due weight to the importance of making the audience laugh as a translation factor in Shakespeare's comic and farcical scenes, but I can only hope that her conclusion . . . 'As in love and war, in a production for the theatre, all is fair . . . in order to achieve a positive response from the audience' is ironical, since her precept could not be applied to a serious dramatic passage, any more than to love or to war . . .

Marking Translations

The short answer, to the student complaining that I have crossed out in red a word in her home work which I now say is the best version, is to say I have simply changed my mind, as all good translators do. However, I admit this can be overdone.

'Don't Like the French . . . Don't Like Their Lingo'

Britten's wonderful opera *Billy Budd* has a scene of race and language prejudice that is as funny as anything in opera I know outside of the *Flute* and *Figaro*. The librettists (E. M. Forster and Eric Crozier) superimpose what I would call universal humanity and other's ideology on Herman Melville's text. The moral purposes of music irradiate the work.

John Weightman

Many years ago, John Weightman wrote at least one rich and brilliant article about translation. His recent piece in the *Sunday Telegraph* (5.6.95) should not be missed. He complains that recent French literary translations are shoddy because (1) titles are changed unnecessarily, (2) introductions and openings are missed out, (3) keywords are left unexplained, (4) gallicisms abound, (5) there are many howlers. Some examples: *les caciques* (leading personalities) incomprehensibly reproduced in the English; *les Universitaires* (university academics), students; *le vicaire savoyard*, the vicarious chimney sweep; *opaque au pékin* (not clear in ordinary language), opaque in Peking. He suggestively compares the translator's work to fitting together the corresponding pieces of a mosaic.

The Run Up to a Translation

Both in translating and in teaching, I sometimes find it useful to tackle a recalcitrant medium-sized sentence by translating it aloud repeatedly from its start up to its difficult/nasty points (*heikle Stellen*), hoping every time that the 'right' word group will suddenly bubble up from my sub-conscious or the word memory stored in my mind. It does sometimes work. If it does not I 'bulldoze over' the gap; at other times I remain tongue-tied, and have to try something else. An example – a feeble example is better than none: *Zur Begründung ihrer Forderungen sagte Franziska Wiethold, Mitglied des HBV-Vorstands, der Einzelhandel dürfe nicht noch weiter von der Entwicklung der anderen Branchen abgekoppelt werden.* 'To justify her claims, F.W., a member of the HBW union's executive committee, said that the retail sector should not continue . . . go on . . . being separated . . . uncoupled . . . disconnected . . . disjoined . . . cut off . . . divorced from the development . . . growth . . . progress of . . . (delete) the others.'

Machine Translation

In a recent issue of *Lebende Sprachen* (1/95), W. B. Barb, the respected chairman of the RWS Group plc, claims that human professional translation is generally more efficient and *cost-effective* than machine translation coupled with post-editing; the reason why 30

German companies use MT systems is that they have been
hoodwinked by their executives, not their translators. Given that MT
and MT research were virtually brought to a halt in 1966 by the
ALPAC report, Mr Barb's letter deserves a full and authoritative
reply.

Translation Studies and Corpus Linguistics

'The emphasis in translation studies has shifted from meaning to
usage, and the notion of equivalence is gradually giving way to that of
norms. The status of the source text has been undermined [*sic*] and we
[who are "we"? who is arrogating "us"?] have managed to make the
leap [*sic*] from source-text-bound rules and imperatives to descriptive
categories.' Thus Mona Baker, announcing her rather late conversion
to Toury and Vermeer (but she writes better) – and even raking up yet
again the polysystem theory of 'another Tel-Aviv scholar' Even-Zohar
from 1979 – in her paper with the above-mentioned title in *Text and
Technology*, a festschrift for John Sinclair (ed. M. Baker, G. Francis
and E. Tognini-Bognelli, John Benjamins, Amsterdam, 1993), which
also contains an absorbing article on Sinclair's contribution to
linguistics ('British Traditions in Text Analysis – from Firth to
Sinclair') by Michael Stubbs.

Baker's statement is naïve: she appears unaware that translation is
entirely concerned with meaning, as is usage, so there can be no shift
therefrom. Further, she implies that the translator should abandon the
search for equivalence, the attempt to discover and transfer the truth of
a text and make do with the mediocre average translation correspondences of a period or a genre which constitute their 'norms'. As for
the source text, is she saying that legal texts, medical reports or
prescriptions, archives, *Othello* (which she introduces so aberrantly
into her book *In Other Words*), Celan's *Todesfuge* . . . should all be
'undermined', 'subverted' (the cant of the cultural relativist) or
'dethroned', as Vermeer has it? She never distinguishes literary from
non-literary texts or language. Her 'rules and imperatives' are
unspecified (her twenty-page article barely gives one example), and
whilst she rightly stresses description, she omits evaluation, in which
she again shows no interest. She produces a ragbag of six 'universal
features of translation', stating rather obviously that many translations
are clearer and simpler than the originals, but these are not aims, as
each task calls for its own solution in this respect. Lastly, she appeals
to a platitudionous remark of Toury's that the source text, its system,
its rules, its norms, its 'textual history' are not affected by the source
text's translation.

I should add that that the corpora in the *Cobuild* and the *Oxford
Hachette* are already assisting translators and I think they will be
invaluable data for translation theorists – without however

constituting a new turn in translation studies; that frequency is an important factor in translation, and I base several fundamental translation principles on it; that corpora risk ignoring rare but key words in the language such as 'incarnadine' and 'fleet' and 'lissom' and 'epiglottis' and 'uvula', as well as the basic but not so common *mots de disponibilité* (i.e. words arranged according to basic topics or domains such as parts of the body, common trees, etc., that should always be available) which Georges Gougenheim identified for CREDIF forty years ago; that there may be a danger of huge up-to-the-minute corpora crowding out smaller more important corpora written or spoken say twenty years ago, and therefore letting Saussure's rigid distinction between synchronic and diachronic texts come in again by the back door; that corpora may inhibit what should be a translator's enormous TL lexicogrammar, which should be there to be fitted into the interstices of the SL. Note in this volume Alan Partington's superb paper which reconciles the synchronic with the diachronic. The translator sometimes has to know how recent, how current, how near to obsolescence a word ('deliver' – joke) or a collocation ('measures in place' – joke) or an idiom ('keep your fingers crossed') or slang ('nosh') or a proverb ('All roads lead to Rome') is, and who (still) uses them.

French Periphrases

Le chef de la diplomatie israélienne (Peres/the Israeli foreign minister), *la capitale norvégienne* (Oslo – is this meant to be a geography lesson'?) . . . is it not time for translators to cure French journalists/'stylists' of their manic fear of repetition?

Acronyms Again

Some acronyms like 'UNO' are stable and have equivalents in all languages except those that resist them. Others such as the German *IM (inoffizieller Mitarbeiter)* are evanescent, time- and culture bound, and could normally only be translated by a full definition: 'an unofficial collaborator with the GDR's State Security Service (the Stasi)', since the acronym is only of interest to the reader if it recurs.

Two French Traps

1. *Merci de*, not necessarily followed by *d'avance*, may be 'thank you for' or 'please' when followed by a present infinitive; (*merci de me faire parvenir* . . . 'please send me'); compare 'thank you for not smoking/please don't smoke'.

Merci de, when followed by a perfect infinitive, is always 'thank you for' (*merci de m'avoir fait parvenir* . . . 'thank you for sending me . . .').

2. *Les coordonnées* is a general noun often meaning (with

'geographical coordinates' and 'location') the 'main details', which can then be particularized according to context: 'your address and phone number'; 'your bank's address and sorting number' (*coordonnées bancaires*); 'your details'; 'where you can find me' etc. Such a 'semantico-linguistic' progression from one particular to abstract to multiple particulars seems unique to me.

Translate Everything

I think university students are so used to having to translate untitled and sourceless little extracts that I continually have to remind them to translate everything: in a newspaper article, straplines (across the top of the page), headlines, sub-headings, by-lines, standfirsts (introductory paragraph in bold), cross-heads, titles, sub-titles, cross-titles, the small print anchors (final paragraph in bold), captions, footnotes, and full detail of the source, including date and year of publication, the latter usually at the head of the translation. Mr Bill Duffin of Cottingham reminds me in an opportune letter that the translator must be the only person, apart from the author, who reads and translates every single word of the original, including the title page, back of title page, ISBN number, preface(s), table of contents, list of diagrams or plates, text, appendices, references, bibliography, all notes, epilogue.

The Best Source

Mr Duffin goes on to write that when available the author of the SL text is not only the translator's best counsellor for ambiguities and references but should also be tactfully consulted when for one reason or another the text has to be corrected or improved. This is a form of criticism which should elicit the author's gratitude.

The DipTrans

It is not sufficiently well known that the Institute of Linguists' Diploma in Translation, which was the brainchild of Peter Foulkes, author of *Letters from Catalonia*, is the only world-wide and international professional examination in translation. It is available in about 45 bilingual combinations, includes options in literature, science, business, technology, and humanities, and a general paper where candidates have to briefly give their reasons for making twelve to fifteen of their translation decisions. Its 'additional advice' on literary translation (viz: 'You should bear in mind the differences in the relevant norms of the source and target languages; natural usage (colloquialisms, slang, phatic language, routine formulations, uncommon metaphors, technical language etc.) should normally be rendered by the appropriate natural usage in the target language. But you respect any originality of syntax, punctuation, vocabulary or metaphor in the source language text, and take some account of phonaesthetic

devices such as assonance, alliteration, onomatopoeia and rhythm')
itself constitutes a methodology and theory of literary translation,
which is fine, but would not be acceptable in all quarters.

Corpus-Based Dictionaries

Having benefited greatly from consulting the *Cobuild English
Dictionary*, of which a new edition, based on new corpora, is now out,
as well as from the first bilingual corpus-based dictionary, the *Oxford
Hachette French-English, English-French*, which recently gave me
the translations 'clean up' and 'reform' for *moraliser (la vie publique)*,
which precisely suited my context, I am still apprehensively expecting
the time, which I hope I shall not see, when such dictionaries are based
entirely on the corpora of the last two or three years and language
becomes bogusly synchronic and loses its roots.

The Translation of Institutional Terms: The Sum

The basic translation procedure for institutional terms is surely the
couplet combining transference with a cultural or functional/
descriptive equivalent; thus, for *la Cour de cassation*, 'the *Cour de
cassation* (the French Court of Appeal)' or 'the final court of appeal in
France'. The actual translation depends on its occasion, including the
form of the communication and how much more or how much less
information the readership is assumed to require. (Unfortunately, there
appears to be no officially authorized translation; the *EB* gives 'Court
of Cassation.')

Colloquial Language

The more colloquial or idiomatic a source language text, the more it
is likely to diverge from literal translation in the target language.
Incidentally, that's why many guide books are so risible, and give
literal translation a bad name.

Redon and Poussin

The Royal Academy is going back to its bad old monolingual
habits. Only one of Redon's haunting and lugubrious pictures (*Les
Yeux clos*) retains its French title. Poussin, the quintessentially French
painter, the Cartesian painter, the painter of the harmony of expressive
design and colour (I was introduced to him by my generous and, after
the cruel horrors of Rugby School, liberating tutor Anthony Blunt),
gave all his paintings English titles, if you are to believe Burlington
House.

Principles of Translation

I suspect that literary translation, first as 'prose', into the foreign
language in the teaching of Latin and Greek, later into modern

languages, always considered superior and more creative than the mechanical 'unseen', has been continuously mistaught by teachers who regard it either as a means of increasing knowledge of the foreign language or as an exercise in good style (in the case of the classical prose, a cunning adaptation or even adoption of a Ciceronian phrase was particularly valued) and never as an accurate rendering of a foreign text, which is what it should be. And for this reason, any transparent rendering of a word, say *ambition* as 'ambition' was taboo.

Paraphrase

Strictly, translation is always paraphrase, since it is an approximation, and only standard terms are exact equivalents. Any deliberate avoidance of perfectly adequate literal or close translations, any unnecessary extended synonym, is paraphrase in the bad sense. Examples: *Es war idiotisch von mir, dass ich ihn ansprach.* 'It was stupid of me to approach him' instead of 'It was idiotic of me to address him'. Paraphrase in the good sense is the closest and concisest possible translation, i.e. explanation, of an SL text segment whose literal translation makes no sense or whose linguistic translation, if it makes no use of extralinguistic (world) knowledge, is likely to be incomprehensible.

XIX
SEPTEMBER 1995

The Equal Frequency Principle of Translation

Any corresponding features of the SL and TL texts should be approximately equally frequent in the appropriate register or discourse; such features include words, terms, collocations, grammatical structures, voice, mood and aspect in verbs, punctuation marks, word or word-class order, metaphors, idioms, phrases, proverbs and phrases. (This principle, adapted from *Approaches*, where it is proposed and discussed with examples, was inadvertently omitted from *A Textbook of Translation*.)

Literary and Non-Literary Language

Unlike non-literary language, literary language, which, however, may be natural and non-innovative, should never be normalized, lexically or grammatically, by a translator. Broadly, literary language is personal to one author, even when it follows the conventions of the time, whilst much non-literary language is 'anonymous'.

Literary language may include or merge with non-literary language. Non-literary language (including the language of literary criticism, cultural studies, linguistics, etc.) normally excludes literary language, except in quotation.

Two Paradoxes of Translation

The more difficult it is, the more interesting it is, and the worse it will be paid (e.g. poetry and other literary translation). The easier it is, the more boring it is, and often, the better it will be paid, by the number of words.

Translators in the EU: an Economical Proposal

The perennial topic in the EU is the increasing cost of translation. In my opinion, all departments of the EU should be given three years notice that their members will be able to speak at conferences in any European language, but that if they require headphones, interpretation will only be available in the three languages of communication (vehicular or working languages), English, French and German. There will be no more relaying, e.g. Danish to English to Portuguese, nor interpretation between languages of minor diffusion and, furthermore, translations will only be supplied in the three languages of communication, unless the translation has legal force.

Juan Sager

Juan Sager, in his book *Language Engineering and Translation*

Consequences of Automation (1993, John Benjamins, Amsterdam) states that the personal letter has virtually been replaced by the phone call [and now E-mail] and that translators rarely now attempt full translations of 'verse' (alas, poor Hamburger, Osers, Morgan, Middleton), and he appears to be unaware of surtitles. However, his subject is the interaction of the language industries with translation theory and machine translation, and to these matters he devotes many categorizations, enumerations and models, which arc too abstract but could all be useful as checklists; he leaves a yawning vacuum in translation examples. His warning to translators is dire: the delays caused by full human translation [not defined] will only be acceptable in special cases of communicative situations. Conventional human translation in industry, commerce and administration will simply be rejected because of its disruptive influence on speed and directness. However, he also states that 'Generally, MT is [only?] applicable where large quantities of text of a few, almost stereotyped, text types on largely constant subject matter have to be provided regularly'. The book contains some useful statistics and has to be read, though the writing is sometimes a bit virus-infected.

Degrees of Excellence in Translation
In principle it is easiest to translate language for universal objects and actions (star, sleep), and hardest to translate language about words and their shapes and sounds (jitter, jell); in between comes language about people and their qualities (a jerk, thrifty). But languages are so illogical and have such strange gaps that more often than not, that's not how translation works out.

Goya
The exhibition of the tremendous and terrible still lives by Goya at the National Gallery (*et praeterea nihil* – and nothing else counts – but it also includes some other interesting Spanish still lives) has all its titles in English. Perhaps this is titfortatting the Prado, but many spectators would want to know the Spanish titles.

Degrees of Translation
One can divide translation topics into five broad categories:
1. Transcultural translation.
2. Information translation, or translation of facts.
3. Social translation, or translation of social science texts.
4. Literary translation.
5. Poetry translation.
In respect of method, as I shall attempt to show, one category begins where the previous one finishes, and there is a gradation from 'detached' to 'close'.

1. In transcultural texts (which include dramatic adaptations, much publicity and propaganda, public notices) where equivalent effect is envisaged, source language cultural expressions and discourses are replaced by target language cultural expressions and discourses.

2. For information texts, the facts are all-important, which suggests that the words can be juggled around at the translator's will. However, if the text is well written, the descriptive and qualitative words that modify the facts, and the syntactical structures and word-order that indicate priorities and emphasis have to be respected. A sentence such as *Grâce à cet ordinateur et son logiciel personnalisé, les médecins disposent désormais du premier fichier médical confidentiel* could be translated as 'Doctors now have their first confidential medical files due to computers and personalised software' or 'The first confidential medical files are at every doctor's disposal thanks to computers and personalised software' but it would be much better left alone as 'Thanks (also) to the computer and personalised software, doctors now have their first confidential medical files'. If on the other hand, an information text is poorly written, the translator has to rewrite and restructure it. *Mon propos ici vise à récuperer la parole qu'ils ont perdue . . .* 'I intend here to redress their inability to express their views'. (Illustrations adapted from Beverly Adab's *Annotated Texts for Translation: French-English*.)

3. For social texts, where I include texts ranging from texts close to the sciences to texts about the arts and the humanities, psychological and cultural nuances cannot be regarded as less important than the facts. These are the texts which require, as their aim, a full denotative translation. A scrap example would be: *L'apparence physique joue un rôle essentiel pour guider l'opinion que nous avons des individus que nous ne connaissons pas. Tous les racismes se nourissent d'ailleurs de ces formes primaires d'identification.* 'Physical appearance has an essential role in guiding the opinion we have of individuals we don't know. Besides, all forms of racism feed on these simplistic means of identification.'

4. Literary translation. The translation is based on denotations, but these are dominated by connotations where they appear. There are other new important factors: the allegorical and symbolic nature of the language; sound (in general terms); personal and emotional language; the shapes of sentences and paragraphs; concision. Scrap example: *Je désirais fortement de toucher terre et n'y parvenais point, faute de savoir où la terre se trouvait.* 'I longed to touch the earth and could not do so, because I did not know where the earth was'. (*Le Défi*, P. Sollers, translated by Jean Stewart. *Penguin Short Stories*, pp. 216–7).

Note that in literary and dramatic criticism texts, the full literary vocabulary may appear, but the other 'new' factors in literary texts such as sound, may be missing.

    5. Poetry translation. Poetry calls on all the resources of language, and, in parallel, these become the factors that the translator of a poem has to consider and hierarchize or prioritize differently for each poem, depending on its specific nature. Thus metre, rhyme, rhythm, assonance, alliteration, onomatopoeia (all) relate to meaning, sound and form. The struggle to reconcile the semantic with the aesthetic (in a natural style as well as in sound and form) is at its most intense and can sometimes only be maintained for single lines.

> *Un brouillard sale et jaune inondait tout l'espace*
> *Je suivais roidissant mes nerfs comme un héros*
> *Et discutant avec mon âme déjà lasse*
> *Le faubourg secoué par les lourds tombereaux.*

> Foul yellow mist had filled the whole of space:
> Steeling my nerves to play a hero's part,
> I coaxed my weary soul with me to pace
> The backstreets shaken by each lumbering cart.

(*Les sept vieillards*. Charles Baudelaire; translated by Roy Campbell).

    Note the brilliant correspondences here, also in sound: *roidissant*, 'steeling'; *mon âme déjà lasse*, 'my weary soul'; *tombereaux*, lumbering; cf. *fourmillante cité*, 'ant-seething city' in the first stanza. The poem is a wonderful translation, but close only by the standards of poetry translation.

    Ironically, information texts, which least need close translation, can be translated most closely, particularly if they are not tied to the culture of the original text; poetry, which is so packed with meaning at the level of syntax, words and sound that it requires the closest translation, is in fact the loosest, usually owing to the conflicting demands of rhyme, metre and sense. (Relatively, it is easier to translate 'free' verse such as Celan's, but in comparison with prose literary translation, this too is more difficult.)

Venuti and Translation

    The Translator's Invisibility, a history of translation by Lawrence Venuti (1995, Routledge, London), has the considerable merit of assembling a great many significant historical facts, references, descriptions and quotations from literary and poetry (non-literary barely appears) translation, and much else, from Horace and Cicero to Lefevere and, too prominently, Venuti. A history of translation it is not, and Shelley, Nabokov, G. Steiner and Louis Kelly are strangely omitted. A thesis and 'call to action' runs through the book, opposing fluency, the transparent, the invisible, the domesticated, the *simpatico*, the Anglo-American hegemony (which we used to call 'free' translation?) and favouring, pardon, privileging, resistancy, foreignizing, deterritorializing, discontinuity, otherness, the German tradition (which we used to call close or accurate translation?) So maybe Venuti is on the side of truth, but the 'valorizing of an élite cultural bourgeois discourse or agenda against the larger, more hetero-geneous culture of the middle and working classes' is depressing.

Bilingual Dictionaries
A common deficiency in bilingual dictionaries is the lack of cross-references in and to both parts of the dictionary. Thus *Wissenschaftler* as 'scholar', 'scientist/scholar' or as *spécialiste* ought to be shown in the G-E, E-G, G-F, F-E-G, E-F and F-E sections. Probably lexi-cographers would not normally think of translating 'scholar' or *spécialiste* as *Wissenschaftler*, but such versions would be appropriate in some contexts.

Dijon and Beaune
Public and historical buildings in these two cities all have descriptive plaques with beautifully close translations into German and English. In one case, *bas-reliefs* is mistranslated as 'low reliefs'. The 'literal' translation is misplaced.

Frankfurt and Saarbrucken
The massive Städel is a small scale National Gallery, and has the minor works of most major painters, but also a superb Holbein panel, the best of Munch's *Jealousy* paintings, a great Beckmann *Frankfurt Synagogue* and Tischbein's notorious androgynous *Goethe in the Campagna*, which dominates the museum. Saarbrucken's (Sarrebrouck) *alte and neue Sammlungen*, also a fine gallery, are mainly approp-riately bilingual.

Styles
In my opinion, it is usually inappropriate to translate official texts using phrasal verbs (unless they are felt as normal social usage) or split infinitives.

Technical Translation
Normally a technical term such as *Verwerfungen* ('faults'!) should be modified with a classifier in translation – 'geological faults' – to ensure that it does not confuse the unwary reader.

Words and Meaning
Meaning does not exist without a potential of words; all words whether in or out of context have meaning, but torn from context many but by no means all words have rather different and often misleading meanings remote from their primary meanings.

The British Centre for Literary Translation

The British Centre for Literary Translation was founded in 1989 by Professor Max Sebald at the University of East Anglia (Norwich NR4 7TJ). Directed by Dr Terry Hale, it annually offers bursaries to translators engaged on a literary or scholarly project, usually for a period of a month. Candidates should apply before January 30 in each year.

The Computer and the Translator

The fact that she is always revising, recasting, changing her mind, correcting, erasing, suggests that the computer with its ERASE, RELAY, DOC PAGE, INSERT TEXT etc. is the translator's one indispensable aid.

Botho Strauss

I take Botho Strauss's article in the *Spiegel* (February 1993), *Anschwellender Bocksgesang*, as an example of obscure and complicated writing that has to be translated as closely as possible, therefore in similar obscure and complicated writing, but with a mandatory preface and notes on almost every line for the 'second' readership (as has been brilliantly done by David Armstrong) since I assume the translator's duty is, inside or outside the translation, to give them some clue to understanding the text.

Translationese and Translatorese

I define 'translationese' as 'interference that distorts the intended sense of an original' therefore the use of a *faux ami* or a 'false friend'. (Example: *génial* translated as 'genial'.)

I define 'translatorese' as the unthinking use of the primary sense of a group, word or collocation, when another sense is more appropriate. Example: *On a beau dire, ils n'apprennent rien* translated as 'one may speak in vain, they'll never learn anything' instead of 'Whatever you say, they won't learn anything'. There is a tendency to regard translatorese as a target language norm, a sub-language created for translation, when in fact it is a sign of a translator's weakness and unresourcefulness.

Translation Mistakes and Their Correction

The translation teacher or critic has to learn to distinguish (1) mistakes due to ignorance or perverseness (I ring or cross these out), (2) unnecessary synonyms (I underline these), (3) 'free' variations, due to a divergent theory of translation (I put '. . . .' under these), (4) valid bits of translation which s/he herself would not choose (I mark these 'OK').

The Translation of Euphemism

I propose 'an inoffensive or embellishing word or phrase

substituted for one considered offensive, frightening or hurtful, especially one relating to religion, sex, crime, death, drunkenness, violence, excretion, mental health and serious diseases' as a fairly comprehensive definition of a euphemism. The purpose of euphemism is to avoid giving offence and/or to conceal the truth. Euphemism is a type of irony and is either standard or original. Euphemisms and dysphemisms (pejorative words) are particularly associated with taboos, the prejudices that are the reverse of universal human rights, and political correctness (the adversaries of PC regard most PC vocabulary as euphemistic). A euphemism may be cultural (sex, ageism) or universal (crime, violence). In matters of death and religion, the element of euphemism cannot be assessed, since they depend on the beliefs of those who use them.

Since translation is an instrument of truth, and translators should be bound by human rights agreements, translation is in principle at variance with euphemisms, although, with safeguards, they have to be rendered accurately. There are many standard euphemisms which have their standard target language equivalents: (perhaps) 'go', 'pass on', 'pass away', *disparaître*, 'go immortal' (Chinese); 'the flower and willow disease' (VD) (Chinese). Note that all languages have numerous and continuously increasing synonyms for sexual intercourse and the parts of the body relating to it and the translator should usually retain their erotic charge, if there is one.

In principle, translators should indicate the true meaning of all euphemisms for disgraceful practices (*apartheid, matador*, 'take out', 'liquidate' etc.), as well as words transferred from another language used for euphemistic purposes, provided they think the reader is unlikely to be aware of them. (I realise that this section is controversial.) (See also 'Euphemism and its Translation' by George Kao in *Translation and Interpretation: Bridging East and West*, edited by R. K. Seymour and C. C. Liu, University of Hawaii, 1994, which has an interesting article on cultural barriers in translation by Nigel Reeves.)

Hybrid and Churn

1. Note that in many languages 'hybrid' is easily confused with 'hubris'; transferred ancient Greek 'u' may become 'y' or 'i' or remain 'u'.

2. The nearest I can get in a reference book to the *Economist's* 'job churning' (contextually, 'continual job switching in order to improve one's career position'), is the colloquial sense in the *Shorter Oxford* 'buying and selling shares to make quick profits'.

Alliteration

If there is any alliteration in the SL text, I suspect that in most cases, it's the first thing that has to be lost in the translation (say *Zittern und Zetern*, 'trembling and wailing') unless there are common grecolatinisms in the two languages.

Allies and Adversaries

Reviewing the course of translation theory in the last thirty years, say since Nida, I find I can count my possible allies on the fingers of one hand, and my adversaries as ten times as many; my true allies are not translation theorists, Raquel Merino Alvarez always excepted, but (I think) the art critic Gombrich, the historian Richard Cobb, the novelist Milan Kundera, the music critic the late Hans Keller (see many previous references). The sharp dividing line is that for me, translation is a weapon of and for the truth (in fact the five medial truths: factual, moral, logical, aesthetic, linguistic). For my adversaries, these truths in translation are either a matter of indifference, or, as some have stated, irrelevant. A second dividing line is the idea that translation determines the dethronement/undermining/subversion of the original (could this be the Bible, the most often translated book, or Shakespeare, since the 'demise' of Marx and Lenin, the most often translated writer, or the A I report on the treatment of immigrants in Germany?). Are these the texts to be deconsecrated? I find the idea puerile. The third contention is that for me, translation studies are evaluative (I'm trying to teach) as well as descriptive.

The T-V Relationship Again: Pronouns of Power, Solidarity and Contempt

Whilst English can only directly translate the pronouns of address of other languages with the pronoun 'you', it has the following supplementary rhetorical translation devices to suggest relations of class, comradeship and intimacy.

1. Formal power relations: sir/madam (rare), Mr Smith, Gov'nor.
2. Informal solidarity relations (of colleagues) John, Mary, mate.
3. Personal friendship: nickname and diminutives.

The actual choice of translation device depends on the particular situation.

The switch from formality to familiarity to show contempt, which is found in some literature (Racine, Hebbel), is now historical.

Translation

When direct translation is not possible, translation has infinite resources of explanation and/or interpretation inside or outside the text, to be used as economically as possible. That becomes the translation.

The Translation of Metaphor: a Synthesis and a Frame of Reference

Type of Metaphor:
1. Dead
2. Cliché
3. Standard
4. Recent
5. Original

Translation Procedure:
1. Use same image.
2. Use different image.
3. Reduce to sense.
4. Adapt standard complex metaphor.
5. Convert to simile.
6. Use couplet of sense and image.

N.B. Metaphors may be universal, cultural or personal.

XX
NOVEMBER 1995

Teaching Translation

Teaching Translation and Interpreting: 2. Insights, Aims, Visions edited by Cay Dollerup and Annette Lindegaard (1994, John Benjamins, Amsterdam) is the best record of translation conference proceedings I have read for some time. Here, at last, are several papers actually devoted to teaching translation, even classroom teaching. Cay Dollerup, for instance, after noting the 'large interface, an overlapping area', between foreign language learning and translation, but ignoring the fact that the cardinal purposes of the two exercises are different (the first, to increase language proficiency; the second, to elicit and transfer meaning from one language to another), gives a fascinating and detailed account of his classroom procedure, which he calls 'the feedback system'. He sensibly insists that classes must first come to grips with 'typical interlanguage errors', and categorizes six of them: (1) text omissions/additions, (2) spelling, (3) punctuation, (4) words/world knowledge, (5) syntax/grammar, (6) expression. (He omits cultural words/world knowledge.) The paper is, I think, too detailed in its distinctions, and rigid in its procedures, but it is rich in examples, also of classroom teaching experience, and is a pleasure to occasionally disagree with.

Andrew Chesterman introduces Karl Popper to the translation class, but as he gives no examples except Pym's experiences, it is more of an introduction to Popper's thought than to the classroom.

Daniel Gile regards 'traditional' (the old dirty word) translation teaching as product-oriented and prefers process-oriented training, whilst admitting deficiencies which a product-oriented approach would rectify! The training is stimulatingly described in stages, but no translation examples are given. Jeanne Dancette, however, centres her discussion of think-aloud protocols on a short paragraph and its translations, and introduces the term 'mapping' (a text or sentence onto a model of reality one is familiar with), and thus is exceptionally enlightening.

Christiane Nord attempts to modify or soften the market-driven skopos theory, that the end justifies the means, with her 'loyalty principle' which shows a little mercy to the undermined/dethroned author; she does not persuade me, but at least she produces several fresh examples. There is a naive and thought-provoking contribution from Manouchehr Haghighi, who after a life of sci-tech translation, was suddenly confronted with 'literature'; s/he ignores the aesthetic/ sonic difficulty and regards 'To be or not to be' as cultural, not a universal issue; s/he appears to think there is no way of handling this speech except 'literally' or by discussing the social and cultural norms of the Renaissance/Shakespeare's time; in fact, whilst Hamlet uses many cultural terms (e.g. slings, bodkin) which have to be treated extra- or intra-textually, the speech is a record of human experience which, to put it mildly, is not confined to one time or one space/place. Lastly, I should protest that sarcasms like 'If you can earn your living translating James Joyce, then maybe there is no problem' (p.308) are not helpful, since they reek of cultural philistinism, the opposite side of the coin of cultural élitism.

Translating in the Dark and Contrast

Just as obscure titles are sometimes clarified when they are repeated word for word within a text, so *Kommunen* may be disambiguated if *Länder und Kommunen* are later followed by *Länder und Gemeinden* (translate as *Gemeinden* or the 'basic local government units'?), and *entrümpeln* is clear (translate as 'clean up' or 'rationalize'?) if it is followed by *und das Steuerrecht vereinfachen* (and simplify tax law).

Mad Translation and Contrast

In a business text, *société de conditionnement* suggests 'a packaging company'. But the context has nothing to do with packaging, and there is a later reference to *conditionnement de l'eau*. Since *conditionnement de l'air* is 'air conditioning', *conditionnement de l'eau* must surely be 'water treatment', but why didn't s/he just call it *société de traitement des eaux* in the first place?

Trade Paper of the Future?

20/20 Europe, a glamorous bimonthly magazine devoted to 'eyewear' – '20/20' is a medical term meaning 'normal acuity of vision' – publishes all its features and articles successively in English, French German, sometimes adding Italian and Spanish; most advertisements are in English, but the mag adds Finnish and Dutch to the quintet, and nicely 'translates' (*Brillen*) *nach Lust and Laune* ('at will') (lit 'according to your pleasure and mood') as (*Brillen*) *te kust en te keur* ('in plenty, of every description', lit. 'at taste (?) and at choice') sensibly concentrating on the alliteration and varying the meaning but keeping it in the same direction.

The titles are in English, whilst the texts of the articles, even the sub-headings, are closely translated, and accuracy only gives way to approximation to preserve naturalness: 'facing a tough economy'; *des problèmes économiques*; den Wirtschaftsschwankungen ausgesetzt(!) 'exposed to business fluctuations'); 'brand awareness'; *sensibilité aux marques; Markenbewußtsein; la notorietà del marchio; conocimiento de las marcas*.

The Eternal Translation Deficit
'Everything suffers by translation', Thomas Paine wrote in 1791 in the Preface to the English edition of *The Rights of Man*.

Teaching and Beginning a Translation Course
What are we trying to do? I suggest:

1. Transferring the meaning of a text from one language to another as accurately and concisely as possible, for a new readership.

2. Keeping the style of the text, which, if the text is non-literary, is likely to be a natural and social style, such as one would find in an analogous text; if it is a literary text, the style is likely to be more personal and intimate; if it is innovative, such a style should be recreated.

3. Where the new readership is unlikely to understand the cultural or technical terms in the text, explaining these outside the text if it is authoritative or official or classical/historical, and inside it if it is informal and not authoritative. (Strictly, the translator should only explain cultural points, assuming the 'foreign' readership will be ignorant of them; but the 'commissioner' may warn that the second readership is ignorant in points of technical or general knowledge, in which case these too have to be explained.)

4. Given that the meaning of the text may be denotative or figurative or pragmatic (illocutionary, persuasive) in various places, ensuring that these kinds of meaning are retained in approximately the same places in the translation.

5. Correcting the text if it is inaccurate, harmful, poorly written or structured – outside it if it is authoritative, inside it if it is not.

6. Bearing in mind that in a serious literary text, the source language stylistic effects should be transferred within the bounds of elegance.

In Search of the Right Collocation
Son européanisme, s'il est moins flamboyant que celui des grands absents de la campagne, VGE, RB ou JD, est fondé sur une vision qui se veut pragmatique de l'avenir de Vieux Continent.

Joke translation: His Europeanism, if it is less blazing than that of the great absent ones of the campaign . . ., is founded on a vision which claims to be pragmatic about the future of the Old Continent'.

Notes

Flamboyant: Blazing, flamboyant, fiery, flaming, ardent . . . only the last one is possible, unless the writer had 'conspicuous' (*flagrant?*) in mind.

Son européanisme. Many languages are fickle in putting or omitting 'pro' or 'anti-' before '-ism' nouns. Here 'pro-European attitude'.

Se veut. 'Claims', 'is supposed', 'is meant', 'likes to think of itself as', 'tries to be', 'professes to be'. (Often a dictionary let-down).

Le Vieux Continent. Typically artificial 'familiar alternative' to avoid the repetition.

Suggested translation: 'His devotion to Europe, although it is less ardent/conspicuous than that of the major personalities not taking part in the campaign, i.e. Giscard, Barre or Delors, is based on a vision which professes to be pragmatic about the future of Europe'.

The Liverpool Translation Conference

The recent conference, 'The Linguistic Foundations of Translation: Literary Translation and the Translation of Sensitive Texts', run by Michael Hoey, professor of English language at Liverpool, and Terry Hale, director of the British Centre for Literary Translation at the University of East Anglia in Norwich, was the richest and most interesting translation conference I have been to for many years. Apart from the plenaries, where a precise and illustrative contribution from Eugene Nida on the difficulties of translating *Matthew 6.9–13*, the Lord's Prayer, was outstanding, there was an abundance of parallel papers, mainly on literary and religious texts, from all over the world and participants were therefore able to pursue their specialist interests. Presentations ranged from the way out: 'Decavalles's rewriting of Eliot's *Four Quartets* in Modern Greek, a rather minor language of a peripheral European country, constitutes a political act of subversion not only of Modernist hegemony but also of Western cultural imperialism with which Modernism has been associated' (Anastasia Anmastasiadou), to an innocuous and innocent description of Djilas's translation of *Paradise Lost* into Serbian, apparently without corruption by his 'Yugoslav Marxism and Communism' (Slobodan Vukobrat). Michael Holman gave a brilliant description of the way that Tolstoy's last novel *Resurrection* was politically and sexually 'sanitized' in various translations. Too many speakers, however, described the subversion of originals as an act of colonialism, militarism, capitalism, etc. uncritically without offering translation examples. Peter Fawcett appeared to take the becalmed polysystems theory seriously, but questioned its validity in contrast with 'the Levyan concept of translatorial personality', meaning presumably Jir Levy's superb translation analysis. Gunilla Anderman's brilliant paper on Strindberg's *Easter* shows how the mistranslation of one (symbolical) flower can diametrically distort the meaning of a play. Derek McCulloch gave a fascinating account of his effort to transpose Patrick Susskind's double bass player into an English culture. Lawrence Venuti, producing only one weak example ('he despatched the sacristan to the headquarters of the Commune' for *mando il sagrestano in comune*) failed to convince me that the

American translator of Giovanni Guareschi's *Don Camillo* novels had
distorted them for Cold War purposes, although it is an interesting
theory which the Göttingen Group might welcome. Most of these
far-reaching papers will be published by the University of Liverpool
next year.

The Clerisy Theory Again

Mr J. K. Morland from Surrey states in the last issue of *The Linguist*
that 'all over the world there are today primitive peoples speaking
highly inflected languages with extremely complicated grammar structures – and not a clerisy (awful word!) in sight'. Who are these peoples?
Who taught them to speak these languages? Have the languages become
simplified (become more analytical, produced abbreviations, shed
inflections) in the course of time, which is the customary process? I
think that all societies have clerisies (learned people viewed as a class)
which normally try to exploit 'the rest'. I don't know why 'clerisy' is an
'awful' word; it is quite an old one, perhaps first transposed into English
from German (earlier Classical Greek *klerisei*) by Coleridge in 1818,
and it is in the *Longman* and the *Webster*, but, surprisingly, not in the
Collins or the *C.O.D.* Behind my conjectural theory I am suggesting that
complicated word-order and inflexions are not part of the precious
immutable cultures of primitive languages which must always be
respected (like suttee? which means 'a virtuous widow'), as some
inverted snobs who revere any old culture maintain.

The Translation of Pauses and Silences

I have sometimes been criticised for discovering an excess of
translation topics, but Gloria Gomez Cortes in an outstanding essay,
discusses the ultimate topic, pauses and silences. Note that the cultural
or the universal quality of the main 'pause' signs, viz. . . . (the Three
Dots, which I have already discussed in *Paragraphs on Translation*,
2nd edition, 1995, Multilingual Matters, pp. 126–7), commas, full
stops, dashes etc., have to be reconsidered by the translator, and that
regular pauses distinguish poetry from all other types of writing.

Janáček and Kundera

It is notorious that the director of the Prague opera, Karel Kovařovič,
held up the production of Janáček's greatest work *Jenufa* for twelve
years after its first night in Brno in 1904, and when he finally agreed to
conduct it, he first 'translated' it to suit the norms of the time by
cutting scenes, eliminating the characteristic word and sentence
repetitions and doubling the orchestration in many places. (The
'originals' of this and other works have since been restored by Charles
Mackerras.) Note, however, that Kovařovič acted in good faith, and
some Janáček specialists such as Jaroslav Vogel and the perceptive

Hans Hollander approved of some of his 'adaptations'.

The well-known novelist Milan Kundera in his *Testaments Betrayed: An Essay in Nine Parts* (translated from the French – *Les Testaments trahis* – by Linda Asher; Faber and Faber, 1995) has now taken Janáček's German librettos adapted by Max Brod, as a model to produce detailed studies of the translations and mistranslations of Kafka, Thomas Mann, Musil and other 'world' writers.

XXI
JANUARY 1996

The Translation of Footnotes

The footnotes of non-literary authoritative texts should normally be closely translated as an integral part of the SL text, with the same references and in the same position. Any additional translators' notes, for the purposes of explanation or comment, to assist the new readership, should be framed: [. . . -Tr.]

In non-authoritative texts, the translator may decide to shorten, summarize or omit the footnotes if she considers them of little interest culturally or professionally, or as already known to the new readership.

In literary texts, explanatory footnotes frequently have to be expanded or added to accommodate the second readership.

(I am grateful to my former outstanding student Rhona Wilson for pointing out that no translation theorist has discussed this topic. Note that the above remarks are tentative, for the reader to react against or to assent to.)

The Translators' Peace International

It may interest some readers to know that the FIDH, the International Federation of Human Rights, is now setting up a team of translators from French to English to translate their publications. The address is Antoine Bernard, executive secretary, FIDH, 17 Passage de la Main d'Or, 75001 Paris, France. Tel 33-1 43 55 25 18, FAX 33-1 43 55 18 80. The corresponding British organisation is the Peace Translation Project in London, directed by Agatha Haun at War Resistance, 5 Caledonian Road, London N1 9DX (Fax: 0171-278-4040 Tel: 0171-278-4040)

The Translation of Pauses

Poetic language normally has regular pauses imposed by the poem's metre. Other pauses signifying silence, hesitation, emphasis, surprise, interrogation, etc. are indicated by appropriate punctuation marks, such as the three dots, dashes, brackets, question and exclamation marks, all previously discussed.

The Uses and Abuses of Repetition in Translation

The translator should bear in mind:

1. The usual effect or purpose of repetition is, in any language, to emphasize. ('He pulled and pulled at the rope'.)

2. Some influential and misguided linguistics/style-setters in any

culture, but particularly the French (culture!), regard repetition as bad
style and avoid it with often artificial familiar alternatives e.g. *VGE
... L'ancien président de la Republique* (Valéry Giscard d'Estaing ...
the former French President).

3. Where a language only has one gender for objects, the SL
pronouns are often replaced by their nouns, in spite of their repetition.

4. It is sometimes useful to strengthen the translation of long and
complicated sentences by repeating a key-noun. For example: *Le PCF
ne veut pas démordre d'un objectif de travail stable, devenu irréaliste
parce qu'inaccessible ...'* The French Communist Party refuses to
abandon its goal of secure employment, a goal that has become
unrealistic since it is inaccessible.' Here the repetition clarifies the
sentence by indicating the subject of the relative clause.

5. Repetition is misused when it is unnecessary and serves no
purpose; it is a not uncommon feature of poor writing.

People Shall Speak Unto Computers ... and be Translated
According to the DTI, eventually speech recognition technology
will enable a spoken message to be received, in written form, on a
computer terminal.

The Importance of Standard Terms
However much a SL text may 'wrap around' a standard term, e.g.
*der berüchtigte Glaubensartikel Nummer Vier in der Parteiver-
fassung*, it must be translated straight: 'the notorious article of faith,
that is, Clause 4 in the Labour Party Constitution'.

The Pointless Pun
When an SL text makes use of a pun, says *Jugendstil* meaning
'youthful style' with a learned reference to *art nouveau* or *le style
Liberty*, which does not work in the target language, nothing much is
lost if the second meaning is lost in the translation.

However, the witty(?) pun in the sentence: *VGE qualife de
défaitistes ceux qui renoncent à reconstruire de fait le monde d'avant
le premier choc pétrolier* ('VGE calls defeatist all those who definitely
give up trying to rebuild the world before the first oil crisis), viz.
défaitistes and *de fait*, is mainly lost.

The Shakespeare Wallah
David Snelling's *Strategies for Simultaneous Interpreting: From
Romance Languages into English* (1992, Campanotto, Udine) is not
only a brilliant book, often on translation as well as on interpretation,
but it is an allusive, rich and educative entertainment with an extraordinary knack of clinching arguments with a pertinent quotation from
Shakespeare. The book consists of an introduction, which distances

itself quietly (*ruhig*) from the ESIT approach to interpretation (i.e. 'forget the words and concentrate on the sense throughout'), and four chapters that reproduce speeches delivered at international conferences in Portuguese, Spanish, French and Italian, each followed by a commentary in mainly parallel subsections, offering an attractive ease of reference.

Snelling writes particularly well on word-order and emphasis; the use and abuse of etymology; the pretentious royal plural – 'a scarcely perceptible shift of subject from the singular to the *plurale majestatis* (p.68), surreptitiously to involve the listener in the speaker's ideological stance' – (can Snelling have been reading the egregious lucubrations, often more relevant to linguistics than to translation, of Mona Baker?); the sub-text ('as I was saying' = 'before I was so rudely interrupted'); the flexible use of gerunds as noun groups ('my being reproached'); the misuse and abuse of media words (as hold-all words) like 'crisis' and 'chaos' in all languages; concision versus prolixity (continuously, with brilliant and witty examples); the use of comment adverbs to open sentences (admittedly, hopefully, thankfully, etc.); the principle of energy or intensity co-efficient, showing how many adjective and verb synonyms are differentiated by their degree of energy or intensity [add formality], e.g. grab and seize (*saisir*), *afferrare* (grasp and clasp). In accordance with this principle, I have long been 'correcting' an insufficiently or an excessively strong word of quality (adjective, adverb, verb, verbal noun, adjectival noun) by marking it with a bracketed upward (↑) or downward (↓) arrow respectively, e.g. 'lar↓ge' or 'mam↓moth' or we↑ak; the importance of compression, particularly by substituting a stronger verb or a stronger adjective for a verb plus an adverb or an adverb plus an adjective respectively; the differences in the nature as well as the conditions of translation and interpretation, which are so often blurred.

Don't fail to get hold of this book from Trieste University, the hub of translation and interpreting, where Snelling has been teaching for many years. (Am I prejudiced? Very well then, I am prejudiced.)

The Translation of Jargon
The word 'jargon' has three main meanings:
1. Specialized or technical terms in a profession, job or other pursuit; such words may be standard, formal or colloquial words. Like neologisms, transferred words and acronyms, they are misused, if employed for purposes of display, conceit, demonstration of superior knowledge, or membership of an élite. They should only be used without explanation if the translator is confident that the readership will understand them.

2. Technical terms unnecessarily replacing simple words.
3. Platitudes, clichés, buzz-words, vogue words, mumbo jumbo, clap-trap.

Formidable (F)
All bilingual dictionaries, except Harraps, 'refuse' to equate *formidable* (F) with 'formidable' (E); but when the word is used non-colloquially and seriously, the French word is equivalent to the English as it is to the Spanish and the Italian.

French Past Participles or Adjectives between Commas
Example: *Sur un autre registre, concordant, le syndicat ...* Possible translation: 'From another point of view that led to a similar conclusion, the union . . .' This construction, which is sometimes over-looked as it is only signalled by the two commas, indicates either (a) emphasis of the adjective/present or past participle, or (b) continuation or contrast. In translation, it is usually introduced by a subordinate conjunction (while, which, that, whilst, although, whereas, etc.) plus subordinate clause as above.

Unnecessary Paraphrase
Unnecessary paraphrase in translation is always wrong in principle, even if it is fairly harmless. Thus in an information text, poorly written at that, why translate *qui n'est pas passé inaperçu* ('which has not gone unnoticed') with the positive modulation, 'has attracted/aroused some interest' or *de gré à gré* ('by mutual agreement') as 'with the consent of all parties', both of which demonstrate a slight difference of meaning, however innocuous? To me it is against the spirit of translation, which is fidelity, which I don't sneeze at. (Note that, in other cases, a positive modulation (*qui ne veut pas* translated as 'who refuses to . . .' may be perfectly justified.) But what is the point of writing something different, when what the author wrote is perfectly all right?

Semi-Neologisms Again
Prefixes such as non-, pro-, re-, anti-, pre-, post-, co-, ante-, bi- and suffixes such as -ist, -ism, -istic, -ation (after -ize), -ish (i.e. 'rather' or 'slightly', but slightly derogatory) can I think be affixed to any roots if they make appropriate sense (who decides? the translator, as always) and s/he should not be told s/he is inventing words, 'the word doesn't exist, etc.

Capitalization in Translation and Elsewhere
In his fascinating article, *The Need for Capital Letters in Translation* in *The Linguist* 34/6/95, D.J. Hunns offers some acute insights into the

interpretation of three literary masterpieces, but unfortunately, at a time when, apparently influenced by the *Economist*, capitalization is becoming rarer, he does not state the principles behind his argument. As I see it, capital letters in English should be used for particulars, that is proper names; the nouns in the names of public institutions; the nouns in the titles of books, periodicals, artistic and musical works; and further, to enhance the importance, often symbolical, of any one person or any object. Even these principles are old fashioned (in the 19th century, capitalization of any abstract noun, or, to enhance the pathetic fallacy, of some natural feature was much more common), but they are particularly designed to distinguish the singular and the particular from the general; they are also approximate, far from hard and fast.

Paul Kussmaul

Paul Kussmaul's second book, *Training the Translator* (John Benjamins, Amsterdam, 1995), is exceptionally useful for teachers and students, mainly of German-English/English-German non-literary translation, as well as of principles and methods of translation. There are also literary examples from *Cosmopolitan*, P.G. Wodehouse and Enid Blyton, but these names show that the genre is not Kussmaul's interest and the complexities of sound, connotations, emotional words (his own section on 'Emotions' is primitive) and even metaphor (a gap?) are barely touched on. The book is well organized, and has chapters on: What goes on in the translator's mind (including sections on Thinking Aloud Protocols, i.e. records of student or professional translators wrestling audibly with their difficulties); Creativity in Translation, which leans on the psychology of thinking as well as Fillmore's 'frames and scenes', Eleanor Rosch's prototype and general Gestalt theory; Pragmatic Analysis, which includes the cultural Factor and Text-types (an excellent case study on manuals and leaflets); Analysis of Meaning, including lexical gaps; Text Analysis (not much) and the Use of Dictionaries, which, like words, all of which are meaningless to Kussmaul – including 'haematology' (?) – are consistently underrated: 'hard' as in 'hard facts', for instance, *pace* Kussmaul, is explained in any decent dictionary; Evaluation and Errors; a Summary of strategies, which ends abruptly.

This is a good and useful book, rich in examples, clear in definitions, widely based in its use of an extensive bibliography, forthright in its value-judgements, making good use throughout of Juliane House's (Halliday's) method of text analysis. It also has too many truisms and redundancies, a rather hectoring tone, and it pursues single difficulties (bed-rooms as 'rooms'; *schliesslich* as 'after all'; *sprechen* and *reden*; 'posture' and 'stance') for too long. It misses the main point of Functional Sentence Perspective for the translator, which is the relationship between word-order and emphasis. This is an engrossing, down to earth book to argue with, though it doesn't say much about classroom teaching methods.

The Sixth Madrid Translation Conference
Miguel Angel Vega, the Director of the Translation Institute at the Universidad Complutense in Madrid, as well as producing a lively magazine *Jerónimo*, has now organized six enormously varied translation conferences in only twice as many years.

Dictionary Words
A 'dictionary word' is a word mainly found in dictionaries. On the whole, these (e.g. *postuler*) should not be used in information texts/communicative translation. Thus if a pretentiously written text states *Mieux, la CFDT postule sur les bouleversements en cours du travail, de ses formes comme de son contenu*, I suggest: 'Further/what is more, the CFDT, the French Democratic Confederation of Labour, is assuming that the radical changes now occurring in both the forms and the content of work will go on', since 'postulating' instead of 'assuming/taking it for granted' would look odd in such a context.

Meaning
Where the meaning of a lexical unit (*esprit*) or of a grammatical structure (*un autre registre, concordant . . .*) is mainly context-based, there is always an element of uncertainty about it. Not uncommonly this element is due to obscure, abstract or poor writing. About the meaning of 'detest' or 'haematology', there is no shadow of a doubt.

A Scale of Semantic Precision: From Monosemy to 'Polysemy'
I propose the following tentative scale for translators:
A. MONOSEMOUS WORDS
1. Standardized or technical terms, or terms of art: these are deliberately monosemized.
2. Monosemous or 'full' verbs (e.g. 'loathe', 'detest', 'discern'). Note that, in general, more verbs are likely to be context-independent and virtually monosemous than nouns.
3. Monosemous adverbs of quality (e.g. 'disarmingly')
4. Phrasal nouns and adjectives (e.g. 'a let-down', 'run down')
5. Monosemous particular nouns (e.g. 'flare path')
B. 'BISEMANTIC' WORDS
6. Connotative-denotative nouns (e.g. 'a dove', 'a hawk')
C. POLYSEMOUS WORDS
7. Connectives
8. General adverbs (e.g. 'frankly')
9. General adjectives (e.g. 'true')

    10. Phrasal verbs
    11. General nouns (e.g. 'chair')
    12. 'Empty' verbs (e.g. 'give' in 'give a hug', 'a salute', etc., 'do',
'go', 'come')
    13. Auxiliary verbs
    14. Hold-all nouns (e.g. 'thing', 'element', 'subject', etc.)
    15. Prepositions
N.B. Most laymen overrate the number of monosemous words and underestimate the role of context; most linguists and translation theorists underrate the number of monosemous words and exaggerate the role of context. I suspect that nine times out of ten, nine out of ten words are monosemous and therefore independent of their contexts, but the more common the word, the more polysemous, and so the more dependent on situational, cultural or linguistic context it becomes.

XXII
MARCH 1996

Poetry and Fischer-Dieskau

'Poetry represents writing in its most compact, condensed and heightened form, in which the language is predominantly connotational rather than denotational and in which content and form are inseparably linked. Poetry is also informed by a "musical mode"', David Connolly has written (and I have written similarly). In the wonderful interview that Fischer-Dieskau gave on Radio 3 on Saturday 23 December, he showed how much more precisely and comprehensively, which is the purpose of setting words to music, the musical mode in poetry can be 'translated', if it is realised by a composer such as Schubert. In *Totengräbers Heimweh*, the words *schwül* and *Grab* appear relatively freely at the end of their lines:

im Leben, da ist ach! so schwül, ach! so schwül
(in life, it is ah! so murky, so murky);
ins tiefe, ins tiefe Grab!
(into the deep, deep grave)

and each rhymed, they have tremendous force (communicative dynamism), so that the singer can bring out their connotations: *schwül*: oppressive (chosen by Bird and Stokes in the F. -D. Book of *Lieder*), sultry, murky, airless, close, muggy, hot, sensuous, has no equivalent in English – the translation yield might be 60%; *das Grab* means 'the grave', with connotations of death, bottomless depth, solitude and also peace but phonetically, the German word, with its [à] and its [p] is enormously more powerful than the soft English 'grave.' Moreover, original or translation, the meaning of both words could never be rendered as finely and as richly as when it is sung by Fischer-Dieskau. (This is a value-judgement; it is personal, not cultural, not universal. I consider it my duty to make value judgements, and I ask any music loving readers I may have, not to accept them, but to test them out, i.e. listen a few times.)

Fidelity in Information Texts

1. How important is fidelity in information texts? The main facts must be rendered, but what about: *Une vaste opération qui mobilisera l'organisation jusqu' en 1996?* I would prefer 'a large scale operation which will keep the organisation busy/occupied till 1996.' Others would leave it at . . . 'will continue till 1996', which is not so 'powerful' but may be all the author meant. How much does it matter? It doesn't.

2. In an information text, the translator normally has to make clear the sense of the whole and every part of the text, leaving all doubts,

obscurities, ambiguities, etc. for footnotes.

3. Translators are still elegantly and unnecessarily recasting/ rearranging clauses and groups within sentences without realising that they are altering, and often ruining, the original emphases.

4. Can anyone be as mad as a translator, e.g. translating *Les cabinets de consultants spécialisés* as 'think tanks'?

5. Only rarely is it justified to translate literal language by a metaphor, since, though it may compress the meaning, it is likely to change the register/style/tone of the message too radically. So *renouer avec l'activité militante*, 'get back to/return to (union) activism', not 'take up their militant mantle once again.'

Translation Examination Papers

Translation examination papers should normally state the source (including the date) of their texts and the purpose and occasion (including the putative readership) for translating them, since all these factors may affect the language of the translation. At present, I know of no standard examination papers that state them all.

Case Grammar Again

Coller à nouveau aux aspirations . . . '(Unions) make contact again with workers' aspirations'. French has a tendency to make verbal nouns into isolated key words (*l'opinion*) where English looks for a supporting adjective or an objective genitive ('public opinion', 'workers' aspirations').

Oblique or Hermeneutic Translation

Some translators will always attempt to fathom the meaning behind the surface meaning of a text, on the grounds that this gives a more comprehensive version of what the author intended. Thus for a sentence such as:

Pour la même raison, ils font d'ailleurs observer que la demande des entreprises est faible, les employeurs étant sûrement gênés par les implications extérieures à leur champ de responsabilité, they may write: 'In the same vein, they are also aware that in a time of recession, employers are not going to concern themselves with questions beyond their control.' I would prefer:

'Furthermore, for the same reason, they point out that company demand for labour is low, as employers are certainly worried by implications that exceed the area of their responsibilities.' Where the original (newspaper) text is as abstract or vague as this, I have to applaud a translator who wants to be explicit, though I would not go as far myself.

The Familiarization Effect

It is usually a part of the revision (a term I prefer to the briefer

160 XXII: MARCH 1996

'checking') stage of translating to ponder and go on repeating an unfamiliar collocation, say, 'his mauve/harrowed/distraught/distracted/ face', which may or may not be a literal translation of the SL text whilst assuming that a non-authoritative text/translation sounds more natural than an authoritative text/translation. Inevitably the more often the segment is repeated the more natural and familiar it will sound.

Translation as Literary Criticism

Ezra Pound memorably stated that there were at least five categories of literary criticism: (1) By discussion, (2) By translation, (3) By exercise in the style of a given period, (4) Via music, the setting of a poet's words, the most intense form of criticism, save: (5) In new composition. Although he translated much and wrote scattered remarks about translation, his idea of translation by criticism appears to have been merely implicit, new composition being a form of translation by criticism (I reverse his phrase), rather than a conscious contrast between a number of new versions and the original.

Several years ago I wrote a piece on 'Translation as a Weapon of Linguistic, Cultural and Literary Criticism (see *About Translation*, Chapter 10, pp. 162–174). Linguistic or literary criticism via translation is retroactive, in the sense that a close or literal translation will show up the most dreadful commonplaces, shorn of the supportive devices of the source language sounds and metre:

Je ne résiste plus à tout ce qui m'arrive
Par votre volonté.
L'âme de deuils en deuils, l'homme de rive en rive,
Roule à l'éternité. (A Villequier. Hugo)

'I can no longer sense anything that happens to me by your will. The soul goes from grief to grief as man from shore to shore, to eternity.'

However, whilst a translation is explicitly an interpretation of its text, it remains for the readers to make their criticism, inevitably influenced by their tastes, but mainly by the five universal medial factors (logic, the facts, ethics, beauty, total language), which I have discussed elsewhere.

Translation the Great Impersonation

Translation looked at in one way is based on the deception that one is pretending to be someone one is not – consciously in literary translation, implicitly in non-literature.

Two Divisions in Translation

For the translator, texts are either literary or non-literary and either authoritative or non-authoritative.

Rendering the Hype

'Translation – a word that covers a host of evils' – thus (=*so*

(German) – it may be noticed I use lovely literal translation quite a lot) Simon Anholt, the founder and managing director of World Writers ('copy and consultancy for international advertising') in a brilliant talk recently, one of an excellent series held weekly as part of Surrey University's Programme for Translation Studies. In the great world of virtual reality, i.e. television advertising, he says, it is sometimes called transcreation, re-evocation, rewriting, co-writing, or even miscalled transliteration. 'Funnily enough' (*strano ma vero, è bello che*), in this trade, the translator's loyalty is to the brief, not to the text, and, says Anholt, the Brits like puns, the French like rhymes, the Germans don't like jokes and only the Brits like irony, understatement and lies and think these funny. Adverts consist of 'facts and noises' and the noises are all cultural: there are no universals.

Another Note on Revision

Normally, do separate checks on: figures, to make sure they are credible and that they fit their new collocations; punctuation, including italics, initially capitalized words and bold face, to make sure it is right culturally and stylistically; proper names and trans-ferred or cultural words, to make sure the TL spelling is correct and that they are adequately understood in translation; acronyms to ensure they are not mindlessly transferred.

Lost in Translation

In an article in *New Statesman and Society* in May 1995, Boyd Tonkin uses this clichéd title (Robert Frost: The Poetry is What gets Lost in the Translation) to retail some interesting statistics: in the UK, 3% of all published books are translations; in other major EU states, there are 25%. Nevertheless, on the evidence of Dr Terry Hale, director of the British Centre for Literary Translation at East Anglia, there is now an immense interest in European literature (Hoeg, Gaarder, Eco having huge sales) after the anglocentric post-War years when literature, according to the strangely misinformed Hale, was dominated by xenophobic Leavis, 'who tinged the equally xenophobic Kingsley Amis', but was recently praised by George Steiner as a great teacher!

Gideon Toury

For close on twenty years Gideon Toury has been one of the most influential figures ('the big names' he calls them!) in the tiny but admittedly international world of translation theory – I myself have one fan in a few countries all over the world, I sometimes say to myself to cheer myself up. Reading his second book, *Descriptive Translation Studies and Beyond* (John Benjamins, Amsterdam, 1995) I think I begin to understand why. There is an air of quiet and modest assurance about the way he writes of whole 'recipient cultures' accepting, hosting, receiving, rejecting or adapting the products of guest cultures according to their 'norms', Toury's key-word. I don't myself think it works like that, so routinely, so monolithically, so polysytematically, according to plan. For long stretches, Toury gives few examples or references (other writers' examples are unsatisfactory, he thinks, because they are not representative) and when he does, as in the case of a Hebrew translation of Goethe's *Über allen Gipfeln*, the most wonderful poem in German literature, he does not discuss its 'adequacy' or 'acceptability' (his opposing concepts of close or communicative translation?) at all; it seems to me that Mandelkern, the Hebrew translator, gets nowhere near Goethe's miraculous sound-combination, but Toury is more interested in the expansion of the translation than in modification of meaning; here he is hardly descriptive, let alone evaluative. Yet strangely, in his last chapter, Toury evolves a series of correlations (but he, who is so anti-prescriptivism and dogma, calls them 'laws') some of which bear a startling and welcome resemblance to mine.

Thus is his: 'The more the make-up of a text is taken as a factor in the formulation of its translation, the more the target text can be expected to show traces of interference' not roughly the same as my: 'The more important the language of the original, the more closely it should be translated' (see my 'A Correlative Approach to Translation', Madrid University, 1995 and other papers). But he writes as a translation scholar, and I as a teacher.

Again, when he writes: 'The most common historical move has been towards greater reliance on the verbal formulation of the source text' (p.271), does Toury mean, as I have frequently observed, that the kind of free and stylish literary 'translation' so often aspired to in the '20s and '30s in at least the UK would not be tolerated any more now, as much due to respect for scientific method as to anything else and never will be? I hope so. 'To be sure, or be that as it may, and of course' (joke – could these be standard translations from the Hebrew?), scholars and others should read this book.

Kafka's *Amerika* Again
1. *Standard and descriptive terms.*
I have already remarked on the transformation of the Statue of Liberty's torch into a sword in the first paragraph of *Amerika*. There is also the difficulty of: *erblickte er die schon längst beobachtete Statue der Freiheitsgöttin, wie in einem plötzlich stärker gewordenen Sonnenlicht.* I think this should be translated as: 'he caught sight of the statue of the goddess of freedom, which he had already observed a long time ago, as though in a sunlight that had suddenly become stronger,' since Kafka did not use the standard term

Freiheitsstatue, assuming that the latter was in use at the time. (1919? No one knows.)

Note also that the two German participial groups (*beobachtet, geworden*), are more forceful and concise (Latin influence) than the more 'natural' English adjectival clauses that translate them.

2. *Long sentences and emphasis.*

Translating a long German sentence, a translator has to distinguish between clumsy word-order imposed by German grammar (the clerisy again), unusual word-order imposed by the writer's emphasis, and at the same time at least to take account of repetitions:

Unten fand er zu seinem Bedauern einen Gang, der seinen Weg sehr verkürzt hätte, zum ersten Mal versperrt, was wahrscheinlich mit der Ausschiffung sämtlicher Passagiere zusammenhing, und musste Treppen, die einander immer wieder folgten, durch fortwährend abbiegende Korridore, durch ein leeres Zimmer mit einem verlassenen Schreibtisch mühselig suchen, bis er sich tatsächlich, da er diesen Weg ein – oder zweimal und immer in grösserer Gesellschaft gegangen war, ganz und gar verirrt hatte . . .

'Below to his regret he found a gangway, which would have shortened his path considerably, locked for the first time, which circumstance(?) was probably connected with the disembarkation of all passengers, and he had to painfully look for stairs which followed each other again and again, through corridors that turned off continuously, through an empty room with an abandoned desk, until he had in effect, since he had gone along this way once or twice and always in a fairly large party, become completely lost'.

Principles and Methods of Translation

I think that a subject called Principles and Methods of Translation (or some such title) should be an essential part of the curriculum of any post-graduate professional translation course/diploma/second degree. However, it would be absurd to fail a student for the whole course simply for failing this one subject if s/he had passed in the rest of the practical translation examinations; but if the student is proceeding to a research degree, say in translation with linguistic/historical/critical commentary which is now and traditionally a proper subject for research, a merit pass in the subject should be compulsory.

The Fifth French-English Dictionary

After the Harrap, the Collins-Robert, the Oxford-Hachette and the Larousse, I am amazed to note the publication of yet another important French-English dictionary: the *Collins-Robert Comprehensive French-English Dictionary, Volume 1* (1995, 1274pp, £35, Harper Collins). This has 400,000 references, 650,000 translations and a 'thesaurus' of

200,000 French synonyms, the latter for the French language learner, but more useful (to the translator from the French) if they had been English synonyms. The dictionary is data – not corpus – based and therefore may be stronger on key-words than on modern words in context but it still has not the courage to give 'formidable' as one of the non-emotive senses of *formidable* (as in *des effectifs formidables*, 'a formidable workforce') and the translations of *moraliser* ('clean up') are inadequate ('make more ethical', etc.). However, *acrimonie* does at least remain firmly monosemous as 'acrimony'.

The NAJIT

The National Association of Judiciary Interpreters and Translations is holding its 17th Annual Meeting and Educational Conference (the two should go hand in hand at all such AGMs) on 17–19 May in Miami. There are sessions on immigrant hearings; varieties of Spanish legalese, to sensitize translators; ethical considerations in court interpreting – do you modify your translations to please the client who has hired you?; the 'bi-lingual event' trials of O.J. Simpson and Queen Caroline of England in 1820; access to justice for non-English speakers in the English (not the UK) legal system. (In AD 2000, 30% of urban Europe under 35 will not be living in their country of origin.) It will be worlds away from the climate of 'Translation Studies'.

Dynamic Equivalence and Beyond

It is a pity that a book co-written by Eugene Nida (*From One Language to Another: Functional Equivalence in Bible Translating* by Jan de Waard and Eugene Nida; Thomas Nelson, Nashville, Tennessee, USA, 1986) is not better known here. (I am grateful to my student Shizoo Yang for referring me to it.)

The book is important since Nida has altered the name of his key translation concept, 'dynamic equivalence' (i.e. attempting to stimulate a receptor's response that is essentially like that of the original receptor's) to 'functional equivalence', on the grounds that the term '"dynamic" has been misunderstood to be merely in terms of something which has impact and appeal for receptors'. Furthermore, this is a fascinating and enlightening book which goes beyond translation to the fields of cultural history, religion, sound symbolism (phonosemantics), mythology and linguistics.

Nida describes his translation method as sociosemiotic: the 'socio-' incorporates the sociolinguistic, and 'semiotic' because 'practically everything about a translation carries meaning'. In fact, in my view, all signs are meaningful: the blank spaces, pauses or not, the diagrams, the pictures the legends, the format, the typeface, the letters, the figures, the linguistic ranks (from morpheme to text), the little illustrations introducing articles in the *Economist*. All have to be accounted for in translation, even if they are sacrificed as of minor importance in the translation.

Nida also has useful remarks on the aesthetic function in translation, which may simply be the equivalent of writing as well (plainly, neatly, attractively) as the source text permits; the categorization and classification of linguistic forms, which may vary from language to language (a whale is not a fish; *un fauteuil* is not *une chaise*; colours and cattle are tricky) – for these, and also for prototype theory, see the attractive and comprehensive *Linguistic Categorization* by John R. Taylor, Clarendon Press, Oxford, 1989; some Christian key-words, like the Lamb of God, which transcend 'sense' in some languages and have to be literally translated. As major functions of rhetoric, Nida includes 'wholeness' (comprehensiveness), aesthetic appeal, impact, cohesion, coherence, focus, emphasis and appropriateness. I regret that he puts more emphasis on the systematic rather than the accurate aspect of scientific method but it is a splendid book, with ample examples.

The Translation of Metonyms

Metonyms are standard terms in which the name of an object or concept is replaced with a word closely related or suggested by one of the two, a term I have attempted to popularize as a 'familiar alternative' when it refers only to proper names (*la Serenissima* as Venice, 'Pompey' as Portsmouth). 'Familiar alternatives' are frequently replaced by their referents in translation, since they are hardly known in the target language. However, when the name of a residence (*l'Elysée*) stands for its occupant (the French President or his office) it may or may not be transferred, depending on the likely knowledge of the term by the readership.

Close Translation

Only deviate from close translation for the sake of explaining (exegesis) or interpreting (hermeneutics) to the new readership.

Lincoln Cathedral

The parallel brochures in German, French and English for Lincoln Cathedral, with its mighty exterior, are nice examples of co-writing but the French get off scot-free from a plea for a contribution, which takes the German and the English six lines each. The only 'through-translated' sentence is:

'The Cathedral exists to show Christianity.'

La cathédral signifie le christianisme

Der Dom besteht als ein Wahrzeichen ('emblem, landmark, symbol'), *des Christentums.*

Repetition in French

In spite of the distaste for repetition in French, the repetition (here of *idées*) may be enforced by its grammar:

La Constitution est un reflet des idées politiques du Général de Gaulle, idées qu'il avait exprimées à diverses occasions depuis qu'il s'était démis de ses fonctions de President du Conseil en 1946.

'The Constitution is a reflection of General de Gaulle's political ideas, which he expressed on various occasions since he resigned his duties as President of the Council in 1946'. (Note again the French pluperfect translated by the English past tense: see S. Guillemin-Flescher, *Syntaxe comparée du français et de l'anglais*.)

XXIII
MAY 1996

The Translation of Philosophy

Peter Bush, Jonathan Reé and Rachael Strange are to be acclaimed for organizing an excellent and wide-ranging international conference on the Translation of Philosophy, the first in my experience, at Middlesex University in March 1996. It soon became apparent, notably in Reé's brilliant paper, how closely philosophy, the universal subject *par excellence*, is intertwined with translation, since its foundation classics were written in now dead languages, and much of the work of later philosophers (Descartes, Spinoza, Leibniz, Bacon, Locke, Berkeley) were either written or suffused in Latin. Philosophy, like law, is cardinally dependent on meaning, and both are notable for keywords and technical terms; from the 18th century onwards, when I think German gradually became, and perhaps is still, the principal philosophical language, Latin and German words sometimes lay behind important French legal words like *relever* and *dépasser* (the notorious contradictory Hegelian *aufheben*, which means both to 'preserve', to 'continue' and to 'annul', cf. to 'sanction'), as Reé pointed out. Reé also considered that 'translators' language' (I assume he means stiff or old-fashioned renderings, like translating *or* by 'now' or *désormais* by 'henceforth'), my 'translatorese', was the result of translators not doing a good enough job; to some extent, the same reservations could be made about 'translational norms'.

The papers are to be published. I would particularly draw attention to the contributions of Duncan Large, R. J. Hollingdale and Carol Diethe on Nietzsche (a superb panel), Lawrence Venuti on Wittgenstein and the present state of translation, Jiyuan Yu on Western philosophy in China, Antonio Gomez Ramos on Jefferson in Catalan, Jean-Michel Vienne on Locke in French, Ulrich Johannes Schneider (Leipzig) on Classical philosophy in German, and Howard Caygill on Kant; a wide range. Not surprisingly, many of the translations give fresh insights into the philosophies.

Fidelity or Servility

Ethics has many apparently contradictory human qualities that overlap (thrift and stinginess, daring and foolhardiness . . .), and servility/fidelity are the ones that cover the virtues and the vices of literal translation. A time may come when '-tion', '-ity' and '-ism' words, which are always grecolatinisms, will intertranslate in most languages.

Translating Universal Idioms

Fingerspitzengefühl has been in the German language since the 19th? century. Why has it remained untranslated into English ('finger tip feeling', meaning 'instinctive/intuitive/fine feeling', 'tact and sensitivity') for so long? Is this not the essence of Walter Benjamin's single *reine Sprache* (pure language) where languages complement and supplement each other continually to cover at least all emotional life that nourishes all intelligence?

Several years ago I translated the closing sentence of a speech by Böhringer Ingelheim's managing director, Wolfgang-Hagen Hein – a brilliant and cultured man, he edited and wrote several chapters in a beautiful volume on the great scientist and polymath Alexander von Humboldt – *Ich wünsche Ihnen eine glückliche Hand* as: 'As we Germans say, I wish you a lucky hand' [acknowledgements to Pauline Newmark]. Surely it is time for the 'As we Germans say' to be omitted?

Elitism and Populism

Neither of these grecolatinisms have yet settled in the international lexicon in their basic sense as the greatest threats to democracy and decent politics: the innate superiority of one person to another and pandering to the majorities respectively.

Hervey, Higgins and Loughridge

The third book in the 'Thinking Translation' series, *Thinking German Translation; A Course in Translation Method: German to English*, by Sandor Hervey, Ian Higgins and Michael Loughridge (Routledge, London, 1995: Teachers Handbook and Oral Texts available from the publishers) is well-named since it is written for a thinking, literate and intelligent readership. Various important translation concepts and topics, beautifully defined in a glossary, but with the inexplicable omission of 'metaphor', are discussed in relation to well-chosen texts, including 19th century German literature and poetry, in which latter an interest is optimistically assumed. The emphasis is on methodology and, refreshingly, the quality of a translation, though the aim of a translation, which might involve theory, is not stated. The book is much too wordy and schoolmasterish – 'These remarks about the need for consultation are not to be taken lightly!' – and many laborious lists of categorizations, e.g. the written genres on p. 123, are not applied to translation examples. A strange reference to Trevor Jones at Cambridge appears to be addressed only and pointlessly to ancients. There is a brilliant chapter on 'Concision and the Adverb' followed by a feeble one on 'Word Order and Emphasis' that shows no knowledge of functional sentence perspective. But this is the only book on the subject in English and is well worth studying.

A Commercialized Theory of Literature

I read desperately and carefully through *Polysystem Studies* by Itamar Even-Zohar (*Poetics Today*, Vol. 11/1, 1990, Duke University Press, 6697 College Station, Durham, NC 27708, USA, for Tel Aviv University) wanting to say something nice about this book sent to me by courtesy of the author and Gideon Toury. And indeed as a wide and sweeping description of what happens to the appearance (*habitus*) and the power relations of a literature when translation is central to it [the Renaissance, my example] compared to when translation is peripheral [the mainstream of French and English 19th century prose and poetry, again my example], it is impressive and assured as a piece of general sociological description; Even-Zohar even hints that translation under the first conditions is closer (he would not use such a word) than under the second, which is not true. What is significant is that he replaces Jakobson's terms/factors in his scheme of communication and language with his own, thus: 'producer' for 'addresser/writer'; 'consumer' for 'addressee/reader'; 'market' for 'contact/channel'; 'product' for 'message'; 'institution, remunerating and reprimanding producers and agents' for 'context'. Thus we are back in the translational business world of Vermeer and Holz-Manttari, although this time we are concerned only with *belles-lettres*, with literature. Further, Even-Zohar warns he will have nothing to do with imagination [*sic*], inspiration [which can, I think, have a precise sense related to a sudden happy intuition], value-judgements, 'masterpieces' (the ironical inverted commas are his own), canonization, or elitism of any kind; I do not think he could ever grasp that the reason why Shopkeeper, Doughty, Racing, Gouty, Check-Off (joke, this is an exercise in translation[1]) are great is that, in this and that instance, they deal excitingly and beautifully and freshly with issues of human behaviour and their reflection in the natural world, issues that are universal in time and space. But up to p. 55, there are no instances here. And in a book of 256 pages, there are no commented translation examples till p. 197. We learn much about the movements of, say, Russian, Hebrew and Yiddish literature at various periods, but little that would help us to appreciate them. Even-Zohar's terminology – his textemes, repertoiremes, realemes, his transitionality (translatability?), void pragmatic connectives (modal particles?), commencitives – is somewhat opaque. Nevertheless, polysystem theory is said to be influential, so judge for yourselves.

Depletion

Even-Zohar refers usefully to Uriel Weinreich's 'depletion' process in language: 'owing to language's preoccupation with its referential

1. Solution: Shakespeare, Dante, Racine, Goethe, Chekhov. (Three of these are Auden's.)

function, various items have been recognized as mere noises rather than
contentfull; they become more 'depleted' the more often they are used'.
Weinreich instances 'take' (a book, a picture, a bath, time), some of
which, in translation, would require more specific verbs. Words like
konnte, insgesammt, jeweilig – usually 'respective', 'at the time', but
better zero in *Die Geschmacksfabrikanten hüten die jeweilige
Zusammensetzung ihrer Aromstoffe als strenges Industriegeheimnis* . . .,
'the flavour manufacturers keep the composition of their flavourings as
a strict industrial secret', and *fromm* (cf. Latin *pius*) sometimes are
better not translated at all since their referential power is so weak.

Translational Defence Mechanisms
    A prudent translator has a certain number of defence mechanisms
available when he is not sure that his translation is correct, or the original
is correct, or that the SL author knows precisely what he means.
Pre-eminent (excuse the pomposity) amongst these mechanisms is the
sly addition of inverted commas in the translation. Thus in an article
describing the effect of a drug on alcoholics: *Der Wirkstoff blockiert die
beim Alkoholiker vermehrt vorkommenden Glutamat-Rezeptoren auf den
Nervenzellen – die Andockstellen sind besetzt und damit für
Erregungsübertragung nicht mehr offen* . . ., 'The drug blocks the
alcoholic's increasing number of glutamate-receptors on the nerve cells.
When these 'docking places' are occupied, the agitation can no longer be
transmitted.' Other such mechanisms are square brackets, *sic*, foot-notes
and the use of comment words such as 'as it were' (I think *Wirkstoff* is
used in the general sense of 'drug', since the strict translation of 'active
substance/agent/ingredient' is too specific or overtranslated here).

The Difficulty of Translation
    In an eloquent article in *The Linguist*'s last issue, Ross Smith has
insisted on the difficulty of translation. Following John Lyons, who
did it for French, he makes an analysis of the 'extreme difficulty' (not
the impossibility) of translating 'The cat sat on the mat' into Spanish.
But translation is not always difficult. Too often in the past I have set
boring business or medical or simple literary texts, or texts with too
many grecolatinisms, or texts with standardized correspondences, as
homework and, in the worst case as exam papers, and regretted having
to scrape up tiny errors in my students' scripts. For the rest, translating
the message rather than the meaning is usually easy. But the more
colloquial, or the more literary, or the more linguistically and/or
culturally remote or the more obscure, the more convoluted, the
source language text, the more difficult will be the translation.

Sensitization to the Meaning of a Text
    One of the first purposes of translation theory is to sensitize

translators and readers to the various kinds of meaning in written language. The most obvious kind is the lexical meaning, whose denotative variant points to the objects and processes of the real or the imagined world, and whose connotative variant indicates the concepts universally, culturally or personally associated with them. Secondly, grammatical meaning, of which word-order is a part, generalizes the objects and processes and clarifies the sequence and the emphases of the actors or arguments in the text; here the translator must be sensitized to whether the grammatical structure is natural ('after doing') or unnatural ('after having done').

Thirdly, punctuational meaning, whilst it basically indicates stops, pauses, questions and exclamations, can also indicate, in its five poly-semous signs: italics, inverted commas, the three dots, capitalization (personification, importance, proper names) and bold face – a variety of moods and comments. Fourthly, there are texts, notably all drama, poetry, speeches, rhetoric and most advertisements, which have sonic meaning, which, in the case of recognized figures of speech, such as assonance, alliteration, onomatopoea and repetition, may be related to lexical meaning (the cry of a person or an animal) but may jar with the sense of the passage and may have to be modified by the translator. Metre and poetic genre are also related to meaning. Such sonic meaning has to be deliberately detected by, if I may adapt Vygotsky's term, 'internal listening' which is not normally operative when reading routine or 'pragmatic' texts.

Lastly, when translators read the source language text, they ask themselves (a) whether they can visualize what is happening here (who is doing what to whom, etc.? or what is the scene?) And (b) would they ever see that sentence/word in the appropriate target language text? They have to be sensitive broadly to the distinctions between person-based literary language ('faltering', 'set to') and object-based non-literary language ('fluctuating', 'about to'); sentences that require and do not require connectives, such as 'further', 'in fact', or the usually dishonest 'of course'; the descriptive and the evaluative senses of a word ('base', *non-précieux* or *sans valeur*); general and particular senses ('scholars', *érudits*, *écoliers* or *boursiers*; 'community', *communauté, communauté expatriée*); modern or historical ('province of Holland', i.e. in the Republic of the United Provinces, pre-1830); modern and obsolete collocations ('mother tongue' and 'English tongue'); indicators for a bibliography ('Walraven 1586:10' = a publication in 1586 by Walraven, page 10); intensified meanings of phrasal verbs ('they got together with', *se réunir pour discuter*); denotation or connotation of a proper name ('Michael Heseltine', M. H. the deputy Prime Minister, or any prominent personality – a clue to the solution of the difficulty may be a parallel proper name in the same text); concept or appliance ('remote control'). There is no word or collocation or grammatical structure to which the translator must not be sensitized.

Une Connaissance Parfaite de la Langue Maternelle

As a translator's main qualification, this is too often followed by a load of commonplaces: (I translate) 'This cannot be overemphasized. How could one possibly savour a translation [which is being compared to a tasty piece of ham!] if it contains grammatical and linguistic errors, not to mention spelling mistakes?' The point is completely missed. Such a *'connaissance'* is trivial compared to the ability to write one's own language well, neatly, resourcefully, individually.

Words, Words, Words

Words, Words, Words: The Translator and the Language Learner, edited by Gunilla Anderman and Margaret Roers (Multilingual Matters, 1996) is an attractive book which distinguishes the approach of first and second language learners and translators to vocabulary studies. The introduction by both editors explains how 'translatology', like linguistics, has in the last three decades taken a turn away from the theoretical to matters relating to purposes, processes and methods, with a foundation in social description as well as in psychological nuances. No one is going to 'solve' the opposition between free and literal translation, but any translator has to take a stand on this issue, and words, in particular the four full word-classes (descriptive nouns, verbs, adjectives, adverbs) are central to the argument. Jean Aitchison ('Taming the Wilderness: Words in the Mental Lexicon') describes how the individual lexicon, which for educated native speakers consists of at least 50,000 active and passive items (Shakespeare used only 30,000 words), is built up from prototypes within categories, which are linked through collocations and the co-ordinates of semantic fields, which usually have surprising gaps in other languages. (Try 'shin', 'knuckle', 'waist'.)

Gunilla Anderman gives a useful review of work on prototype theory, in particular that of Neubert and Snell-Hornby, who both situate prototypes as primary representatives of certain categories, with slight but marked differences in various languages. (Most words are either over- or undertranslated, more, or less, particular in their relation to their correspondents); 'empty' or nuclear verbs (go, do, see, know, etc., which translate differently according to their collocations, e.g. 'Know A from B', 'know better than to'); 'translatorese', e.g. automatic 'first learning' translations of 'arrive', *déjà, avoir beau, or*; John Ayto gives an invaluable statistical and descriptive review of neologism creation, which is too often the criterion mentioned in the blurb of a new dictionary; Paul Meara discusses vocabulary acquisition and Margaret Rogers reviews dictionaries, which I think she underrates, at any rate in their modern forms, thesauri and computer storage of words, such as the Surrey workbench. I attempt to illustrate the vast abundance of English, its lexis, its grammar, and the huge concentration of its lexi-cogrammar, its twenty-two model verbs, its mainly monosyllabic and Germanic phrasal words (e.g. 'Run down' in three word classes), all so often precipitating a translation loss. I do not mention its phonology, its unique consonant combinations, its apparently exceptional five diphthongs (due to the great Fifteenth Century Vowel Shift), its triphthongs, its sometimes unreproducible h, w, q, d, ch, all of which may cause translation losses. It is a pity there is no extended discussion of the merits and disadvantages of corpus-based reference books. The book is free from jargon; 'the real world' (yuck, of money-making) does not get a single mention. It fills many gaps and will interest language teachers, translators and linguists.

Interpretation Theory

It is normally assumed that interpretation is distinguished from translation in being spoken to spoken. In fact, since interpreters often get printouts of the speeches/papers they are due to interpret, anything from a few days to just before the conference starts or the paper is read, or the speech is made, interpretation is often a combination of spoken to spoken and written to spoken. Particularly for important texts, the interpreter relies on the printed version modified by the definitive spoken version. The critical third stage of translating – revision – goes by the board, though if the translation of the paper/speech is published later, the interpreter may have an opportunity of revising it. Therefore the gap between translating and interpreting is narrowed, but the title of the well-known book by Seleskovitch and Lederer, *Interpréter pour traduire*, remains misleading.

The Familiarization Effect Again

The familiarization effect, of which I wrote two issues ago, may also assist in giving near-functional equivalence to a close but strange sounding translation such as 'Shall I compare thee to a summer's day?' (Shakespeare) (which at first sight is unflattering in Arabic – 'spring' has sometimes been substituted for 'summer', writes my Arabic translator, Dr Hasan Ghazala, of Al-Fateh University in the Libyan Tripoli – but usually 'summer' is retained in the Arabic), since the reader will gradually become familiar with the context and the sound of the sonnet.

Semantic Depletion Again

A translator has to bear in mind that a conceptual word that becomes less frequently used is apt to lose one or more of its meanings. Thus, in my opinion, in spite of the *Concise Oxford Dictionary*, 'individualism', which may have a positive meaning (making independent decisions; a belief in the sanctity of the individual and individual conscience) or a negative meaning (a doctrine which encourages selfishness and social conflict), surely, no longer means 'egotism' or 'self-centred conduct'.

First Names: a Cultural, but Potentially Universal Fact

I think the translator should assume that, in the anglophone or 'Anglo-Saxon' countries, colleagues, at least in civilized firms, organizations and institutions, now call each other by their first names, from the first meeting, irrespective of gender, age, pay and 'rank'. In the thirties, this was already so in the English theatre world, in the male working-class and in Labour and Communist Parties.

Great Art: One Person's Definition

Great art, which for me is first and foremost accompanied singing, and then music without singing, and then poetry and dramatic poetry, and then tragic drama, and then drama and 'comedy', and then the novel or the short story, and then Goya's *The Shootings* (*Los Fusilamientos*), and then painting and sculpture – is art that makes me cry. Normally, however well I know the song, I need the translation with the text, to read it as I hear it.

Teaching Translation in Universities

Teaching Translation in Universities: Present and Future Perspectives, edited by Penelope Sewell and Ian Higgins (published by the Association for French Language Studies with the Centre for Information on Language Teaching and Research (C.I.L.T.) 20 Bedfordbury, London WC2N 4LB, 1996) is a useful and realistic miscellany about (unfortunately) mainly French teaching in French and British universities, though it would have benefited if the authors had been asked to distinguish between literary (rarely discussed here) and non-literary translation, interpretation and translation, as well as day to day and authoritative texts. The editors note the difference between the ESIT method, here poorly represented by the trite Karla Déjean Le Féal, who fails to produce a single translation example, and the sensitive approach of the rich and stimulating Michel Ballard, without explaining this difference. Further, the confusion between translation used for the purpose of transferring meaning, as opposed to foreign language learning, is mentioned but not clarified. Malcolm Harvey makes many subtle distinctions between French and English usage; Florence Mitchell is sensible but verbose and frequently banal on 'effective reading'. The Brighton trio, Critchley, Hartley and Salkie, begin by condemning abstract theory, but indulge in abstractions like 'knowledge engineering' and 'text-handling'; however, they later comment on some interesting material, though they use execrable jargon. The book, like the Brighton chapter, is lively and combative, and deserves a wide readership.

Surtitles for Foreign Plays

I understand that in some countries surtitles, i.e. sub-titles displayed above or alongside the proscenium, as initiated for operas in Toronto in 1983 – see Michael Kennedy's *Oxford Dictionary of Music* for further details, and all translations of musical terms – are now being used in preference to booth-interpreters for foreign play performances in Britain.

Translation Gain

The question whether a translation can ever be better than its original is I think mainly a non-topic. In brief, I think the translator of advertising or tourist material will always try to make the text better than the original, though transferring all the facts, and this is frequently possible. It is likely that a brilliant writer will instinctively improve the quality of the translation of any kind of information text. Strictly, a non-literary authoritative text, e.g. a law or an official statement can only be improved in translation if the target language has greater lexical or grammatical resources than the source language. It is usually agreed that Baudelaire's translations of Edgar Alan Poe and Rilke's of Louize Labé are superior to their originals, but given that a translation of a literary text is intended to be faithful, this raises the question of the nature of translation. In any event, a good translator may in this or that passage express herself better than the original, either because she grasped the author's thought rather better, or by taking advantage of the target language's neater and/or richer linguistic resources. Certainly some authors have sometimes modestly stated that one of the translations of their books is better than their original. (I apologise for the lack of translation examples, which I hope to remedy, in this paragraph.)

The Alpha and the Omega of a Translation

More important than reading the text before translating it, is to read your own version of it at least three times after completing it, once on its own, once clause and word for clause and word, comparing it with the original, once reading it aloud for sound, once checking the original for punctuation, capitalization, italics, tenses, metaphors . . .

Parafraud

In an outstanding article in the *Times Higher Education Supplement* of 20 October 1995, 'Dr Peccadillo and Assorted Sins', Harold Hillman has coined the useful term 'parafraud' [add: 'parafraudster', 'parafraudulent'] for a case when a writer propounds a theory whilst he knows that there is strong evidence or objections against it, and suppresses or refuses to mention them; or, as Hillman puts it, 'unwillingness to enter into proper dialogue with people with whom one disagrees, or who have challenged one's findings, assumptions, theories or published opinions'.

Cultural Functions of Translation

Cultural Functions of Translation edited by Christina Schäffner and Helen Kelly-Holmes (1995, Multilingual Matters Ltd) is, together with an interesting editorial by Christina Schäffner about the relationship between culture and translation, a record of two seminars held at Aston

University, the first beginning with a paper by Lawrence Venuti on Translation and the Formation of Cultural Identities, the second beginning with one by Candace Séguinot on Translation and Advertising: Going Global, both concluding with outspoken and skilfully summarized debates. Venuti wraps up his argument in favour of fidelity in literary translation by considering how translation creates possibilities for cultural resistance, innovation and change, all at the risk of destabilising domestic institutions and subverting domestic ideologies! but his references, unfortunately always without translation examples, are fascinating. Candace Séguinot demonstrates a wide knowledge of modern advertising. The book is educative, and should go into paperback.

The Paradox of Poetry Translation
Poetry is the most concentrated of all forms of literature and all of its components as written and spoken are important and should in principle be closely, individually but cohesively reflected in translation. In fact, because it has so many ingredients of meaning and expression which other kinds of writing lack, it is the prime instance of loss of meaning and of expression in translation. There is an admirable example of the attempt to capture all the meaning, commented by Richard Holmes in *Footsteps: Adventures of a Romantic Biographer* (Flamingo, 1995), in Gérard de Nerval's haunting sonnet, *El Desdichado* (The Wretch/the Poor Devil), strangely mistranslated by Holmes as 'The Disinherited':

Je suis le Ténébreux, – le Veuf – L'Inconsolé,
Le Prince d'Aquitaine à la Tour abolie:
Ma seule Étoile est morte – et mon luth constellé
Porte le Soleil noir de la Mélancholie

Holmes's prose 'translation': 'I am the man of shadows – the man in the shadows – the man of darkness – the man lost in the dark – the shadowy man you cannot see. I am the Widower; I am the Unconsoled, the disconsolate, the grief-stricken man. I am the Prince of Aquitaine (that region of south-west France between Bordeaux and Toulouse, through which the rivers Garonne and Dordogne run). I am the Prince with the abolished, shattered, stricken or blasted Tower; or the Prince standing by that Tower. My only Star is dead, burnt-out, extinguished – the noun is feminine. And my star-studded lute, or my lute marked with the constellations or the zodiac signs; my lute carries, or is emblazoned with, the Black Sun of Melancholy or Melancholia' (pp. 211–2). So much for a few senses. Now what about the form, and the sound, which are two more kinds of senses, which together all make up the meaning?

The Altered Ego
In *The Guardian* of 4 July 1996, Denis MacShane MP makes an

interesting analysis of parallel texts by Sir James Goldsmith, pointing out the striking differences between the English and the French versions beginning with the author 'James'/'*Jimmy*'. The English is anti-EU, the French anti-American. The French version advocates the break up of European states (even Bavarian independence!), but this is missing in the English version. This instructive and pioneering analysis only fails in distinguishing 'primitive' from 'primal' as translations of *primitif* (languages), though the author's views are all too clear.

German Literary Language

The distinction between literary and non-literary language is, I think, clearer in German than in English or French; since the Romantics, and later particularly Wagner, there is a link with medieval language: *Leib/Körper/*body; *Wonne/Entzücken/*delight; *Heiland/ Erlöser/*saviour; *Wurm/Schlange/*snake; *Gram/Kummer/*grief. How much more forceful and risibly preposterous is the Wagnerian vocabulary than modern literary German!

From here we move straight to the equally absurd but now so much better written language of tourist advertising. Take this, from the Opal Coast (between Calais and Boulogne, in case you didn't know!):

Im Nord-Pas de Calais sind vom Mittag bis Mitternacht die Himmel wie
In the Nord-Pas de Calais the heavens are like fairy-stories from morn to
Märchen: der bewegbare Dekor einer Schein-Leben Szene. Ein Himmelskörper
midnight: the moveable decor of a scene that resembles life. A celestial
ist der sichtbare oder abwesende Schauspieler, dessen schillernde Maske
body is the visible or the absent player, whose shimmering mask
zwischen goldgelb und silberfarben wechselt. Hier haben die Steine eine
alternates between golden yellow and silver. Here the stones have a
Seele. Sie sind das Antlitz der Vergangenheit.
soul. They are the countenance of the past. (My translation).

It is unlikely that this smooth piece is a translation from the French; apart from *Antlitz*, the language is normal sound usage; only the content is silly. However, much publicity now goes over the top:

Le moutonnement ample des champs est dominé par les hauteurs où s'accrochent fièrement les villages. Les sites surprenants des carrières de marbre obligent le regard à plonger vers les entrailles de la terre.

'Villages proudly nestled into the heights dominate vast fleecy fields. The surprising sites of marble quarries attract the eye into the bowels of the earth'. (Published translation).

No howlers here, but original and translation seem equally daft.

The T-V Relationship Translated into English

The T-V relationship, which is proverbially difficult (impossible!) to translate into English, can in fact be handled by using various resources, which I have already listed, but primarily by the alternation of first names with forms of address plus surnames. Thus Monika and Thomas Nenon, in a fascinating article on 'The Devil in Thomas Mann's *Doktor Faustus*: Reflections on Untranslatability' (see Marilyn Gaddis Rose's *Translation Perspectives V* (1990, SUNY at Binghamton, USA), point out that when the Devil says '*Du bist*' . . . to Adrian Leverkühn, the '*dare*devil'(?!) hero, a translated reply such as: 'Who is saying *Du* to me, I ask angrily,' can hardly achieve equivalent effect; only a paraphrase along the lines of 'Who dare address me by my first name?' would allow the reader to understand immediately the issue here.'

Three Museums

There are two new museums on the Opal Coast. The largest professes to be the only one in France to give a full history of the Second World War. It has many impressive *maquettes* (models), videos and voice-overs. The numerous captions are all translated into English, but barely a single one is without a mistake, which is usually grammatical, e.g. prepositions, articles, plurals, word order, plus misspellings, so that the text is always comprehensible, but irritating rather than funny ('The fightings prolonged themselves'). 'Arms' were mistaken for 'weapons', 'seamen' for 'marines'.

The second museum, on a wonderful site on Cap Blanc Nez, tells the history of the Channel Tunnel, and has a wealth of captions, documents, newspaper articles, all gloriously in the original French, nothing ever translated. And Calais has a magnificent museum building with fine sculptures (Bourdelle as well as Rodin), and good bilingual notices, but dreadful post-post-post modern dense 'blank colour field' art with a 'painting' of Goethe which the museum should be ashamed to hang.

Internal Translation

'Internal translation', the successive use of a foreign language to supply a word for an object, where the earlier word has become out of date, has a peculiar fascination: thus, cul-de-sac(E) for *impasse*(F); 'small carafe'(E) for *pichet*(F); clique(E) or coterie(E) for *chapelle*(F). Rather more surprising is when words like 'dilettante', transferred from Italian in 1733, and 'amateur', transferred from French in 1784 retain their basic (lover) and their derivative meanings (dabbler, non-professional,) throughout long 'careers' in English. Internal translation, like internal investment, is strong when it makes use of the unique nuance of a foreign language (wealth), and weak when it trades too long on its own poverty (lack of resources).

Translation

1. Translation is educative, because, usually with the help of the familiarization effect, it helps you to express the lacunae of meaning for the first time in your own language.

2. The language of translation is internationalisms; it is useful when it facilitates accurate translation; it is pernicious when used to undertranslate, rounding off the edges, deculturalising, abstracting.

3. Translation of a linguistically interesting text that relies on norms and stock dictionary versions is mediocre.

A National Languages Commission?

I warmly commend Professor Gareth Thomas's essay 'The European Challenge: Educating for a Plurilingual Europe', which can be obtained from the Faculty of Languages and European Studies at the University of the West of England, Bristol. With a wealth of significant statistical and factual detail, distinguishing clearly between linguistic fluency and cultural familiarity, Thomas shows that the place of foreign language teaching in the educational system is uncertain, incoherent and inconsistent, and that standards are low in many areas where interlingual communication is essential. He recommends a Languages Commission to formulate a comprehensive Action Plan for lifelong learning for all sectors of the nation.

In my opinion, a Commission, which usually reports and then disbands, is not enough. A permanent National Languages Council, with a developing and progressing policy as well as clear terms of reference, and with a powerful research unit, such as I suggested for South Africa, which is starting one, is required. The Centre for Information for Language Teaching (CILT) already has the embryo of a research unit, and the DfEE (the Department for Education and Employment!), the DTI (Department of Trade and Industry), the employers, the universities and the language associations could contribute powerfully to the Council's formation. I cannot help observing that whilst a combination of tourism, travel and the media has ensured that the public face of most countries has been changed in a generation by translation (notices, posters, titles, brochures, guides, in public and private buildings, means of transport, institutions), many language experts and authoritative personalities pay little attention to translation, and they still conflate or confuse it with language speaking or writing.

-less(E), -los(G) and *Mit-*(G)

The three Germanic affixes appear to be unique in being affixable at will to any appropriate noun/verb and in gradually moving from the physical to the figurative and from the particular to the general.

Go for the Contrast

If you have *privates Gespräch* ('private conversation') collocated with *pathetische Rede* ('speech', or here, why not 'discourse'?!) the meaning of *pathetisch* (pompous, ceremonial, impassioned?) is imposed by *privat*, and you may not find it in a dictionary.

XXV
SEPTEMBER 1996

Translating and Revising Non-Authoritative Texts

I assume on principle that any well-written text should be closely translated, but the less important the content, the less closely it *need* be translated, and again, the less authoritative and the worse written the text, the more the translator would want to write it better, and in fact in her own normal and personal style.

George Steiner, Art and Morality

For too many years now Dr Steiner, a specialist in *Gruselgeschichten* or giving you the creeps, has been moaning that art has no effect on morality and behaviour, and that a few of the worst Nazi war criminals loved music. What are the facts? All art has a moral and an aesthetic aspect. Many people can ignore or overlook the moral aspect. For them art may be just a drug (an opium), a relaxant or a stimulus to sense delight. They may be or become criminals, or even harmless sensualists. Sade may have inspired criminality, but I do not think Sade is art. 'Everyone' knows that Frank, the Nazi butcher of Poland, listened to Bach. Not so well known is that he said that hearing the St Matthew Passion again, he repented of his racism and his crimes. I believe that art has generally a good effect on people, and that Beethoven's Fifth Symphony has not got its place in world history as an inspiration for victory for nothing. When Sean O'Casey wrote,

'The thinkers, poets and brave men say with us:
No more shall the frantic wakeful mother watch
Her child's new body shrink away from freshness'

I think he was broadly right. Wilde, Auden and Vaughan Williams wrote that art changes nothing, and I think their work disproves it. Schnitzler's *Liebelei* is said to have been responsible for the abolition of duelling in the Austro-Hungarian Empire.

Word Changes

The quickest word changes are geographical: Bombay has become Mumbai, Madras is changing to Chennai. Normally, translations should give the present name first, the old one following in brackets.

Capitalized Words

A translator meeting a capitalized word, which is normally a cultural word, in the source language text, has to consider whether to add explanatory information to the target text, intra- or extra-textually, provided one accepts my definition of translation as the transfer of the

meaning of a text from one language to another for a new readership.
The first criterion is whether this information will be of interest to the
new readership. King Abdul Aziz, the virtual founder of Saudi Arabia,
was an important person, but in the context of 'the King Abdul Aziz air
base in Dharan on the east coast of Saudi Arabia', he is merely the
name of an air base, and therefore of no conceivable interest to the
readership, first or second, nor of relevance to the topic of the text,
which was the terrorist bomb attack on June 25th. The second criterion
is whether the text is authoritative or not, and whether the extra
information can be inserted neatly. In a sentence from Evelyn Waugh's
Brideshead Revisited: 'She was about to stay with her aunt at her villa
in Cap Ferrat', Cap Ferrat, nearly fifty years after the novel appeared,
probably has a denotation (cape in the Alpes Maritimes) and a
connotation (warmth and luxury) not known to most readerships;
should the translator add 'in the South of France/on the French
Riviera/not far from Nice' to 'Cap Ferrat' in the translations, information at present denied to the English readership? I think so.
Occasionally, by default translation, the translator may simply
'interpret' the meaning, adding the SL term as a curio: thus in Howard
Jacobson's *Coming up from Behind*, 'his specialism was the Long
Novel', the translation into another language could be 'his specialism
was the 18th and 19th century English novel (Fielding, Richardson,
Dickens, Thackeray, Hardy, etc.), which he (pretentiously) called the
Long Novel'. Alternatively, it could be translated as 'the Long Novel'
simply as evidence of the character's pretentiousness.

The Back Translation Test: A Variant

Surely the best rule of thumb to check whether a word of quality
or manner (adjectives, adverbs, verbs, adjectival nouns, verbal
adjectives, verbal nouns) is being translated beyond its reasonable
semantic range is to look it up in the appropriate TL-SL (the second
part) dictionary? (You have to make allowances for particularly
context-bound words – in idioms, collocations, specialized texts, etc.).
But normally, I don't think *bequem* (easy-going, comfortable, lazy,
indolent) will stretch as far as 'idle' (*faul, müssig*), nor *verstiegen*
(extravagant, fantastic) as far as 'eccentric' (*exzentrisch*), and most
dictionaries would confirm this. Too often a translation in the first part
of a bilingual dictionary is not reproduced in the second part in a
reversed and appropriately qualified form, as it should be.

Sound

A translator need not bother much about sound with a non-literary
text, except to avoid alliteration and too abrupt or too long sentences,
and to ensure that the text reads naturally. For literary texts, she must
be constantly aware of the sound of the clauses and the words in her

mind, and for poetry, sound becomes a primary criterion throughout the poem.

A Diagram of Metaphors and Their Translations

The following diagram should be added both to *Approaches* and *A Textbook of Translation*:

TYPE	TRANSLATION PROCEDURES
1. Dead	1. Same image
2. Cliché	2. Different image
3. Standard	3. Reduce to sense
4. Original	4. Adapt images (extended metaphor)
5. (Metonym)	5. Sense plus image (Mozart method)
	6. Simile (weakened metaphor)
	7. Deletion (for redundant metaphor)

Note that the two columns are independent of each other (the procedures do not directly relate to the types) and that my so-called 'recent metaphors' were (idiotically, inexplicably) in fact metonyms, which are imaged objects.

Translator Anonymous

Thomas Mann's *Little Herr Friedmann and Other Stories* reprinted in 1988 as a Penguin Modern Classic acknowledges no translator. No comment.

James Ensor

James Ensor's fine painting in the Ostend Fine Arts Museum, *My Dead Mother*, is translated as 'The Artist's Mother in Death'. Why?

A Thomas Mann Puzzle

In the S. Fischer Verlag 1916 edition of *Der Tod in Venedig*, p.88, a sentence, referring to Aschenbach, reads:

Sein Geist kreisste, seine Bildung geriet ins Wallen, sein Gedächtnis warf uralte, seiner Jugend überlieferte und bis dahin niemals von eigenem Feuer belebte Gedanken auf.

By the 1954 edition (*Der Tod in Venedig und andere Erzählungen*), *kreisste* had been changed to *kreiste*. In the *Gesammelte Werke Bd. VIII*, p.490, 1960, revised 1974, *kreisste* had been restored; similarly *die duldenden Klänge* had become *die dudelnden Klänge* again (p.506). Both translators therefore relied on the earlier edition.

H.T. Lowe-Porter: 'His mind was in travail, his whole mental background in a state of flux. Memory flung up in him the primitive thoughts which are youth's inheritance, but which with him had remained latent, never leaping up into a blaze'.

David Luke: 'His mind was in labour, his store of culture was in ferment, his memory threw up thoughts from ancient tradition which he had been taught as a boy, but which had never yet come alive in his own fire'.

Kreiste ('his mind spun, revolved, rotated, kept circling, whirled') is possible, but I think a continuous birth process is slightly more likely, and I suggest:

His mind was in labour, his whole make-up (constitution) started to shake (become agitated, waver, slip, totter), his memory cast up age-old (time-old, primaeval) thoughts, which had been handed down from his youth and which had never till then been quickened (enlivened) by his own fire.

This is as near as I can get to what Thomas Mann wrote, and I don't think it is more 'absurd' than the two published versions. I admit my reading of *Bildung* is controversial.

Amazingly, the Fischer Verlag has continued to ignore its own *Gesammelte Werke*, and has retained *kreiste* in its 1991 and 1995 reprints of *Der Tod in Venedig und andere Erzählungen*.

(My student Catherine Law, has made a substantial study of metaphors in *Death in Venice* in her M.A. dissertation, has spotted the two discrepancies mentioned and some others, and has contributed substantially to these comments.)

The Translation of Slang

I am dissatisfied with the dictionary definitions of slang I have seen, so here is my attempt: a slang word is a colloquial word or expression for a common object or activity (the more common these are, the more numerous the 'familiar alternative' slang words), often associated with strong feelings, usually of limited duration, and therefore typical of a certain period and of a particular age group, or, decreasingly, gender or social class. Slang is also used in the sense of jargon or argot when referring to informal language specific to a certain profession, trade or age group. It sometimes begins as an abbreviation for the standard word (mob, sec, mo', bus) and, rarely, becomes standard itself (boss). Some colloquialisms such as *tiens!* 'you know', *magari, ja*, with broad meanings depending on context, are not classed as slang. There are various degrees of vulgarity in slang, often associated with social class rather than the traditional topics of sex, religion, mental and physical health and excretion. Slang includes both 'swear words' and the so-called four-letter words related to sex. It is sometimes punctuated by inverted commas. The distinction between colloquial/*familier* and popular/working class/ *populaire* in slang is now difficult to maintain. Examples of slang are: phiz, phizog (both dated, for a face); phoney, phony, bogus (fake), *bidon*; bash (a. a heavy blow, b. a party), no French equivalents?

In handling slang, the translator has to pay particular attention to the frequency and the period of the word, since uncommon or dated slang in the translation jars like unsuitable dialect. Slang can sometimes be literally translated – *Woher wissen diese Schweine, vor wem ich gekniet bin?* (How do those swine (not 'pigs') know, who I prayed to?), Willy Brandt said of the people who attacked him for kneeling in the rain before the Warsaw ghetto memorial, saying one should pray to no one but God (I thank my student Suzanne Hart for this example) – but this is rare, as many slang words are neologisms or abbreviations. A corpus-based dictionary of slang, using the one-to-five diamonds of frequency signs initiated by Cobuild, and distinguishing between new, vogue, dated, obsolescent and obsolete forms, would be useful.

A Controversial Book
Successful Polish-English Translation: Tricks of the Trade by Aniela Kornzeniowska and Piotr Kuhiwczak (Warsaw, 1994, and obtainable from the School of Comparative Literature at Warwick University) devotes half its 'space' to questions of translation theory before concentrating on translation from Polish. It is an exceptionally lively, 'reader-friendly' (if I may coin a word) and widely allusive book, and contains abundant translation examples. There are many examples of execrable literally translated Polish which are not 'cultural', but bureaucratic jargon in any language, and have to be rewritten in accordance with universal aesthetic criteria.

Budapest
There were over 400 eager participants at the recent translation and interpreting conference at Budapest, (brilliantly organized by Kinga Klaudy) where Eugene Nida read an inspiring paper on Principles of Discourse Structure and Content in Relation to Translation, emphasizing the role of cohesion and sound with lively examples. Sirkku Aaltonen's view of British theatre translation, poised between a pariah's 'literal' and a master's distortions was arresting but exaggerated, and Jeremy Munday read a perceptive paper applying systemic linguistics to a piece by Garcia Marquez and its translation. The range of the contributions was wide.

Minimal Translation
The useful term 'minimal translation' was coined by Pal Heltai in a rich and exceptionally funny paper; a minimal translation is contrasted with a vital translation (*Hamlet*, an aircraft maintenance manual) and covers translations as purely illocutionary acts, e.g. where translations must be seen but not read; produced quickly, however badly; are translationese but intelligible; are used only for language learning.

Pal Heltai has a great future as a translation theorist or as a second Buster Keaton.

Leipzig

At the seventh big conference, *Grundfragen der Übersetzungs-wissenschaft*, held at Leipzig, which is perhaps the 'mother' of modern translation theory, Albrecht Neubert haunted and dominated the conference by his absence. However, he sent a paper with the longest title I have ever seen: 'Translation Science and Translation Teaching: Tensions and Opportunities (*Chancen*), Obstacles and Possibilities, Conflicts (*Gegensätze*) and Common Features (*Gemeinsamkeiten*), Isolation and Unity (*?Gemeinsamkeit*), etc.' which was distributed but not discussed. Neubert, like Mary Snell-Hornby, quoting Lars Berglund's notable paper, 'The Search for Social Significance' (1990), in *Lebende Sprachen*, which stated that, apart from my work (*sic!*), translation theory was of no use to professional translators, appears to be obsessed by the gap between translation theory and practice, and his own lengthy paper, which is unrelieved by instances, does not narrow it.

My opinion is that in many cases, translation 'scholars' are more interested in the history and 'archaeology' of translation than in its present or its future, so the gap there is inevitable. Further, if writers on translation would write better, irrespective of their languages, would produce abundant two- or more language translation examples to define their terms as well as their translation principles, laws, theories, theorems – this is coded language indeed, – ideas, theses, propositions, etc., and would teach translation, would themselves translate, would state whether they were discussing literary or non-literary translation (Hatim and Mason, for example, appear to ignore all the differences), the gap in many other cases would disappear.

Das Ruhrgebiet im Wandel

Das Ruhrgebiet im Wandel is the title of an excellent article in *Lufthansa Bordbuch 5/96*. The translated title, 'Revival of the Ruhr', is suitably upbeat but inaccurate. 'The Changing Ruhr' is semantically accurate but 'perspectively' (from FSP) incorrect. So, I think, 'The Ruhr on the Move', which is the Essen translator Cornelia Stockinger's, not mine, gets it right. So much for translating into one's away language!

A Distinction

Target text oriented translation theories and studies are propounded from the perspective of the translation historian or 'scholar', who examines as objectively and descriptively as possible the 'actual/real' translations of the past, evaluates them, and may attempt to formulate the 'laws' governing them as though they were immutable. They may also have to take into account the source text oriented perspectives of some translators. Source text oriented translation theories, principles and methods are propounded from the perspective of the translation teacher or trainer, who looks critically at the translations of the past, which she often uses as examples, and attempts to secure all kinds of improvement from translators and translation students, usually and broadly for the sake of accuracy (not 'correctness') and elegance. Historians and teachers are concerned both with literary and non-literary texts, though historians are likely to put more emphasis on literary texts. Desirably, both translation historians and teachers are concerned with moral and aesthetic values.

XXVI
NOVEMBER 1996

Capitalized Words Continued

It is, I think, regrettable that in the 'Vienna Declaration' of July 1 (see *The Linguist* 35/5, p. 158), it was decided to retain capital letters at the beginning of German nouns (they were abandoned by Stefan George, the fine poet and best of all German translators, particularly of Baudelaire and Shakespeare), so that German cannot make particular use of these for God, names, titles, personification, symbolization or emphasis, as can most other European languages. The tendency to personify abstract nouns of human qualities and the features of nature, often as women, has declined in this century, and translators normally only retain their capitalization in religious or historical texts (e.g. in *The Pilgrim's Progress*, and *The Rights of Man*). There is also a general tendency in British English (see *The Economist Style Handbook*) to reduce the use of initial capital letters.

Categorizing and Evaluating Translation Errors: a Task for Examiners and Book Reviewers

The categorization of translation errors is firstly subject to one's personal theory of translation, and secondly to whether the errors occur in a literary or a non-literary text.

If it is thought that every translation serves its own purpose and there is no such thing as a good or a bad translation, the question of translation errors does not arise. The view that there are no moral or aesthetic values implicated in the composition or assessment of a translation now has a certain vogue, particularly amongst theorists of literary translation (but see also B. Hatim and I. Mason, T. Hermans, etc.), who simply 'accept' most translations as historical or professional phenomena without attempting to assess them). Moreover, if a script clearly follows a theory of translation that differs from that of the examiner (e.g. avoiding the use of 'the same words' – see below) then the examiner must take this into account in marking, and not indulge in repeated penalization.

In both literary and non-literary translation, at a professional level, a major or a gross or a basic error (or a 'howler') may be defined as the mistranslation of a common word, idiom, structure or sentence, due plainly to the translator's ignorance: thus *arbre* (shaft) translated as 'tree'; *aus hartem Holz* (made of stern stuff, tough, as 'out of hard wood'); *ha tanti amici quanti nemici* (he has as many friends as he has enemies) as 'he has as many enemies as he has friends'.

A medium or a standard error is the mistranslation of a word or idiom that should be known, that should be in the translator's passive vocabulary: thus *holzen* (to hack, in football) as 'fell'; *tour de table* (a pool, in finance) as 'round table'; the misspelling of an important technical term (oxydation' instead of 'oxidation').

A minor or slight error is the use of a synonym where there is an obvious one-to-one translation: thus *excellent* (excellent) as 'first class', which is *de premier ordre*, or the misspelling of a common word, or a slip (in an exam).

In literary texts, the seriousness of these errors might be modified by considerations of sound, ambiguity and the failure to distinguish figurative from non-figurative language, but since the individual words and the style of language used, as opposed to the facts, are more important in literary than in most non-literary texts, the seriousness of these errors could also be aggravated.

Whilst it is always easier to distinguish a bad from a good translation (i.e. one can usually tell if something is plainly wrong, but not so easily when something is right, given that translations are often only approximations), the negative element has to be assessed analytically; the positive element, where the text is considered as a whole, is equally important, and I have for long been criticizing the few reviews of translations that are published for concentrating exclusively on translator's errors. Timothy Buck has rightly exposed the howlers in H.T. Lowe-Porter's translations of Thomas Mann's works, but the theory of translation implicit in her work (which may have stemmed from her publisher, Alfred Knopf) allowed her an extraordinary freedom to recast and abbreviate her original texts, and it does include some accurate and lyrical translated passages. Usually the positive element in a translation can be assessed through 'impression' marking which focuses on paragraphs and takes note of *trouvailles* or inspired clearly imaginative renderings, possibly the following from *Death in Venice*:

Wie irgend ein Liebender, wünschte er zu gefallen, und empfand bittere Angst, dass es nicht möglich sein möchte. Er fügte seinem Anzug jugendlich aufheiternde Einzelheiten hinzu, er legte Edelsteine an und benutzte Parfums, er brauchte mehrmals am Tage viel Zeit für seine Toilette und kam geschmückt, erregt und gespannt zu Tische. (p.75) (1912)

'Like any lover, he desired to please; suffered agonies at the thought of failure, and brightened his dress with smart ties and handkerchiefs and other youthful touches. He added jewellery and perfumes and spent hours each day over his toilette, appearing at dinner elaborately arrayed and tensely excited. (H.T. Lowe-Porter, 1928)

Here I would say that the correspondences for *wünschte* (literally, wished), *dass es nicht möglich sein möchte* (that it would not be possible), *bittere Angst* (bitter fear), *aufheiternde Einzelheiten* (cheering details), *brauchte viel Zeit* (needed much time) and *zu Tische* (at table) are 'happy'; that 'elaborately arrayed and tensely excited' is nicely balanced and counterbalance the sound-play of the original (*geschmückt, erregt, und gespannt*, embellished, excited and tense); and that whilst the 'smart ties and handkerchiefs' are gratuitous, they do no harm.

Literary Titles

I have already remarked that up to perhaps this decade, many literary translators appear to have considered themselves exempt from the normal principles of translation (i.e. the search for equivalence/s, accuracy and elegance) particularly where titles are concerned, and to have preferred to be 'creative'. Thus Kafka's *Die Verwandlung* (1912) was translated by Edwin and Willa Muir (1961) as *Metamorphosis* and by Stanley Corngold (1972) as *The Metamorphosis*, and it was only in 1992 that Malcolm Pasley translated it more accurately as *The Transformation* (*The Transformation (Metamorphosis) and Other Stories*, Penguin Books).

In fact, a Germanic or 'simple' monosyllabic Romance noun is required to translate *Verwandlung*, but only a verb ('to turn into') exists. If Kafka had 'meant' *Metamophosis*, a zoological term, or *The Transfiguration* or *The Transsubstantiation*, both religious terms, which some critics, who give a religious interpretation to the story, have favoured as translations of the title, he could have used virtually the same words in German. Instead he used a simple non-technical word (shades of Freud), for which 'transformation' is the nearest equivalent. Note that the prize-winning books in the recent *TLS* Literary Translation Competition all had closely translated titles, e.g. *His Mother's House* for *Casa Materna, Extinction* for *Die Auslöschung*, but the winner's title (Albert Cohen's) *Belle du Seigneur*, was simply transferred by David Cowan, the translator; this seems a cop-out to me, even though a literal or 'semantic' translation of the title is quite evidently impossible, and an approximate but adequate translation could only be worked out through the book's context. The original title, in brackets, could, however, remain on the title page below the translated title.

Similarly, the title of Janáček's masterly opera *Osud* should be translated as *Destiny* at least until the opera is as well known as *Die Götterdammerung* or *Cosi fan tutte*, since, when it is transferred it sounds like a personal or place name. However, it is now 'safe' to simply transfer *Les Liaisons dangereuses* at least into English.

Konstruktives Übersetzen

Konstruktives Übersetzen by Hans G. Hönig (Stauffenburg,

Tubingen, 1995) is a somewhat uneven book. A critical and sane look at many examples of defective German – English and English – German non-literary translation is intercalated with numerous passages of ponderous and pompous pedagogy that amount to nothing better than platitudes: e.g. 'A realization, which is obtained from a text analysis preparatory to translation, is the fact that this listing was written for medical experts; hence a strategic measure can be derived for competent translators: they must review self-critically, whether their stock of knowledge will allow them to . . . (p.88)'. I think the most sensible way of reading this book is to start at the examples and then read Hönig's comments as in the case of many other similar books.

The Same Words
    An I.O.L. examiner complains that too many translation candidates in French deliberately avoid the use of the 'same words' – s/he calls it 'an unwillingness to use obvious words'; what reasonable alternatives are there, in most contexts, to, say 'describe' for *décrire, beschreiben, describir, descrivere*, or to 'ambitious' for *ambitieux, ambicioso, ambizioso?* Yet in the often excellent *Pédagogie raisonnée de l'Interpretation* by Danica Seleskovitch and Marianne Lederer (Didier, 1989), the flagship in the field, the authors, who persistently identify interpretation with translation and regard themselves as translatologists, advise students 'never to repeat "the same words", since, "however similar they are in English and French, they are always (*sic*) so subtly different that it is preferable to avoid their use if one does not want to run the risk of saying something different when one wants to say the same thing. It is preferable to mistrust all friends as one cannot hope to know all false friends' (p.142). Never could there be a greater encouragement to inaccuracy.

Translation Theory Always a Step Behind
    It is truly pathetic that translation theorists who used to pick up the latest craze in linguistics to apply it to their own writings, are now – see for instance the handsome review *TradTerm* 3 (1996) published by the University of Sao Paulo in Brazil, which is so full of Derrida and Foucault as well as of their epigones, their inferior imitators – piling into deconstruction, post-structuralism, feminism, post-imperialism, ideologism, etc., long after these have ceased to be mainstream.

Translation Unchanging
    'Update your models', the participants at the recent huge conference in Budapest were urged. The remark was misguided. Essentially, translation does not change, any more than art or linguistics. Giotto is no more outdated than Shakespeare or Velasquez. What changes, what dates, is the dress, the expression, but the issues remain

the same: all translators have to take a stand on how to value their originals, how to handle their readerships, how closely to translate. It's a question of the occasion of the translation, not of updating.

Postilions Struck by Lightning

An amusing article, *La Plume de Ma Tante* by Andrews Eames in the British Airways in-flight magazine *Business Life* (October, 1996) reminds the reader that whilst most phrase books have superseded the 'minty imperiousness' of 'Boy, it is going to rain, put up the side sails' for Java, 1923, some still have a distinctly 'remember-who-won-the-war-aroma', 'Have my luggage fetched from the station' (Collins German, 1970). Certainly, the tourist and the traveller are always the customers, but surely all phrase books should begin with the phrases: Please, Thank you, Excuse me, I beg your pardon, notoriously and significantly difficult as the first one is to translate into French.

Further, they should make abundant use of contrasts or oppositions of all kinds:
1. Human qualities: good/bad; kind/unkind.
2. Material qualities: thick/thin; long/medium/short.
3. Action: work/idle/idle
4. Reversal and negation: do/undo; go/return.

Note that a third 'neutral' term is sometimes available.

Lastly, they should include a list of practical word formation 'conversion' rules, a set of reach me down Grimm's laws, e.g. for Spanish approximately:

Spanish	English
h (hambre)	f (famished)
h (hastiado)	g (disgusted)
ue (cuestar)	o (cost)
ll (llenar)	pl (plenty)
ll (llave)	kl (cl) key
t (vitoria)	ct (victory)
ch (hecho)	ct (fact, feat)
ch (hacha)	x (axe)
-cc- (acción)	-ct- (action)
-b- (goberno)	-v- (government)
-g- (lagrima)	-ch- (lachrymose)
esc- (scama)	sc- (scale)
est- (estazione)	st- (station)
esp- (espacio)	sp- (space)
-ie- (diente)	-e- (dental)
-ch- (derecho)	-gh (right)
-d- (vanidad)	-t- (vanity)
-idad (universidad)	-ity- (university
-ismo (socialismo)	-ism (socialism)

-ista (socialista)	-ist (socialist)
-eza (grandeza)	-ness (greatness)
-ble (notable)	-ble (notable)
-cion (nación)	-tion (nation)
-bil (mobil)	-bile (mobile)
ll- (llano)	fl- (flat)

For additions, see the invaluable Basic Vocabularies for the Romance Languages in Frederick Bodmer's *The Loom of Language*, a fine book.

Note also that intervocalic double s, m, n, t, in English are often singular in Spanish.

Whilst many phrase books still retain rather old-fashioned injunctions, or reverse roles ('You should not travel for at least three days'), most take into account that they are teaching culture as well as language, even if the Berlitz Arabic Phrase Book for Dating 'Do you mind if I sit down here? Are you waiting for someone? May I take you home?' etc. would not be welcome in Iran or Saudi. Any phrase book might take a leaf out of the Insult Dictionary, which translates *Tenga le mani in tasca, porcaccione* (Keep your hands in your pockets, you fat pig) as 'Get your slimy hand off my bottom', which is a good example of compensation as a translation procedure (*porcaccione* → slimy).

Units of Meaning: the Morpheme and the Musical Note

When words are set to music, the unit of meaning contracts from morpheme to note, and a modulation, a change of note or even the prolongation of a note can express a new message. Thus music is more concise and economical than language, and a composer such as Schubert can express the passing of a whole world in a song such as (Schiller's!) *Die Götter Griechenlands (wieder, lebenwarmen)* or *Dass sie hier gewesen (Düfte, Tränen)*. But at a time when there are a wealth of splendid singers (Christoph Prégardien, Matthias Görne, Bo Skovhus, Wolfgang, Holzmair, Thomas Quasthoff, etc.), it needs a singer who is acutely aware of the tiny units as well as the large ones to achieve this denseness. (This para may be nonsense, but if it leads one reader to listen to the two songs again, it is justified, whether she waits for the next concert at the Wigmore Hall mecca, or, less patiently (patience being a vice), gets hold of the Fischer-Dieskau tapes/records/CDs.)

It's Good to Talk

'The phrase "It's good to talk" is an understatement', says Karen Burdett, language expert of A & C Exports in Spalding, Lincolnshire. But there's more to exporting than telephone enquiries, though these may come first, and the rest, publicity material, sales literature, manuals, contracts, all depend on translation.

XXVII
JANUARY 1977

Translation and Meaning
The third volume of the Maastricht-Lodz series of translation conferences has now appeared (*Translation and Meaning*, Part 3, edited by Marcel Thelen and Barbara Lewandowska-Tomaszczyk, Hogeschool, Maastricht, 1996), and although it is heavy (600 pages!) it could not be more thoroughly and efficiently indexed. This volume focuses on practice (whilst the Lodz volumes are on theory), and there are useful groups of essays on particular topics which specialists can consult: terminology, court interpreting (for which, see also the brilliant article in the current *Proteus* published by the NAJIT, NY), corpus linguistics (Laviosa-Braithwaite), lexicography, MT and MAT, teacher training (Adab), the scenes and frames model, languages for special purposes (LSP), translation of poetry and religious texts (Ronald J. Sim, a fine contribution), translation assessment (Kirby), and, for all translators, metaphors (Mandelbilt, Rakusan on animal metaphors, Thelen, with discussion and comments). The most controversial paper is Nicholas Round's on 'Translation, Cultural Influence and Semantics: Notes Towards a Theoretical Divergence'. Round states that in modern translation theory, nobody has much use for equivalence; but as far as I know, Snell-Hornby alone maintains this view and she has been much criticized (by at least Wilss, Neubert, me); secondly, translation is inherently target-oriented, which literally but only sometimes figuratively is a plain statement of fact. Round is however sceptical about the statement: 'Most theorists (from Even-Zohar to Derrida) – [which sounds like Katharine Hepburn running the whole gamut of emotions, or translation theory, from A to B] – tend to agree that the stranglehold of source-oriented theories [Nida, etc.?] has been broken.' It is a provocative and discursive essay which should be read, but some examples would have clarified the argument.

Teaching (Translation): Some Further Points
1. After answering a question, I sometimes ask: Have I answered your question properly/completely?, as a check.
2. Spelling. At least in Europe, English and French are the two dual languages, written and spoken. For this reason, I spell out and speak all new words and collocations. Spelling gives more emphasis than the OHP (overhead projector) or the white/blackboard.
3. Digressions/excursuses. I do not hesitate to make digressions, even at length, provided (1) I believe the whole digression is useful

educationally; (2) I know how to revert to my proper subject seamlessly.

4. If I get no questions, the class is a failure. If as often the students are too timid (the majority are always girls), *I* have to ask the questions. The risk is sometimes of too much opinion and not enough new knowledge, in this case, translation examples.

5. In translation classes, invented examples are better than no examples.

Stages of Translation

I doubt whether any foreign writers, apart from the Greek dramatists and the Latin poets have ever made so great an impact on British literature as have Ibsen and Chekhov (and later, in drama only, to a lesser extent, Strindberg, Pirandello, Sartre, Genet and Brecht); they were virtually chapters in the history of British drama, whilst hardly any other translated foreign dramatists influenced it at all.

Stages of Translation (edited by David Johnston, Absolute Press, 1996), with contributions by Jeremy Sams, Ranjit Bolt, Nick Dear, Edwin Morgan, and others, has the merit of showing that the 1980s, due perhaps to the widening of so many international communications and the stimulus of the opening of the National Theatre in 1976 (*endlich einmal*, at last), were a hive of translation activity for the theatre. It is a disappointing book, long on loose diffuse tape recorder 'writing', short on translation quotations, let alone examples, with too many pieces by 'translators' like David Hare who work from literals which lose all the richness and the sound effects of their originals, but a few useful contributions with the concision of writing like Eivor Martinus, Anthony Vivis, and Gunilla Anderman. Unfortunately it barely touches on the large number of great classical (dare I say 'canonical'? No, it's too trendy) non-English plays that are unknown to the Anglophone public.

Translation Theory

Translation theory is the identification, generalization, diversification, contextualization, variation and proposed solution of particular translation difficulties.

The Museo National de Bellas Artes of Buenos Aires

This splendid museum has an extraordinary picture, one of five by Goya, called *Escena de Guerra* ('War Scene'), but also, in some books, *Escena de Bandidaje* ('Bandit Scene'), presumably because the subject may be either. This picture has some common features shared with the great Prado picture, *The Shootings of the 3rd of May*.

The titles of all pictures in the museum are in Spanish and English (but *El Repos de Diana*, presumably *Le Repos de Diane*, becomes

Diana at Rest, which confuses the functional sentence perspective and any index of titles). A pity the third language titles in the museum were not added where appropriate.

Translational Ranks

My revised translational ranks are as follows:

1. Text (book or article or segment).
2. Chapter or section.
3. Paragraph.
4. Sentence.
5. Clause.
6. Group or phrase.
7. Collocation.
8. Word or term (in either case, simple or compound).
9. Morpheme (prefix, suffix, root).
10. Punctuation mark.

These should appear in the left-hand column of my general frame of reference; the central column is occupied by contextual factors, the right-hand by translation procedures.

Notes: 1 to 10. In principle, top-down precedes bottom-up when the language of the text is less important than the content; when language and content are equally important, bottom-up and top-down are equipollent.

6. These may be nominal ('a nice morning'), verbal ('could have done') or adverbial/prepositional ('quite calmly', 'on a warm day').

7. Terms have to be translated by standard TL terms; if they don't exist in the TL, by descriptive words.

The Infinite Paradoxes of Translation

The infinite paradoxes and contradictions of translation arise because at bottom the translator is pretending to be someone she's not. Further examples:

1. The easier the text, the better paid the translator (being paid by number of words).
2. Therefore the harder the text (poetry), and the more time consumed, the worse the translator is paid.
3. The more linguistically and referentially challenging the text, the worse it's paid.
4. The more boring the text (statistics plus grey factual language), the more useful it often is, and the better paid.

Can a Translation Ruin a Literary Text?

A bad translation can 'ruin' a poem or a play, but I think it takes a lot for a translator to ruin a short story or a novel. Witness the notorious 'mistranslations' of the Russian classics, Camus, the last volume of Proust (*Le temps retrouvé* so badly translated by Stephen Hudson as

Time Regained and then brilliantly translated by Andreas Mayor as *Time Found Again*), and now Thomas Mann, which didn't do much harm to the reputation or sales of these authors. I suspect that the 'force' of the novel usually comes through, and besides, three quarters of the translation will usually be all right. However, this is not an argument against retranslations. All translations should usually be into the modern language, and masterpieces should be translated after a generation, hence David Luke's translation was overdue and 'owing' to Thomas Mann anyway. Note too that Thomas Mann wrote that he wanted his books to be translated as literally and accurately as the foreign language would allow.

Trio

At a fascinating conference on translation issues recently organized by the Oxford University Department of Continuing Education, Edith McMorran, the animator of this and previous 'Trio' (Translation In Oxford) events, suggested that words were like banknotes (always changing in value and currency on the foreign exchanges, I assume), and gave some fascinating examples of neologisms such as 'cool' (maximum of approval with the minimum of emotion, from jazz?), 'streetwise' (resourceful and capable in crowds and cities?), 'politically correct', 'ramshackle' (all over the place, in a poor state). These words (except for the last one) fill the endless lexical or grammatical gaps in their own and later in other languages; being centred in the qualities of persons rather than things, in adjectives rather than nouns or verbs, they are the touchstones of literary texts and their translations; inevitably, they are often transferred together with componential analysis or paraphrase in translation. Edith McMorran also said, memorably, that a good translation makes you aware of something in the source text that you hadn't noticed before.

The poet Peter Dale brilliantly illustrated Dante's cool language in describing the horrors of the *Inferno*; the taboo language in Peter Crimp's translation of *Le Misanthrope* (with *Britannicus*, the best and most serious play in French literature?) was somewhat overdone; and Terry Hale (apart from pursuing his misplaced attack on Leavis and Leavisites for being responsible for the dearth of literary translations in this country – in fact, Leavis included a paper on Dante and a subject from French literature in his curriculum for an English literature degree, surely a far-sighted and unique proposal, nor had he the influence on London publishers and the literary world with which Hale credits him) – Terry Hale gave an interesting account of the European intertextuality of the detective novel.

The Proportion of Translations in Book Publishing

Terry Hale also produced some statistics showing the number of book publications and translations in European countries in 1991; these showed that whilst UK and Germany had the largest number of total publications (67,000), Germany had five times as many translations (14%) as UK; Netherlands, Italy and Spain (25%) substantially exceeded France's (18%) rate of translations; Portugal (44%) and Greece (36%) translated more than other countries; UK's (and Ireland's) translation record of 3% was incomparably the worst. Hopefully, five years later, after several new translation prizes, the active encouragement of the Arts Council and the *TLS*, and the foundation of the British Centre for Literary Translation at Norwich (UEA), the situation has improved.

Modern Translation Studies and Literature
'Translators', writes Theo Hermans in his abstract for a paper given at the recent seminar on literary translation run by Piotr Kuhiwiczak at Warwick University, 'anticipate, negotiate and manipulate the expectations about translation held by their prospective audience'. I do not understand how one can negotiate or manipulate expectations when one has not even met one's readership, but it is a strange way to talk about serious literature which is what translation is generally held to be, even by the Manipulation School. 'Readers respond to translated texts by measuring them against their expectations of what translation ought to be or do.' Readers do nothing of the kind; not knowing the source language, they can't measure anything, and are interested in the text as literature rather than as translation.

Moreover, such terms as norms, models, systems, strategies and polysystems, so common in Translation Studies, all suggesting a reductive scientific approach, are more suitable to the business of nonliterary translation than to the appreciation of literary translation, which should be marked by the sensibility and intelligence which can detect expansions, contractions, distortions and even enrichments of meaning in the translation, of which the writer of the original was never aware, in respect of the original. Thus perhaps, in the last paragraph of Thomas Mann's *Death in Venice*:

Minuten vergingen, bis man dem seitlich im Stuhle Hinabgesunkenen zu Hilfe elite, which I would translate as: 'Minutes passed before anyone hurried to the assistance of the man who had slumped sideways in his chair', the 'untranslatable' 'slumped' for *Hinabgesunken* has a sense of feebleness, helplessness, sickness, heaviness, suddenness and above all a quality of phonosemantics or onomatopoeia – sl-: *slip, slide, slither, -lump*, dump, thump, rump, crumple, a heavy fall or body – which, I think, is missing in Helen Lowe-Porter's and David Luke's 'collapsed' or the otherwise perfectly acceptable and literal 'sunk down sideways into his chair'.

Or again, however one handles the puzzling and extraordinary:

Seine Bildung geriet ins Wallen (line 13, page 50, Fischer Verlag dtv): 'His whole mental background was in a state of flux' (Lowe-Porter); 'Its store of culture was in ferment' (Luke).

'His mental structures started to disintegrate', my version – note the wide differences of interpretation – the translation is bound to point to a contraction of meaning in respect of the original owing to the lexical gaps in English when faced with the German words *Bildung* and *das Wallen*.

The Translation Examiner's Problem

Every translation examiner has to determine the extent of the gap between her preferred translation of a segment of the text and the variants of what she will admit as valid translations, which may consist of near-synonyms and will cover the ambiguities and alternatives of the segment's meanings. It needs a lot of tolerance to move away from a version that stands out as a *trouvaille* (a find) to a more humdrum but acceptable rendering. She has to bear in mind that the candidate translators have no opportunity to defend their versions or discuss alternatives, which is one good reason for requiring candidates to annotate a dozen points, to explain and defend their versions as a compulsory part of at least one of the translation papers in a professional examination.

Vogue Words

When a word increases rapidly in use, as has the French word *réflexion*, it is soon likely to proliferate in a growing number of non-technical meanings, thus: thought, thinking, consideration, remark, comment, complaints, criticism, study, reflection, forethought. Five of these translations from the 1994 Oxford-Hachette, all of which are heavily context- and collocation-dependent, did not appear in the 1972 Harraps. Compare the word 'deliver' in 1996, which has expanded 'produce what one has promised' ('deliver technologies') to meet all promotions and politicking; or the supreme hold-all word, 'problem' (trouble, illness, disability, difficulty, question, hitch, defect, disaster, etc.). 'No problem', an apparently genuine official said to me in Bombay Airport after midnight when I asked him how to get to my hotel. Five minutes later, in a 'taxi', I was staring at two daggers confronting me on my left and right.

XXVIII
MARCH 1997

Genres

When a literary work is converted to another genre, e.g. translation, film, drama, music, opera or ballet, much of the original is lost, but the cinema can explicate psychological and physical details, and opera can dramatize and intensify all the range and sequence of emotions.

Thus *Death in Venice* has been enriched by its complements, the film by Luchino Visconti (1971), and, incomparably, the opera by Benjamin Britten (1973).

Notes on Literary Translation

1. The more serious the text, morally and aesthetically, the more accurately and economically it should be translated, reflecting the thought, style (idiolect rather than variety of language), emphasis (through functional sentence perspective), and as far as possible, particularly in poetry, the rhythm and sound of the original.

2. The more important the language of a text, which is on a scale from poetry (where every word and feature are important, but paradoxically, there are so many factors, that close translation is most difficult and denotatively least likely or possible) through the short story and the novel to tragedy, drama, comedy and farce, the last four being actively affected by their audiences, the more closely it should be translated.

3. A deviation from normal SL social usage, whether lexical, idiomatic, or grammatical, should usually be reflected in the translation.

4. A word, whether key-word or leit-motif repeated in the source language text, should be repeated, never replaced by a synonym, in the translation.

5. An original universal metaphor should be translated literally; an original cultural metaphor should retain as much of the original image as is possible consonant with the situational and linguistic context bringing and making the meaning clear to the second readership.

6. A standard metaphor should be translated by its standard equivalent or, failing that, comprehensibly adapted.

7. Humour and irony must be reflected in the translation, sometimes at the cost of literal or denotative meaning.

8. If the dramatist intends the audience to cry or to smile or to laugh at a certain place in a play, the translator must do likewise, sometimes, in the case of broad laughter, at the cost of a faithful linguistic translation.

9. Sound should be reflected in onomatopœia and compensated in assonance, but may have to be sacrificed in alliteration.

10. Essentially, literature, *belles-lettres*, is about individuals and their actions, while non-literature, *Sachbücher*, is about objects and movements. The salient features of literary texts are the human qualities expressed in adjectives, adverbs and nouns of manner. These are the more sensitive components of language, readily changing in meaning in response to their situational and linguistic contexts: thus, 'cool' (*branché*, *super*) or 'streetwise' (*dégourdi*).

11. Sound, linguistic rhythm, speech-rhythms, colloquial language and linguistic innovations are fundamental factors in literary language from poetry through drama to fiction, and have to be recreated in the translation.

12. Literary language is basically the recording of spoken language, a dialogue between writer and reader ('Reader, I married him'), or between the first and the second person singular. Non-literary language is basically third person singular, impersonal or passive.

Service Translation

Translation out of the home language or the 'language of habitual use', sometimes known as 'service translation' (both terms were originated by Anthony Crane) needs reconsideration from time to time, and the following reflections are (hopefully) pertinent:

1. As developing countries increasingly require translations, service translators may be the only ones available.

2. In information translation, a poorly written translation that is full of translationese is better than no translation.

3. An intelligent and sensitive 'non-native' translator is always likely to produce a better translation than a silly and insensitive 'native' translator.

4. A 'non-native' translator translating informal or colloquial texts is likely to betray the text.

5. In principle an experienced 'non-native' translator handling information text should have her work revised by a 'native' speaker; literary texts should only be translated by 'natives'.

6. In the provision 14(d) in the Translator's Charter adopted by the Fourth Congress of FIT (the International Federation of Translators) in Dubrovnik in 1963:

A translator should, as far as possible, translate into his or her own mother tongue or into a language of which he or she has a mastery equal to that of his or her mother tongue, 'into his or her own language of habitual use' should replace all words succeeding 'translate'. NB In the above remarks, 'native' is used in the sense of 'with the target language as language of habitual use'.

Translation Theory and Criticism
Normally, anyone writing a piece of translation theory or criticism should produce his own translations of any examples that he quotes or makes up. This is not so much to show his ability as a translator or his professionalism, as to give concrete and plain evidence of his argument. Nothing is so clear and reductive of abstractions as a translation example written by a translation theorist.

Grecolatinisms Again
Translators have to bear in mind that usually an English grecolatinism is not used so frequently as its Romance language counterpart: thus *préfiguration* certainly means 'prefiguration' (Oxford-Hachette), but it may translate more persuasively in the context as 'advance indication', 'indication' or 'warning'.

Reference Books
I am again amazed by the inadequate number and range of reference books which candidates bring with them to their professional examinations; apart from mono- and bilingual dictionaries, encyclopaedias, thesauruses, dictionaries of quotations and modern quotations, etc. are essential. The most common mistake is to bring only dictionaries, forgetting that translation is a referential and cultural as well as a linguistic exercise. There is no need to bring a dictionary of neologisms; if the reference books are up-to-date, there will be no difficulty with *criminogène* (conducive to crime) or 'regenerate' (slum areas). The Institute's International Diploma in Translation examination usefully asks candidates to list reference books used, which has shown that too many annotations have been confined to grammatical points and recasting of sentences.

Two Kinds of Paraphrase
The good kind of paraphrase is when the translator has to 'circumscribe' the meaning because the target language does not have the words or the target culture does not have the objects, customs, etc. that translate the source text adequately (e.g. translating *un tout autre visage de la banlieue, révélateur, au sens photographique du terms, de la cité du futur* as 'Another aspect of the suburbs, revealing, like the developing of a photograph, the city of the future' (my translation). Note I have translated both senses of *révélateur*, but split it into two unrelated words).
     The bad kind of paraphrase, both in literary and non-literary texts, is when the translator unnecessarily attempts to improve on the source language text, usually by overtranslating (showing off extra knowledge), or undertranslating (using abstractions), although a close translation is all that the reader needs. (*Les autres y décèlent une*

fatalité: 'The others show that nothing can be done about it', in lieu of 'The others show that this is an inevitable occurrence'.)

The Translator's First Loyalty

The translator's first loyalty is neither to the writer nor to the reader but to the truth.

I have to explain this declaration. First, the declaration is 'potential'; it is only pertinent when the occasion arises, when the truth is threatened. Secondly, the truth is fivefold: the truth consists of the assertion of the physical facts, of logic, of social and personal morality, of beauty and of the convergence of pure language; these are universal, therefore non-cultural truths. Thirdly, the translator, if called upon, usually intervenes extratextually rather than intra-textually, but this intervention is an integral part of the translation. Fourthly, this is a programme, now called a 'mission statement' but it underlies all the fine translations of the past. Fifthly, it is at variance with the ideas of most modern currents of thought about translation, which are cynical and deterministic; they assume that translators are always the slaves of the linguistic norms of their time and the servants of their publishers, formerly their patrons, the commissioners of their jobs, etc.

Needless to say, any translation of substantial length is to some extent affected by ideology, culture, norms. But a good translator is aware of them and attempts to reduce their influence as much as possible.

Minimal Translation Again

A correspondent in the *Times* of 26.12.96 reports that in the world of European cycling, European cultural integration is a few kilometres short of perfect; he is shocked because on his new cycle lock, *Cet antivol est fourni avec trois clés. Assurez-vous d'en donner une à une autre personne* ('This lock has three keys. Don't forget to give one of them to someone else') is translated as: 'We supplied three keys. Please give one to your mother in case you lose the other two'. In fact, the strangeness of this adequate minimal translation may ensure that as a speech act it is successful.

The Principles of 'Leavisism'

In view of Dr Terry Hale's baseless suggestion that Leavisism is responsible for a xenophobic attitude to literature which hampered the publication of translation during Leavis's lifetime, here is an attempt to define the philosophy of F.R. Leavis's works:

1. 'Leavisism' is both an attitude towards literature that takes literature as seriously as life and a rigorously intellectual and intensely feeling method of literary criticism.

2. The quality of the language is the central element of, in particular, literature and popular writing, and also of all educational subjects.

3. Literature has a moral and an aesthetic aspect. It is both a comment on human behaviour and a beautiful and delicately realised artefact. It appeals to intelligence and to sensitivity at the same time.

4. Literature is 'the (concrete) words on the page'.

5. Literature is free from the clichés of language and the platitudes of thought.

6. Literature is based on human themes rather than human characters.

7 It is important to 'place' and to discriminate between major and minor works of literature. Minor works stress the aesthetic rather than the moral and are to be enjoyed.

8. Literary criticism is the response and responsible judgement of one person; it benefits from discussion leading to agreement on major issues and to disagreement on details.

9. Literary criticism is the close, concise and detailed analysis of a text, and in particular of the interweaving of its moral and aesthetic elements.

10. The personal and public life of a writer of literature has no place in literary criticism, although it may offer some correlative evidence.

11. A work of literature essentially re-echoes vocal sounds and speech-rhythms. If it sounds like a book, it is 'dead'.

12. A work of art remains 'contemporary' in every period. It interprets and is representative of the life of its time and, in a further moral degree, of all times. (Morality is progressive; it does not change.)

13. It is the literary critic's duty to make value-judgements, supported by arguments with numerous telling quotations from the text (illustrations are not enough), and giving the contrary arguments where pertinent.

Technical Terms or Descriptive Words

Do not translate any word (e.g. *écroulement*) by (with? as? the dictionaries are no help) a technical term ('landslide', 'earthquake'), until you have first looked the technical term up in the TL to SL half of your dictionary. If you find it gives another word (*glissement de terre, tremblement de terre*), translate *écroulement* with a descriptive word, e.g. 'crumbling/collapsing object/building'. A TL to SL dictionary is always useful for the purposes of back-translation which is normally a part of any checking or revision process in translation. Note also that a descriptive word is a general or hold-all word which often includes one or more technical terms; technical terms are essentially narrow forms of descriptive words.

Urban Feature

In an 'educated' text, the name of an urban building (*Palais Richelieu*), whether it still exists or not, should usually be transferred into the TL text, but in roman type.

The Giggle

No translation should make you giggle because it sounds daft or unnatural, unless you think that was the author's intention. Take the sentence, *A ce jeu, elle aura dû être récréee bien des fois*, referring to the history of the *commedia dell'arte*. I don't know what *à ce jeu* means here. *Jeu*, like *jouer*, has a hundred meanings. If you translated it as 'at this game', it would be ridiculous. If you translated it as 'in this form', then it makes sense, but 'form' is too far away from *jeu*. So, by default translation, I suggest 'In this improvised form, it must have been newly created many times'. As a general hint, I suggest that if you read a segment aloud, it helps to detach it from the source language text and brings it to reality; you'll soon know if it makes you giggle.

Art

It is a quality of great art to get better every time one listens to (reads, looks at) it, and discovers new things in it, provided one spaces the listening. And the end of the second act of *Figaro* gets more hilarious and more moving into the bargain. *In giardino*, 'In the garden', *In dem Garten* – never has translation been so irrelevant, so unimportant, so minimal.

Translation and Research

Whilst doctoral theses on this or that aspect of translation theory or consisting of contrastive translation criticism are no longer rare, it is unusual to include the candidate's own translation of a text as a component of such a thesis. Such a doctorate should, I think, consist of:

1. A preface covering current thinking about the translation of this text-category;

2. An introduction to the particular text and its translation, substantiating the translation method to be adopted by the candidate;

3. The text and its translation;

4. A detailed translation commentary;

5. A conclusion, assessing the validity and the semantic loss of the translation.

I am assuming that the text chosen should be 'scholarly' (*dottorabile* – joke – cf. *papabile*, candidate for papacy), rich and complex; that it should be a serious and dignified piece of writing; that in length it should be between a quarter and a third of that of the whole thesis; that it should require extensive research ('pyramids of notes' as Vladimir Nabokov put it) to enable the candidate to translate it appropriately, and that it should have one or more of the following characteristics: it should be of historical and/or literary interest; it could be a distinguished text that urgently requires retranslating, since the previous translation is misleading; it should make an original contribution to its subject; it should be linguistically original and/or exceptionally difficult; it should be wide-ranging, polysemous, allusive and imaginative. Since translation is often maligned as a mere craft in some academic circles, the existence of such a degree should help to establish the academic respectability of translation. In the 19th century, German and British classical professors such as Housman were engaged in similar work, but before the time of doctorates in the humanities.

XXIX
MAY 1997

Mirages and Trials of Exam Marking

Why does what seems wrong in a silly script, one that in places makes no sense, suddenly appear at least interesting and subtle in an intelligent script?

The Linguistic Paucity of French

Given that among languages with a European base, English is the largest and French one of the smallest, it is not surprising that many common French words each cover the meanings of a plethora of English words; that so many common French words also have technical meanings (*révélateur*: develop; *arbre*: shaft – but so has the English 'tree'); and that many normal non-literary words also have colloquial meanings (*génial*: great, cool).

Schiller and Spender

Schiller's *Maria Stuart* has been turned into English at least seven times in the last forty years (though I think that only Jeremy Sams at the National last year has had any success with it). The first time was in 1959 when it was 'freely translated and adapted', and shortened to under two thirds of its length, into verse by the poet Stephen Spender.

In a stimulating preface ('On Translating Schiller's *Maria Stuart*'), Spender first points out that he has translated not only the German words but also the German interpretation of English history, which, unlike the English one, casts an abhorrent light on Elizabeth. Secondly, he justifies the freedom of his translation by maintaining that Schiller wrote in 'word-groups' and clauses, whilst the individual words were not so important. He does not suggest, as I would, that Schiller's stature as a poet is thereby diminished. I would say that a poet who writes in word-groups and clauses writes in clichés – try Schiller's *Wilhelm Tell*.

Despair of a Translation Examiner

On the one hand, there's the cynical brigade preaching the undermining/dethronement/manipulation/subversion of the author/ source text, presumably encouraging the student-translator to never translate a word by its obvious meaning, so that *résidence* becomes 'dwelling'; on the other, there's the student who, convinced that the Collins-Robert is the 'only' French dictionary, always translates by the first word s/he finds in it, so that *simulacre*, though there's a choice of 'pretence, sham, imitation, representation, simulation, mock-up, mockery', etc., automatically translates as 'enactment', simply because it's the first word under *simulacre*, though it makes no sense in the context.

Language and Culture

From a translator's point of view, culture is deposited in language, e.g. when personification is converted to gender or historical periods into tense systems, but, fortunately, culture is only one component of language, the component that makes translation so difficult. The universal component of language is the dictionary or the first part of the *Petit Larousse*; culture is relative and is the encyclopaedia or the second part of the *Petit Larousse*. If a translation is going to be even approximately accurate, it must turn a cultural phrase like *les trente glorieuses* into a linguistic phrase like 'the boom years of 1945–75', or into the minimum of what will be understood by the prospective English readers.

Idiolect

My situational neologism, 'speakable', – 'are you speakable now?', 'Are you free, not too busy to speak to little me, gaping as you are so earnestly so interminably into that computer screen?' – has for long been an item in my idiolect, an 'idiolectalism' – all idiolectalisms are neologisms, but there are many more neologisms than idiolectalisms – and is usually understood and accepted, though I am then exposed to the quick retort, 'Yes, I am, but you're unspeakable'. The German 'translation', *sprechbar*, though also a neologism, sounds natural to me, since *-bar* is more easily transferable than *-able* or *-ible*, but I suspect that *parlable* and *parlabile* (but shades of *papabile*, 'suitable for high office') would be resisted by most 'native' speakers. The negatives of 'speakable' should be 'not speakable' (temporarily) or 'non-speakable' (permanently), not 'unspeakable' (joke).

Note also my grammatical neologism, 'I'm *me*', meaning, 'I'm not like you or anyone else', 'I'm always better and more reliable than you or anyone else' (joke). Translate as *Je suis moi, Io sono io* (not *sono io* which is normal Italian), *Jetzt bin's ich*.

Fear of Using the Same Word

Why do so many exam scripts have 'threat', 'menace', 'idea', 'unpleasant image' (*sic*), 'fear', 'shadow', 'prospect', 'spread', 'thought', 'ghostly suggestion' (*sic*) as the translation of *spectre* (*du chômage*), from candidates who know perfectly well that *le spectre* means 'the spectre', when 'spectre' is the only accurate translation, since none of the ten 'synonyms' are strong or spooky enough? Is it to be creative rather than servile, or to subvert/undermine/dethrone/ explode the source language text? At any rate when *le spectre* means 'spectrum'/*spettro/Spektrum/espetro*, the 'same' word would not have been avoided, though sixty years ago some purist Germans would have translated it as *Farbenbild*!

In my opinion, the choice between using the 'same' or a 'different' word when translating does not arise, since normally the sole aim of translating is to find a sequence of equivalent contextual meanings; these include sound meanings, but apart from poetry, literature and persuasive texts, the latter have rather a low priority.

The Gap Again

(See 'The Translation Examiner's Problem', *The Linguist* 36, 1/97, p.25.) For *travail précaire*, I want 'casual labour'. Time and time again, I get 'job insecurity'. Both translations are accurate, both make sense in the context, both demonstrate different aspects of the same reality, and both are 'right' or as near as makes no matter.

The Hilarity of Mistranslation

I wonder if any other kind of examiner is ever treated to so many good laughs as I am! Take, for *La banlieue se trouve à la pointe de la réflexion* (say, 'The suburbs are at the forefront of discussion'), 'The suburbs are at the tip of consciousness'.

Cité, Grand Ensemble and *Banlieue*

Cité, grand ensemble and *banlieue* are peculiarly French cultural/ institutional terms which would normally be transferred and glossed in a technical translation on town-planning, architecture or cities; however, I don't think they make/are making sufficient impression on anglophones to warrant them being transferred as prospective items in the English language for general purposes. In non-technical contexts, both *cité* and *grand ensemble* could be translated as 'housing development' or 'housing estate', and *banlieue* as 'the suburbs' (but not 'suburbia', which is too cosy).

The Mobled Queen

I am surprised to find that neither the *Collins* nor the *C.O.D.* cite 'mobled' ('muffled'). Any topos, any word, in *Hamlet* should be in a standard modern dictionary, since *Hamlet* is an essential part of modern English.

Vaskulitides

Whilst the medical suffix '-itis' (F. *-ite*) meaning 'inflamation of' occurs in many languages, its plural '-itides' is much rarer. Thus the German *Vaskulitides* can be translated as 'forms of (small vessel) vasculitis'. If they are *zum Teil vom Typ Schoenlein-Henoch*, they can be translated as 'partly of the Schoenlein-Henoch purpura type'.

Note that academic German, which has the *Faust* legend running through and dominating it, has a greater weakness for Grecolatin fossils than Romance languages or English. This weakness is confirmed and satirized in the delicious hocus-pocus of Thomas Mann's *Dr Faustus* and vigorously attacked in Goethe's *Faust*, which is a fierce condemnation of academicism and book-learning.

DMW 1992, 117.Jg., Nr. 33 125

The above typical reference or first line heading of a German trade, professional or academic journal – it headed a paper on *Polyalgia rheumatica und Grippe-impfung* ('Polyalgia and influenza vaccination') which I translated – should, I suggest, by typically translated as: *Deutsche Medizinische Wochenschrift* (*DMW*), the German equivalent of the *Lancet* and the *British Medical Journal*, 1992, Vol. 117, No. 33, pp. 125–6.

I have transferred the acronym DMW for English readers, since it may be useful to them if they are medical professionals or academics.

Incidentally, the top heading is in such small print that the translator is in danger of overlooking it, though the source is normally an essential component of information for the reader. The name and hospital address of the author are in small print in the bottom left hand corner of the first page, and in my translation I transferred them unaltered to a line immediately below the title. All the key-words in the article are translated into English in the bibliography/references at the end of the article; a medical translator should always read the bibliography before starting to translate the text, since it will probably include the English translation of so many of its key-words.

Populism and Democracy

In my experience, the concept and key-word 'populism' has in recent years been used in a new sense which is not recorded in the dictionaries: 'populism' now means government at all or any level by majorities or by the force of numbers; the free play of market forces in the political field, resulting in the rule of Gresham's Law, where the bad drives out the good. Populists always, often deliberately, confuse populism with democracy, which is a delicate system of checks and balances, where minorities as well as popular opinion always have to be taken into account. The contrast was pellucidly illustrated in the *Guardian* of 22.2.97 in the exchange of 'letters' between the populist Barbara Cartland and the democrat Richard Hoggart.

The Five Cobuild Frequency Bands

John Sinclair, the editor of the Cobuild Dictionary claims that these bands, ranging from the 700 words with five black diamonds to the 8000 with one, are of 'immense importance' to language learners and lexicographers. They are equally useful to translators, and will be even more so when they are extended to some bilingual dictionaries.

David Connolly and Odysseus Elytis

I warmly recommend *The Oxopetra Elegies* by Odysseus Elytis, translated by David Connolly (Harwood Academic Publishers, Emmaplein 5, 1075 AW Amsterdam, 1996), which includes a superb preface. Connolly states that in Elytis' poetry, 'the words themselves as sounds and images precede, or are at least as important as, their own cognitive content. To ignore the words in favour of the "spirit" or the "message" is to ignore the essence of his poetry. My approach is to attempt as close a correspondence as possible in the target language to the original word or phrasal unit, which is here the basic translation unit. I abandon this procedure only when the result was clearly unnatural in terms of utterance in the target language or unsatisfactory in terms of poetic effect.'

I would like to suggest that this is the only way to do justice to great and serious poetry; that paraphrase *à la* Robert Lowell or Tony Harrison may be interesting, brilliant, thrilling, refreshing, etc., but it is not translation.

Irresistible English

English has triumphed where Esperanto failed, and become the international language. Given that it is financially so rewarding, all the national establishments and a vastly increased number of working people are going to know English. But unless other countries start making their own Toubon laws, as in France, and all institutions ensure that public notices, leaflets, guides, labels, etc. are multilingual, not just bilingual (vernacular and English), the world is going to be immeasurably culturally impoverished, and the Cola-McDonald culture will swamp the world. The French, crying out that to 'surf' is *naviguer*, 'E-mail' is *le courrier e*, and the 'Web' is *la toile*, are in a wilderness. The topic ought to be on the agenda of the United Nations Assembly as well as UNESCO. There has to be at least a second working language for each world region and, again, Britain must have a national language policy and a National Language Council.

The Small Print

The translator must account for, without always translating, every word, letter and sign on the page – not only the overplayed text – but, in particular, the small print, which, if she thinks it is small for deceptive purposes, she should italicize or print in bold.

The Difference

An extract from Susan Bassnett's article on 'The Translation of

Literature' in *The Linguist* of Vol. 36, No. 3, 1977 (p. 72): 'My concern here is not to demonstrate which of these versions is the 'best' or 'worst', for such considerations are culture-bound and will inevitably change as tastes change across time'. The implication here is that standards of translation are largely a matter of taste. I think this degrades the status of translation. Translation is, or should be, a noble profession concerned mainly with seeking the truth and not with manipulation or taste. Otherwise the article is controversial and instructive.

In my first book (1978), I wrote that translation is always partly science (the truth and accuracy of the cognitive meaning, tested partly by a comparison with reality and partly by the process of back translation), partly a skill or craft (the grind or graft of the process), partly an art (writing well, assisted by inspiration and luck), and partly a matter of taste. The proportion – the *dosage* (French) is a more accurate word – which is notional, of each of these factors depends on the text, the translator, as well as the type of text, and therefore varies. Normally, the scientific factor is around 70 per cent, and the taste factor around 5 per cent for close translation, 10 per cent for informational texts, 15 per cent for 'persuasive' texts, where the message is more important than the meaning. Taste always plays a part in the translation of non-standardized language, but it is always a minor factor in good translation; this is my guess; it can only be hazarded.

Translation by Factors

Translating by Factors by Christoph Gutknecht and Lutz J Rölle (SUNY Press, Albany, USA, 1996) is an extraordinary book. Purporting to discuss translation, the authors, who are experienced linguists, make a comprehensive and detailed comparative study of the modal verb systems of English and German, and virtually skew all their topics round to illustrations of these systems. However, the 'factors' implicated (misleadingly, the term is not used in the mathematical sense) are discussed in detail. The authors are in fact cognizant of a large portion of the translation literature, but they show little interest in the definition, the process or the purpose of translation. There are plenty of references to 'the client', but no evidence that either author-linguist has ever come across one.

A book that comes to its conclusion with the sentence: 'Researching into TL speech-act felicity relative to different kinds of factor sets potentially demanded by the client seems [!] to be a promising path towards a theory of translating successfully' and the note: 'Every translation is motivated in some way or other!' [the exclamation marks are mine!] and the last inevitably modal example: 'He must be able to come', which hardly has Firth's 'implications of utterance' . . . such a book is rather strange.

Incidentally, Christoph Gutknecht is the author of two brilliantly entertaining and instructive books, *Lauter spitze Zungen* and *Lauter böhmische Wälder* (C.H. Beck, Munich, 1997) both happy combinations of etymology and linguistics, which are also well-indexed and useful background books to translation to or from German and several other European languages.

XXX
JULY 1997

Bethlehem and Hebron

I recently taught at Bethlehem and lectured at Hebron University on aspects of translation. I hope that Bethlehem, where St Jerome spent the last thirty-four years of his life, will soon have the second (after Bir Zeit) translator training course in Palestine. Hebron University has endured political occupation and military rule for too long.

Adaptation as a Form of Translation

Many people make a strong distinction between translation and adaptation which is untenable. If adaptation is defined as an attempt to reproduce the approximate meaning of a text, using a different form but the same theme and plot transferred to the target culture, then the critic can proceed to make a finer distinction for himself, which could be useful provided it is openly stated.

Ellipsis in Translation

Penny Sewell discussed ellipsis in translation at the recent conference on Foreign Language Teaching and Translation at the Institute of Germanic Studies in Russell Square, Bloomsbury, and I have done so in the course of a chapter on Case Grammar in *A Textbook of Translation*. Ellipsis is grammatical when it is a feature of one language as against another: *lo so*, 'I know'; *laisse à désirer*, 'is faulty'; *le difficile*, 'the difficult thing'. Ellipsis is semantic when the target language text has case-gaps which need to be filled, particularly in the instance of pronouns (*lui* is what?), or nouns such as 'the mobile', 'the establishment', 'the killers', etc.

Juliane House

I warmly recommend Juliane House's *Translation Quality Assessment: A Model Revisited* (1997, Gunter Narr, Tübingen), the sequel to her *A Model of Translation Quality Assessment*, written twenty years earlier. After a detailed critical review of the main streams of translation theory in the intervening years (according to her: literature-oriented or manipulation school; deconstructionist and post-modernist; functionalist; linguistics or discourse oriented), she then revises and to some extent simplifies her own model, the Hallidayan translation criteria. Still based perhaps too rigidly on the overt-covert translation opposition, it is distinguished by the 'cultural filter', ignoring the kind of correlation ('the more cultural the source language text, the more "covert" the translation') which might keep it in balance. Her discussion throughout is exceptionally intelligent and often pointed, though always tactful: 'the more target-audience-oriented notion of translation appropriateness, which is a recent shift of focus in translational studies' [where the customer is king, the source text is undermined, the truth is at a premium?] 'is fundamentally misguided' (p. 159).

Juliane is sometimes too economical with her examples, but she compensates with detailed studies of four texts and their translation, one of which, from Daniel Goldhagen's international best-seller, *Hitler's Willing Executioners: Ordinary Germans and the Holocaust*, is of outstanding interest.

Even its title in the translation, *Hitlers willige Vollstrecker* (which means 'executors' rather than 'executioners', *Henker*) 'modifies' the original, as the *Spiegel* initially pointed out. Juliane abundantly substantiates the argument in a careful analysis, showing how Goldhagen's repeated and violent attacks on 'the German population' are softened (*geglättet*) throughout the translation. Not surprisingly, Goldhagen, the title of whose book alone is, in my opinion, sensationalist, silly and racist, defends the translation: further, 'a claim was made that the publisher had imposed the changes for political and marketing reasons'. However, I don't think Goldhagen need have worried about his German royalties. Juliane's book should be read for many reasons, and particularly because it illustrates, here paradoxically, the intimate link between truth, morality and translation. Her conclusion, stating the importance of evaluating a translation, where a personal judgement is supported by reasoned arguments and copious parallel quotations from the texts, flies in the face of much modern translation theory (Merino, Wilss and Neubert are outstanding and honourable exceptions), and is masterly.

A Mismatch

'League of Nations', *Société des Nations* (*Società delle Nazioni, Sociedad de Naciones*), *Völkerbund* ... the absurd mismatch of standard terms seventy years and more ago, compared with the straight and literal 'UN' over fifty years ago charts in a scrap example the progress of translation and lexicography. Fifty years ago, Cassell's was still giving *Volk* as the second sense of 'nation'; the identification of 'league', *Bund* and *société* must have created some legal nightmares; 'community' or 'organisation' in their appropriate morphologies could have replaced them adequately.

Translating

In borderline cases (*cas limite*), do not look up a word of quality (i.e. adjective, adverb, adjectival noun) in a bilingual dictionary, without afterwards, looking it up first in an SL monolingual dictionary, and then in the TL-SL half of the bilingual dictionary. Thus, if you translate *gauche* as 'uncouth' or 'ham-fisted', check these in the E-F section to assess the difference from the heart of the meaning of *gauche* within the collocation, say *un malotru*.

Translation as Detection

On an official card leaving blanks after *Nombre y Apellido, C.I.,* and *Direccion*, the acronym *C.I.* was not recognised. The most obvious assumption was *cifra de identidad*. This collocation did not appear under *cifra*, but, under *identidad*, there was *carnet de identidad*, translating as 'identity card'.

Reference Books Again

Translation being concerned with three domains of life: reality, language and the mind that spans the two, these domains are approximately related in three types of reference books: atlases, gazetteers, encyclopaedias, topic or subject (e.g. science, geology) dictionaries, dictionaries of national biography, all of which cover reality; mono-, bi- and multilingual dictionaries, thesauruses, dictionaries of synonyms and antonyms, linguistics, usage, etc. cover language; dictionaries of general and modern quotations, the arts, psychology, etc. cover the mind. All three types must be distinguished and readily at hand for the translator.

The Impossibility of Translation

The myth (in the primordial sense, a legend that explains true situations and is a value-bestowing area of belief) of translation's impossibility has usually been confused. A pragmatic message within a text can always be transferred from one language to another, but the full meaning can only be partially or approximately transferred. As the great Jakobson pointed out, 'cheese' is not *sir* (Russian), since the ingredients are different. And the failure to distinguish literary from non-literary translation is the main source of the confusion, since non-literary texts tend to monosemy, and literary texts to polysemy.

Explication and Back Translation

Vinay and Darbelnet gave the 'classical' definition of explicitation: 'a process which introduces into the TL certain details that remain implicit in the SL, but which are consequent on (*se dégagent de*) the [linguistic] context or the [extralinguistic] situation'. I assume that any explicitation of an authoritative text should in principle be given outside the translation, however much it is required by the reader of the translation. Either in the course of revising or criticising a translation, the 'explicitation' component is 'unveiled' in a back translation.

Gerald Finzi

The booklet for the Chandos (CHAN 8936) CD, Finzi's Choral Works (Finzi Singers, Paul Spicer), has a useful introduction to the composer in English, French and German, all well written, though the German gives up on Finzi's visionary texts (just *Texte*, why not *visionäre Texte*?), whilst the French tries *textes chimériques* (wild, fanciful), (*textes de visionnaire*?), which is way out. Yet the booklet inexplicably provides no translations of the texts, which I think are essential.

Gerald Finzi (1901–1956), a quintessentially English (the country-side, poetry, folk-song) composer, of Jewish-Italian parentage – and this 'racial' contradiction heightens the tension – produced some fine choral (*Dies Natalis*) and orchestral (cello and clarinet concertos) works, but I think his most valuable contributions to music are his numerous (over fifty) settings of Thomas Hardy's poems. *The Dance Continued* (*Regret Not Me*) is shattering.

Travail Précaire

Janet Fraser has written to say that *travail précaire* in industrial relations and labour law contexts is now almost universally rendered as 'precarious employment', which she wittily describes as a 'legacy, I fear, of the Eurospeak phenomenon', but which I would quote as an instance of the fifth medial factor, the convergence of language and languages, 'because it covers not only casual labour (i.e. recruited directly by the employer) but also fixed-term or variable hours contracts and temporary work, i.e. all those workers not on open-ended full-time contracts'. This widening of sense is, however, not yet confirmed in the second edition of the Oxford-Hachette (1977).

Serious Money

The fashionable financial sense of the word 'serious', where all the fat cats are seriously rich, debases the meaning of the word, unless it is used ironically, and usually it is not. Far better to use it, as Benjamin Britten did, in the sense of deserving thought, care, consideration, and related closely to the moral sense, *per serio, per bene*. German has no worthy equivalent for the adjective (a 'serious' person), though the adverb *ernst, im Ernst* collocates adequately with *nehmen*.

Trio and Yves Bonnefoy

The last meeting of Trio (Translation Research in Oxford), or, according to Professor Malcolm Bowie, whose sane impact on foreign language and translation teaching and examining at Oxford is still eagerly awaited, an arcane reference to K.563 (German K.V. 563 = *Köchel-Verzeichnis*, Köchel's Index number), which translates as Mozart's Divertimento for string trio in E Flat, the least diverting and most serious and bleak divertimento ever written – a masterpiece) . . .

the last Trio meeting was devoted to Yves Bonnefoy's poetry and translations.

Personally, to appreciate poetry or poetry translation, I have to have the poem or the poem and the translation to read in front of me, and so Bonnefoy's reading of his Yeats translations into French without any handout was virtually lost on me . . . he strangely assumed that all Yeats's poems were famous and would all be familiar to his large audience. He also managed to read a long and rather abstract paper on *La communnauté des traducteurs* without giving a single translation example, which might indeed have clarified his concepts.

However, I was richly compensated by Michael Edwards's detailed and brilliant analysis of his own wonderful translations of Bonnefoy's quiet, moving and paradoxically concrete poems, an analysis which referred continuously to the poems and translation handout. The translations look deceptively literal:

> *Es-tu venu par besoin de ce lieu,*
> *De ce lieu seul, ravin, porte dressée*
> *Au-dessus du levant et du couchant . . .*
> *Comme passe la barque d'un autre monde,*
> *Entre, je te permets presque une halte.*
> *(La Voix, qui a repris)*

> 'Should you have come for need of this place,
> This place alone, ravine or doorway lifted,
> Above the rising and the setting sun,
> As the keel passes of another world,
> Enter, I allow you almost a pause.'
> (The Voice, speaking again)

Michael Edwards illustrated the extraordinary reserve riches of English: the ubiquitous synonyms: the alternative nouns (*porte*, door, doorway; *buisson*, bushes, shrubs, brushwood; *herbes*, meadow, grass; *seuil*, threshold, doorstone; *chênes clairs*, light-leaved oaks); the versatility of the -ing forms (*marteaux*, hammering; *emplis de larmes*, brimming; *froissements*, rustlings), all also often available to the non-literary translator. Michael Edwards also convincingly demonstrated what I would call 'the Translation Exception', where a close translation is (a) inadequate, (b) sounds feeble, when he translated *dans ce buisson* as 'in gorse, in tamarisk'. 'The Translation Exception', in my opinion, does not exist in non-literary translation, and is in fact one of the 'defining' (the cliché irks me increasingly) features of literary translation.

The Phonosemantics of Irritation and Curiosity

I suggest that *sekkieren* (note the Austrian *-ieren*, which enlivens many French roots in Austrian German colloquial language) is more expressive than *reizen*, which is more expressive than *irriter*, except when Racine uses *irriter*: *C'est là ce que je veux, c'est là ce qui m'irrite* (*Phédre* 1.453): 'That's what I want, that's what excites/inflames me.'

The paucity of French words tend to heighten their expressiveness. Again *neugierig* says indefinitely more than 'curious', which says more than *curieux* but less than *curioso*.

Personal Coordinates

The semantic range of my English transfer(ence) of the French expression *mes coordonnées* (i.e. 'my coordinates') would normally include my address, phone number, e-mail number, fax-number, income-tax and national insurance number. Surely it is absurd that such a useful expression should remain confined to the French language?

AN AFTERWORD, OR A LOOK INTO THE FUTURE

I am more concerned with the future of translation than its past. I want a mission statement for translation, not long descriptive pseudo-objective studies of the deviousness and manipulative nature of translators in the course of history.

As I see an increasing number of languages becoming increasingly important throughout the world, I see translation as an instrument and a channel which can contribute to clarity, order and precision. Speaking is too often prolix, unstructured, noisy, populist; writing should be economical, quiet, reflective. Translation first into and then between four of the world's working languages, gradually less dominated by English, is going to contribute towards international communication, comprehension, and friendliness.

Ironically, the two fundamental issues of translation remain the same now as they have always been, and therefore a perceptive statement about translation now is no more out of date than Schubert, Giotto or Shakespeare can ever be out of date.

The first issue is that between 'free' and 'literal' translation, on which every translator or translation critic has to take a position. This opposition is sometimes stated in terms of indirect or direct, secondary or primary, domesticating or foreignizing, covert or overt, communicative or semantic translation, but it can be summed up as the difference between those who instinctively prefer to generalize elegantly and those who prefer to particularize every detail, which may be clumsy.

In principle, the more important the grammar and the words of the original text, the less it is amenable to generalization when it is translated.

The second issue is the stance of the translator. Here there are three main options:

(a) The translator's only purpose is to render the text transparently, adapting it to the readership's likely cultural and educational level.
(b) The translator follows the favoured translation norms of the time.
(c) The translator follows option (a), but modifies her version intra- or extra-textually, depending on whether it is authoritative or not, where it does not conform to the factual or moral truth of its subject, to logic, or to the principles of good writing, since it is

221

normally her job to inform the readership accurately and agreeably.

I think that teachers, translators, and translation theorists should be concerned with the improvement of translation standards.

Paul Meara, the Chair of the British Association of Applied Linguistics, has recently called for research into 'the problem of vetting the standards of translation papers objectively'. At a time when standards and values in translation and in literature are being widely challenged, this call is welcome. The difficulties inherent in such research must however be recognized. To begin with, whilst translation is mainly an art, a skill, a craft and a science, it is usually 5 to 10% a matter of taste, which can hardly be assessed. Secondly, there is enormous disagreement about the nature of translation, only touched on in the well-known and often quoted twelve apparently contradictory statements made about it in T.H. Savory's *The Art of Translation* (1968), all of which, however, can be reconciled.

Thirdly, whilst I, but not some others, think that the essence of translation remains the same, a translation is dynamic: no two translations of the same piece are identical, and each translation, reviewed after one day or after ten years, is also likely to change. Conscious of these factors, when I was responsible for the marking of a college's degree translation papers, I insisted that each paper by marked by two examiners, and where appropriate, the marks be discussed and reconciled by them. As far as I know, this is rarely done.

I welcome Paul Meara's call, but in my opinion, the criteria of such difficult research cannot be 'rigorous' in the sense that many linguists like to prate about ('with the utmost rigour') but must be approximate and flexible, and must allow for aberrations and inspirations; further, such criteria cannot be the same for authoritative and non-authoritative, nor for literary and non-literary texts or translations.

In fact, I suspect that many methods of assessing public translation exams are chaotic and contradictory, and a wide-ranging survey of current practices can itself do nothing but good, and will at least show up some craziness and narrow some gaps.

I closed my last volume with a reference to the vast areas – tourism, packaging and the world of refugees, detainees, deportees and exiles – of which at least many university translation training courses do not take sufficient account. (The Surrey Police is to introduce multilingual leaflets and notices for minorities within its area, in November 1997 – hopefully the only authority without them.)

Perhaps this book should close with a celebration of Mistranslation through howlers, the cause of so much deflation of pompousness, and punning, Freudian slips, and hilarity.

INDEX